Healing Corrections

D1564607

Healing
Corrections
The Future of Imprisonment

Chris Innes

Northeastern University Press
BOSTON

Northeastern University Press
An imprint of University Press of New England
www.upne.com
© 2015 Northeastern University
Manufactured in the United States of America
Designed by Dean Bornstein
Typeset in Minion Pro by The Perpetua Press

For permission to reproduce any of the material in this book, contact
Permissions, University Press of New England, One Court Street, Suite 250,
Lebanon NH 03766; or visit www.upne.com

Library of Congress Cataloging-in-Publication Data

Innes, Chris.
Healing corrections : the future of imprisonment / Chris Innes.
    pages cm
Includes bibliographical references and index.
ISBN 978-1-55553-846-0 (cloth : alk. paper)—ISBN 978-1-55553-847-7
(pbk. : alk. paper)—ISBN 978-1-55553-848-4 (ebook)
1. Corrections—United States. 2. Correctional psychology—United
States. 3. Prisons—Social aspects—United States. 4. Organizational
change—United States. I. Title.
HV9471.I556 2015
365'.973   dc23
                    2014039398

5 4 3 2 1

To Abbie for her love, support, and, most of all, patience

CONTENTS

INTRODUCTION

How I Got Here

All books are autobiographical. They may not recount the personal history or experiences of the author, but they are molded by that history and those experiences. My own life, not coincidentally, has spanned a very peculiar period in the American justice system. I say that this has not been coincidental because my birth, in 1951, places me squarely in the Baby Boom generation. In the past sixty years much has happened and the broad social changes that have transformed American society have been profound. These changes have been called "the unwinding" by writer George Packer to describe how "the coil that held Americans together in its secure and sometimes stifling grip first gave way."[1]

As these changes unrolled through the decades, they also transformed our system of justice, including corrections. For the record, by "corrections" I mean the whole business of supervising all of the people involved in the criminal justice system because they have been accused or convicted of a crime. This includes anyone who is detained or incarcerated in a jail, a prison, or some other secure facility and anyone being supervised in the community, whether pre-trial, during probation, or during post-incarceration supervision, as in the case of parole (including places where it has been "abolished"). While I review the trends in the field over the past few decades, the subject of this book is the role corrections will play in the coming decades, hence the subtitle: "The Future of Imprisonment." What I mean by "healing corrections" is a longer story but will unfold as we precede through this book.

The book is addressed to correctional professionals, decision makers in criminal justice, and any others with a serious interest in the possibility of a fundamental change in corrections and our system of justice as a whole. In the following chapters I show that our way of responding to crime is so fragmented that the only real solution is a significant change in the cultures of corrections and our justice system. I present a model of organizational culture and cultural change that is practical and workable for real organizations, including prisons, jails, and community corrections agencies.

For most of the past four decades, I have been an active participant at the national level in the research on and the policy debates about the American criminal justice system. I started studying victimization, crime, and corrections in 1977 while I was a graduate student at the University of Michigan and managed a project funded by the Law Enforcement Assistance Administration to archive computerized criminal justice data.[2] By 1985, I was working at the u.s. Department of Justice as a corrections researcher and over the years served at various agencies in varied research and management jobs. During my federal career, I worked at the Bureau of Justice Statistics, the Federal Bureau of Prisons, the National Institute of Justice, and finally at the National Institute of Corrections. I started writing this book (on my own time) while working at the National Institute of Corrections.[3] I retired in 2014 after twenty-nine years of federal service.

My government career afforded me a position from which I closely watched developments in American corrections at all levels. I have worked in this book to exploit the advantages that point of view provided me, while also mitigating the biases it brings with it. Many readers will detect a slant toward institutional corrections, especially prisons, in this book. This is partly autobiographical (since prisons have been the focus of most of my work), but also practical. Because state prison systems are limited in number and corrections policy is often driven by prison policy, there are much better data and much more research on them than on local jails or community corrections agencies (of which there are many thousands, of every size, type, and description). In addition, prisons are where the money is, where the cultural symbolism of punishment is centered, and therefore, in my view, where the fulcrum of change rests.

One of the people you will meet later, the consultant and trainer Peter Garrett, once told me when I asked him to tell me his story that we should be very careful when we tell stories about ourselves. This is because our stories tend to be much more sensible and coherent in retrospect. Be that as it may, I would like to believe that I have matured to the point where I can see a little more clearly now than I could while I was still in the thick of the corrections business. Many, many choices we made over the past few decades seemed reasonable, even necessary, at the time but now can be seen as a string of steps in the wrong direction. I also know that somewhere and sometime along the way in my career, I developed the capacity to be deeply shocked by the things that human beings can do to each other, both in breaking the law and, it turns out, in enforcing the law.

And I realized I had participated in one of them: America's extraordinary use of the justice system to manage the symptoms of a complex set of interconnected and profound changes in our society, while leaving the underlying problems themselves unaddressed. Mystics tell us that Truth is revealed to us in an instant, like a flash of lightning on a dark night. But more ordinary understanding grows apace in its own time. And while it often feels as if we are too late wise and too soon old, there is no other way. By the time we have mustered even a small collection of insights, our only option is to share it with those who still have the time and energy to make use of it; the alternative is simply to live with our regrets.

I have reluctantly come to believe that our habitual ways of thinking about the policies and practices of our justice system have become self-defeating. The whole range of options we routinely offer in our ongoing debates about crime, punishment, and rehabilitation are counterproductive because the system has become a problem in itself. Reducing the level of dysfunction in this system will raise the level of dialogue in our society about it, and I hope this book will contribute to that goal. The alternative is the never-ending stream of initiatives aimed at reforming rather than transforming the justice system. Nearly all have devolved into efforts to find more cost-efficient, intrusive ways to maintain and preserve existing institutions and cultural structures that are in fact unworkable.[4]

What makes the solutions unworkable is that they are the products of fragmented cultures and systems that do not work themselves. The notion of fragmented cultures and systems, along with their opposite, coherent ones, is an essential background theme of this book. The idea is that our individual and collective ability to make things happen as we intend them to happen is far more difficult under fragmented circumstances than when our systems and organizations are coherent. We feel isolated from each other and alienated from our lives. A coherent system is one that makes sense and has meaning; the path from point A to point B is clearer to us. When we are living a fragmented life or within a fragmented culture, however, it takes much more psychological, human, and social capital to produce whatever results we want. Not only are more resources required to accomplish something, but success becomes more uncertain and unintended results are more likely. The solution is to heal the fragmented, incoherent system so that we can connect with each other in meaningful ways.

To heal in this sense is to make something whole. This is as true for the living cultures of organizations as it is for living creatures; both are complex systems with identifiable, functioning parts that make up the whole. Whether our liver or our organization's business office, a complex system fulfills specific functions in the service of the goals of survival and growth. When an organization is fragmented, it is not working as a system made of subparts so much as a collection of disconnected pieces, like a pile of fragments left after a machine is destroyed (or a body is dissected).

The idea of wholeness and using holistic approaches has many versions, of course, but the one I will rely on comes mainly from the physicist and philosopher David Bohm (1917–1992). In addition to making important contributions to quantum theory, he spoke and wrote extensively about how the process of knowing things affects what we believe and how we can, but very often fail, to communicate with each other.[5] He also proposed the cure, Dialogue, which through a curious series of events that I will trace later, found its way into prisons. Bohm's view of wholeness is subtle. The whole as he envisioned it is not a mash-up of everything all together as the universal One, in which everything causes everything else simultaneously everywhere and everywhen. Instead, he talks about parts of a whole versus fragments that might have been (or could be) parts of a whole. Bohm said that a part is "intrinsically related to a whole," but a fragment is not. To fragment something is to break or smash it. Bohm wrote, "To hit a watch with a hammer would not produce parts, but fragments that are separated in ways that are not significantly related to the structure of a watch."[6]

Our usual way of thinking about things, said Bohm, produces pervasive fragmentation because we insist on thinking of wholes as if they were only a collection of parts. But this way of thinking and talking leads to more grief than we realize. It may be true that the universe at some transcendental level is a unified whole, but that does not mean our particular corner of the universe is not fragmented or smashed up. At our level, wholeness is variable—from highly coherent and pragmatically meaningful to so fragmented and incoherent that we can barely make sense of it.[7]

Our current system of justice is one of the things we can barely make sense of. Altering the cultural dynamic that stymies our ability to constructively address ways of changing the justice system requires a national dialogue that can challenge the tacit cultural patterns of the system and American culture. We are experiencing what could be a historic moment in our collective understanding of how the contradictions of and between our social, legal, and economic systems can be used to catalyze fundamental changes in order to re-create our justice system and redefine its role in society. One source of this change must be a transformation of the culture of corrections, which will, in turn, initiate a shift in our society's relationship to both the people who work for and those who literally live within our justice system.

Among the factors that fragment the justice system (and continue to drive high incarceration rates) are the cultural functions and symbolism of punishment. Whatever our opinions about the necessity or wisdom of punishment, I do not anticipate that the American criminal justice system will abandon it soon. And whatever the size or reach our correctional system may have in the future, it is not going to suddenly disappear. We may need prisons, jails, probation, and parole to help us deal with people we do not know what else to do with, but that does not mean we must keep millions of people under supervision or spend billions doing it. In an imperfect world, justice will never be perfect, if for no other reason than that once harm has been done it can never be wholly undone. At the same time, we should not magnify the effects of that harm more than necessary by our response, even if respond we must.

In this, I agree with Barack Obama, who said in his Nobel Peace Prize acceptance speech, "To say that force is sometimes necessary is not a call to cynicism—it is a recognition of history, the imperfections of men, and the limits of reason." Obama was addressing the use of force in the international arena, but his message applies equally to the use of force and punishment in our search for a justice system. A government's power to punish is so awesome that it must be tempered by the knowledge of our own human failings. Nor should we accept that the basic American belief in the possibility and power of redemption has been lost among our people. Martin Luther King, Jr., said, "He who is devoid of the power to forgive is devoid of the power to love. There is some good in the worst of us and some evil in the best of us." Both our limitations and potentials as human beings living together, insofar as we choose to allow them, can obscure our vision or unleash our strengths.

Infusing the policy debate with moral urgency is exactly what needs to happen. As philosopher Kwame Appiah demonstrated in his 2010 book, *The Honor Code: How Moral Revolutions Happen,* dismantling the beliefs under-pinning a social institution is the first step.[8] Appiah analyzes such apparently disparate moral revolutions as the end of foot binding in China, the ban on dueling in Europe, and the suppression of the Atlantic slave trade. He found that the crucial stage in a successful moral revolution is attacking, even ridi-culing, the cultural assumptions and symbols of an institutionalized practice such as foot binding. In other words, it makes the practice "dishonorable" by revealing its unexplored and indefensible roots. In the case of our crimi-nal justice system and mass incarceration, this would mean challenging the underlying cultural assumptions that give the system its credibility. But the tacit knowledge that makes a dysfunctional system appear sensible has been discussed before. Finding and applying a new approach and demonstrating that it can work are what remain to be done.

Another person you will meet later is Harold Clarke, who introduced the idea of healing to corrections. Clarke is a respected corrections leader who has worked with four state departments of corrections, most lately in Virginia. By 2014, he had already served a combined twenty-five years as a director, more than any other active director in the country. During that time, he discovered in Dialogue a vehicle for achieving healing environments in corrections settings. He told me, "If you apply the principles and practices, then you begin to think together. And when you're thinking together, you are able to learn together. And it is only through learning together that you can change your reality jointly and that's what I call then creating new meaning together, creating new realities together."[9] As I discuss later in this book, this process has, in fact, begun in the Virginia Department of Corrections and has produced measurable changes in attitudes and behavior among staff, in-mates, and people under community supervision.

While I hope to do many things in this book, there are some things I avoid. Unlike many who have written about American corrections, I do not issue a ringing indictment of or call for the immediate abolition of the sys-tem. I do not disparage the field of corrections or the dedicated and talented people who do its work. I do not discuss the many debates surrounding the supposedly conflicting goals of using "sanctions" (better known as punishment) versus rehabilitation. I see punishment and rehabilitation, if they are different things at all, as differing approaches to social control, not conflicting philosophies. You will not find here a sermon on the history, research, or necessity of using "What Works" or "Evidence-Based" practices in corrections and crime control. There is also very little discussion of a distinct "inmate culture" in prisons and jails because, as I define culture, there is no such thing. All of these issues have been addressed numerous times by other writers, many of them better equipped and more able than I. The simple reason for avoiding these topics is that there is no evidence that a choice between one solution and any of the others is really possible or what the American people want.

What this book *does* do is provide a framework for understanding how cultures work in organizations, especially corrections, and propose a guide to generating fundamental changes in them. This book describes correctional cultures as they really exist and examines the process by which the culture of corrections can be changed. On the basis of my experience in this system, I believe that it is possible. It can be done by creating a healing environment within correctional facilities and agencies. Accomplishing this will require focusing on correctional workforce development and the use of innovative practices to help people working in correctional settings to communicate with each other and with people under correctional supervision in constructive and compassionate ways. And a transformation in corrections will, over the long run, help to shift our society's relationship to our system of justice as well as the people working or living within it and beyond it.

The ideas and insights in this book arise from my experiences in working with other corrections professionals. Especially important has been the work I did during my tenure at the National Institute of Justice as director of the Justice Systems Research Division and then at the National Institute of Corrections (NIC) as chief of the Research and Information Services Division. The backbone of this book is based particularly on the work I did at the latter. This included work on organizational culture, which began long before I arrived in 2006, and especially on the Norval Morris Project, which I led during my years there. The Morris Project was a unique effort to accelerate the uptake of knowledge new to the field by systematically searching for research literatures that could be translated into correctional practice.[10]

The goal of these projects at NIC, and the reason the agency funded them, was to produce knowledge that could be applied across the field of corrections. For that goal to be realistic, any model or framework had to fit the realities of correctional organizations as they exist. One of them is the typical turnover of staff at all levels. For example, the average tenure of a state department of corrections director is less than four years, so any initiative has to be fully implemented within that time span.[11] The work will not be done during that period, it never will be completely done, but there must be tangible progress with measurable results to keep it going under new leadership.

The second prerequisite of a usable model is that it be cheap. Few agencies have the time or money to invest in a costly initiative. Intensive, consultant-driven interventions are too expensive and time-consuming given the ongoing operational demands of a correctional agency. That means agencies have to depend on a lot of do-it-yourself initiatives run by their own staff. Dialogue works in this environment because it embodies a set of skills and practices that can be used by anyone. They have been introduced to executive and line-level correctional staff in several agencies, and only a few days of initial training are required for staff members to get started using a cascading model that spreads the practices across the organization.

Still, reading this book will be much easier than doing the work of healing the cultures of corrections, our criminal justice system, or society. All are deeply fragmented. It took us decades to create this ultimately dysfunctional and incoherent system, and it will take decades to re-create it in new ways. One of the themes that recurs with depressing frequency in this book is that everything I propose that you do will be very hard work. It takes a serious investment of time, energy, and courage by many people in an organization to even get this process going. If you are in a senior leadership position in an organization just starting the process, it will be left to your successors to continue it.

I should probably also tell you now that another thing I do not do here is explain exactly how you can create a healing environment in your own organization. This is because there is no single, step-by-step recipe for changing the culture and creating a healing environment for every organization. I have a framework to offer, but the details have to come from the people living within a culture; only they can change their culture because a healing environment is not a thing; it is a place. It is a cultural container within which people can talk and think together, discover a shared understanding of what they are doing, and decide together what their future should be. The solutions for each organization have to emerge out of the process as people go through it together.[12]

Given my experience in communicating with practitioners and decision makers, I have tried to make this book easy to use.[13] It is roughly divided into four parts, which are organized, to some degree, on the basis of my own life experiences. The first part, comprising chapters 1–3, reflects my background in research and policy and is about the recent history of corrections and the way organizational cultures work. The second part, which includes chapters 4 and 5, examines closely the results of a project I became involved in at NIC that assessed the cultures of prisons across the United States. The third part, chapters 6 and 7, reports on a second project at NIC, the Norval Morris Project, and the work by the Virginia Department of Corrections to apply a dialogic approach to change. In the fourth part, chapter 8, I return to the future of corrections.

By design, there is not much theory in this book. There is a framework for thinking about cultures and how they work, but it is pretty much descriptive. I think ideas are worth something only if they help us organize what we think we know into a coherent understanding that allows us to take actions to get what we think we want. If the ideas work for that purpose, that is good enough. John Dewey put this a different way when he proposed a pragmatic test for the usefulness of any inquiry by asking, "Does it end in conclusions which, when they are referred back to ordinary life-experiences and their predicaments, render them more significant, more luminous to us, and make our dealings with them more fruitful?"[14] This is the test I use in this book; does a way of thinking and talking about living cultures help people in those cultures work and live better together? In short, does the inquiry illuminate us? Wholeness and the use of Dialogue do just that.

If this all seems too theoretical, I have another, more personal way of looking at wholeness: public service does not mean anything unless you assume wholeness is real. If everyone were a separate, semi-independent piece of our society, why would anyone risk his or her life for a general good, such as public safety? Anyone who does exactly that has already settled the question in a way that theoretical debates never can; your actions say you are connected to others and committed to their welfare. When you go through the sally port at a prison or jail or march up to the door of a parolee's home not knowing exactly what is on the other side, you have made a statement about your commitment to others that is much stronger than any philosophical argument will ever be.

Finally, in the interest of full disclosure, I want to note that one of the main forces throughout my adult life has been my practice of Buddhism. I have been motivated to write this book by an aspiration to practice compassion. Buddhists, of course, are not alone in placing compassion at the center of their spiritual life and striving to make it the driving force behind their everyday actions, nor is the practice of compassion limited to those who follow a religion.[15] I have never felt that there is an essential contradiction between my professional work in corrections and my practice of compassion. Although some may be shocked to hear this, I believe that the essence of correctional practice is compassion. Public safety, protecting people from harm, and preparing people who have done harm in the past to return to their families and communities are the mission of corrections. To me, that makes compassion the essential core of correctional practices.

Healing Corrections

CHAPTER ONE

How Many Tragic Ironies Are Too Many?

On March 19, 2013, while I was in the process of writing this book, Tom Clements, the affable and compassionate director of the Colorado Department of Corrections, was assassinated. In a statement to the department staff the day after Clements was killed, Colorado governor John Hickenlooper said of him, "He was unfailingly kind and thoughtful, and sought the 'good' in any situation. As you all know, in corrections that is not easy . . . I am so sad. I have never worked with a better person than Tom."[1] When I saw the governor some weeks later, he still looked genuinely sad when I mentioned Tom. A couple of months before his death, Tom had run into Frank Bruni, a journalist who writes for the *New York Times*, in a Colorado diner and struck up a conversation.[2] Bruni wrote shortly after his death, "Clements knew his business, cared about it and was someone to whom we owed a debt of gratitude. He wanted us safe. And in the service of that, he worked in a byway of the government that a great many of us pay insufficient heed to."

During his conversation with Bruni, Clements talked mostly about "administrative segregation," the high-security units that most American prisons use to isolate from the general inmate population people who are especially difficult to manage, even in a prison setting. Clements told Bruni that he believed administrative segregation was overused, and unwisely so, because it was an easy (but by no means cheap) way to deal with difficult people who were repeatedly disruptive. For his article, Bruni also interviewed Governor Hickenlooper, who said that Clements had been working toward a "transformation within the culture of the entire prison system away from solitary confinement into actual preparation for reentry into society." During his two-year tenure as director in Colorado, Clements had reduced the number of inmates in administrative segregation by 50 percent.

The last conversation I had with Tom Clements was in Houston, Texas, just a few weeks before he was killed. We were both attending the semiannual combined meetings of the Association of State Correctional Administrators and the American Correctional Association. The major topic at both meetings was the use, and sometimes the abuse, of administrative segregation as a way of managing troublesome people in prisons. Clements played a central role in those meetings as an articulate, reasoned, and principled voice in the discussions and formal presentations.[3] Colorado had also been involved in a very ambitious attempt to transform its community corrections operations, which had, Tom admitted, failed. I was especially interesting in talking to Tom about creating healing environments and using Dialogue as a way to build them. Although he was busy preparing for a presentation that afternoon, he took the time to talk about my ideas. When I described the pitfalls of trying to transform an organization without engaging all of the staff and how such attempts so often led to failure, he told me, "That's what happened to us." We agreed to continue the conversation about working together on a possible initiative in Colorado and wished each other safe travels back home. That was January 28, 2013.

On that very same day, Evan Ebel, age twenty-eight, was released on mandatory parole from custody after serving an eight-year sentence for robbery and assault. While in prison, Ebel had been involved in a white supremacist prison gang called the 211 Crew. He had spent most of the past several years in administrative segregation and was released directly from there to the street. After his release Ebel was suspected of having killed Nathan Leon, a father of three who worked weekends delivering pizzas, on March 17, 2013, in order to get Leon's Domino's Pizza jacket. Two days later, he was suspected of being the person who shot and killed Clements. When Ebel showed up at Clements's home, Tom may have thought he was opening his front door to a pizza delivery man who had somehow got lost. Three days later, Ebel died in a shootout with police in Texas. When he was pulled over in Texas, he shot and wounded a patrol officer, then led other officers on a Hollywood-style chase in which he peppered them with shots before he crashed his car and emerged from the wreck shooting. Media reports quoted Decatur, Texas, police chief Rex Hoskins, who intoned, "He wasn't planning on being taken alive."

As it turned out, Evan Ebel was not even supposed to be on the streets. He had been released four years too early because a 2007 addition to his sentence for assaulting a correctional officer had not been properly recorded. And, as a convicted felon, he was not supposed to have a gun either, but a suburban Denver woman was subsequently arrested for allegedly buying one and giving it to him.[4] During all this time, Ebel was under strict parole supervision, which included daily check-ins and electronic monitoring. He had been compliant with the conditions of his parole from the day he was released until March 14. On that day, his ankle bracelet sent a tamper alert and he stopped checking in. On March 17, the day Nathan Leon was found dead, a parole officer visited Ebel's home and decided he had absconded. A warrant was issued for his arrest on March 20, one day after Tom Clements was shot and the day before Ebel was killed by police in Texas.[5]

Evan Ebel did not have the history most people would associate with a career criminal.[6] The son of a Denver oil and gas lawyer, he grew up in a middle-class suburb. When he started engaging in threatening and violent behavior as a teen, his parents sent him to special camps in Utah, Jamaica, and Samoa for children with behavioral problems. His mother wrote, "Some people may blame us for what has happened to Evan. I can only say that his dad and I had to make hard decisions when he was younger hoping to avoid where he is now." His father, testifying before a legislative committee hearing on administrative segregation, said, "He'll rant a little bit. He'll stammer. He'll be frustrated that he can't find the words. And I let him get it out, and eventually, because I'm his father, he will talk to me." One of Clements's signature initiatives was to develop step-down units that would ease the transition of inmates who had spent long periods of time in administrative segregation back to the general prison population or into the community.

Evan Ebel was just as concerned as Tom Clements about what would happen to him if he were released directly from segregation. "Do you have an obligation to the public to acclimatize 'dangerous' inmates to being around other human beings prior to releasing them into society after they have spent years in solitary confinement and if not why?" Ebel asked in one of the many grievances he had filed while in custody. Clements had asked a similar question during an interview in 2012. He said, "You have to ask yourself the question—How does holding inmates in administrative segregation and then putting them out on a bus into the public, [how does that] square up? . . . We have to think about how what we do in prisons impacts the community when [prisoners] leave. It's not just about running the prison safely and securely."[7]

What are our answers to these questions? The Colorado system was operating normally, even well by most standards. Evan Ebel was one of about eight hundred people released each month from the system, and he was being monitored closely. As an inmate, Ebel had been difficult to work with. He was associated with a gang, had a history of assaulting staff, and was disruptive. Tom Clements was doing the right thing and for the right reasons. Many things could have changed the course of events and stopped Evan Ebel: if the programs he had taken part in as a teenager had worked; if his sentence computation had been done right; if a step-down program had been available; if he had not been able to get a gun; if the tamper alert on his electronic monitoring bracelet had been responded to more quickly; even if there were better ways to deal with difficult inmates or the attempts to change the way parole was done in Colorado had been more successful. But three men were dead. When we stop and think about how our society should respond to the Evan Ebels in our world, is there anything that comes to mind that we have not already tried with mixed results?[8]

Is Mass Incarceration the Problem?

Many people, both inside and outside of corrections, recognize that our use of incarceration and community surveillance in all its many forms has been a catastrophe for millions of people and thousands of communities. How this happened is the product of what I call the big squeeze in American corrections and is the subject of the next chapter. Briefly, the big squeeze is a combination of ongoing population pressures, continuing budget constraints, and political polarization and gridlock at all levels of government. The hallmark of the big squeeze is that while crime rates have fallen dramatically, incarceration rates have hardly changed. The system has become disconnected from its public safety mission and is self-perpetuating. Even two recessions since the crime drop began in the mid-1990s have produced no more than token attempts to end what has become known as "mass incarceration." Modest efforts at reforming the system have routinely ended up reinforcing its reach. This has all been driven by the changes in sentencing practices that began in the 1970s and were themselves the product of a dark brew of expressive punishment, cultural defensiveness, and partisan warfare.

Some believe that the problem with corrections is just that the system is too big. They advocate reforming the system by focusing on mass incarceration and ways it might be reduced through sentencing reform, programs designed to reduce recidivism, diversion programs for special populations, and the like. All of these programs are good and useful and should continue. But even those who argue against mass incarceration and propose dramatic cuts in prison populations acknowledge that many people will still be imprisoned.[9] In the United States, a 50 percent reduction in the number of prisoners would still leave hundreds of thousands of people incarcerated. The total correctional population in this country is very slowly declining, and it will continue to decline. But the end of mass incarceration, when it comes, will create a future for imprisonment that is vastly different from the one we now know. The truth is that a downsized system could be worse than the one we have now; some of the most shocking excesses in our history took place in much smaller systems.

The main driver of correctional work is the sheer volume of time, energy, and money involved in managing an ever-changing population made up of millions of people under the supervision of hundreds of thousands of correctional staffers at a cost of many billions of dollars every year. Many pressing operational issues—such as segregation housing (both for administrative purposes and for disciplinary cases); special populations (people with mental illnesses, women, those with chronic diseases, the elderly, etc.); policies, practices, and special conditions ("super-max" prisons, sexual or other abuse by staff, crowding, violence, etc.)—push correctional policy. None of these issues are going to simply disappear if the system shrinks. We could not build our way out of the population expansion, nor can we simply unbuild our way out of a population contraction. Crime and punishment are not going to go away.

The Future of Imprisonment

Whatever form the future takes, American corrections can and should be prepared for a much different role. This is not because we have failed—we may have succeeded too well—but because the time has come to redefine our mission and remake ourselves in the service of a new vision. What we were called upon to do during a period of rising crime rates and an expanding system is not what we must do in an era of falling crime rates and a shrinking system. To meet this challenge, something more is needed than tweaking sentencing laws, adjusting good or earned time, introducing yet another behavior change, reentry, or resettlement program, or employing ever more refined and cost-effective techniques designed simply to "manage offenders more efficiently."

Harold Clarke, director of the Virginia Department of Corrections, put the dilemma this way: "We're in the business of creating public safety, and we know quite well how to build secure institutions. We know how to operate secure institutions . . . We have to do better than to simply incapacitate. And so, how do you do better than that? You do better than that by addressing the deficits, the needs of offenders and staff. And to address the deficits and needs of offenders and staff, you have to create the conditions for that to occur. And the conditions that need to be created are those, in my vision, that are readily in existence in a healing environment where the needs of staff and offenders are being addressed. So I am sold on the concept. I think it's a human thing . . . We have to evolve in our industry. If we don't evolve in our industry, it's going to be because of our lack of initiative and because of our lack of courage to do the right thing and our desire to embrace the past."

Like Clarke, I believe corrections must transform its cultures from the inside out and, in so doing, change the dynamic of the justice system and of American culture. To do that, corrections must heal itself, by which I mean make itself whole, and in the process become both a healing profession and a healing force in society. Transforming correctional cultures will mean fundamentally changing how people working in corrections talk and think together. Out of this dialogue, an environment will develop within correctional facilities and community corrections agencies that will generate a different future for those who work for and live within corrections. This future would not be defined by endless tragic ironies piled one upon another, but by the vision of people like Tom Clements, who saw so clearly that we must bring an end to our easy (but by no means cheap) ways of dealing with people like Evan Ebel.

Given the amount of financial, human, and social resources our justice system consumes and all the direct and indirect costs it incurs, including enormous opportunity costs, everyone in our society is affected by it in countless ways.[10] Many more people are "involved" in the system than just those accused or convicted of a crime. These include their families, friends, neighbors, and communities, as well as victims and their families, friends, neighbors, and communities (who usually belong to the same overlapping groups of people). This turns out to be many more people than we typically think of whose lives are fundamentally affected.[11] In fact, everyone in our society and beyond is touched in one way or another through the complex, interconnected networks of effects that operate in our world.

Also included, of course, are the people who work in the system. The public image of corrections has often been very negative, and the people working in corrections are routinely portrayed as uncaring, inflexible, or obsessed with punishment. In fact, the nearly universal acceptance of the principles of evidence-based practices and reentry programs has transformed the outlook of the corrections field over the past thirty years. The professionalization of the field during this time and the maturation of correctional practices have created a system that would be unrecognizable to anyone not long ago. This is why one of the main avenues for progress will be the correctional workforce. I know that not all the people working in corrections will immediately respond positively to this approach, and some never will. But my experience of past attempts to change correctional organizations is that they have had no trouble finding enthusiastic support among enough people to be viable from the beginning. When the Virginia Department of Corrections asked in its Healing Environment Initiative for twenty-four volunteers to spend one day a week working as trainers and coaches, it received more than three hundred applications.

What Is Healing?

When people first hear about the idea of creating a healing environment in corrections, they often misunderstand its meaning. What are being healed, and thereby become healing, are correctional cultures themselves. These cultures have become fragmented under the pressures of conflicting demands, limited resources, and the inevitable stresses and strains of correctional work. Correctional work is very difficult and routinely inflicts a great deal of wear, tear, and sometimes trauma on anyone doing it.[12] It is also more dangerous than other work. In 2011, the rate of work-related, nonfatal injuries or illnesses among correctional workers that caused them to lose a day or more of work was 544 per 10,000 workers. This is four times the rate for all workers in the United States. In that year, they suffered 254 per 10,000 work-related injuries caused by assaults or other violence (the equivalent figure for all U.S. workers is 7 per 10,000). From 1999 to 2008, an average of eleven correctional workers died on the job each year. More recently, 40 percent were killed in transportation-related accidents and 25 percent were homicide victims.[13]

In this context "healing" means to make whole by providing support and assistance both in repairing the psychological, emotional, and physical damage that inevitably comes along with working in correctional settings of all types and in empowering staff to build a better work environment. This is very different from the idea of healing as a kind of cure for a workforce that is somehow sick or needs to be fixed. We have to be careful when we talk about healing cultures that we do not fall into the trap of thinking this is about sick, diseased, or unhealthy cultures. In Virginia, where the idea of creating a healing environment is central to efforts to effect change, some staff members reacted to the idea by asking if management thought they were sick. (The answer "You're not sick, your *culture* is" does not play very well, either.) What is being healed in this case is the pervasive fragmentation that is common to many organizations and systems, including corrections.

Fragmentation of a system is not like an infectious disease or trauma. If anything, if we want to use an analogy from medicine, the concept that probably comes closest is inflammation. According to one definition, "Today it is believed that inflammation is part of the nonspecific immune response that occurs in reaction to any type of bodily injury . . . In some disorders the inflammatory process, which under normal conditions is self-limiting, becomes continuous and chronic inflammatory diseases develop subsequently."[14] So a culture that is pervasively fragmented is really irritating, and if it goes on too long it becomes a chronic and painful part of life.

What Is Culture?

In chapter 3, I review in detail what organizational cultures are and what makes correctional cultures different from other types. Culture, as I define it, is the network of ongoing interactions between and among all the people participating in that culture. It is made up of the patterns of communication between people as they live and work together, negotiate their social reality, and define their identity. Cultures are learned and have the practical purpose of helping people manage their daily lives together. This way of thinking about organizational cultures is different from the way they are usually described as a collection of values, beliefs, attitudes, and so on. This is important, because the reason most attempts to change organizations fail is that they try to change cultures by trying to alter the surface things (like our assumptions, values, beliefs, norms, paradigms, and mental models) that are really expressions of the underlying and less visible patterns of interactions taking place between all the people throughout the organization.

Most of those who write about organizational culture and change offer a definition of culture that refers to assumptions, beliefs, attitudes, and the like but do not bother to define what "assumptions," "beliefs," and "attitudes" are. They end up prescribing ways to attack false assumptions, correct distorted beliefs, and challenge resistant attitudes as if it were obvious how to do that. The truth is that assumptions, beliefs, and attitudes do not change; the cultural processes that create them, if altered, will produce different ones. Culture is made up of the pattern of interactions between people living and working together. It is the sum total of all they have learned and are learning together as they survive and thrive together in daily life.

Every culture has to solve two problems if it is going to survive, much less thrive, in any physical or social environment. The first thing people have to do is work out how much they will look inward at their own needs and how much they will have to keep an eye on the world outside. If people's needs are not being met, they will not have or keep a commitment to the group. But if no one is paying attention to the external environment, the people in that culture will not recognize and adjust to the changes occurring around them. The second thing they have to work out is how much stability or control they need to keep life and limb intact versus how much latitude they can give people to do their own thing. Individually and collectively, we make this choice, whether consciously or unconsciously, by our own will or not, because we embrace the world we find ourselves in or because we are resigned to what we are given. However it happens, in the end the people in a culture adopt the style that works for them. The culture an organization adopts will determine whether it succeeds in its mission, however that mission and its success have come to be defined.

An organization competing in the marketplace may use an outwardly looking, competitive culture to turn a profit, while a prison will adopt one that focuses on internal operations and uses hierarchical controls to preserve and maintain security and public safety. A culture with a hierarchical style focuses on rules, specialization, and accountability to produce an organization that functions smoothly and reliably. The type of leader you would expect to find in a hierarchical organization would focus on directing operations, coordinating and monitoring activity, and maintaining discipline. Such organizations define success in terms of efficiency, timeliness, consistency, and stability. This is essentially what being a warden requires.

Bradford Bogue, a longtime trainer and consultant in the corrections field, has pointed out that corrections shares a number of attributes with other high-reliability organizations characterized by complex, tightly interconnected processes intended to position the organization so that it can respond instantly to potentially catastrophic events.[15] Bogue's review of the literature on high-reliability organizations identified the key characteristics of such organizations. Besides corrections, other examples include air traffic control, nuclear power plants, air and rail transportation systems, aircraft carrier deck operations, combat operations units in general, and firefighting units. All these have similar cultures because they deal with situations in which a small problem can quickly become a large crisis, at which point it is too late to think about what they might do. In chapter 3, I examine Bogue's view in greater detail within the context of correctional cultures.

The Prison Culture Project

The understanding of cultural types I have just described is more formally known as the Competing Values Framework. It was developed by Kim Cameron and Robert Quinn, professors at the University of Michigan's Ross School of Business. It assumes that every organization must balance the emphases it will place on the competing values of an internal versus external focus, on the one hand, and between structure and control versus flexibility and agility, on the other.[16] The Competing Values Framework is the framework the National Institute of Corrections (NIC) used in working with correctional agencies across the country on cultural issues.[17] The Prison Culture Project was conceived in 2000 by Susan Hunter, then chief of the Prisons Division, to explore ways in which the idea of organizational culture could be used in the field of corrections.[18] Part of the project was the development and use in dozens of prisons of a cultural assessment using official data, interviews or focus groups, and extensive observation across several days and different shifts. The long-running project was funded by NIC through a series of awards made to the Criminal Justice Institute (CJI), led by George and Camille Camp.

Each assessment resulted in a detailed report intended to help the warden and executive staff at each facility to get a clearer picture of their organizational culture.[19] Overall, the problems that the assessment team found in the two dozen prisons visited were remarkably consistent across the country. The most common problems were related to fragmentation and included poor communication, lack of trust, lack of respect for and between staff members, absence of recognition of staff performance and achievements, and unclear expectations, apathy, and ambivalence toward change. Other problems, usually found in tandem with the effects of fragmentation, included corruption, excessive use of force, sexual misconduct, and the effects of the code of silence (co-workers covering for others' misconduct). In chapters 3 and 4, I review the results from the early period of the project. It was during this time that the assessment team routinely administered the questionnaire that Cameron and Quinn had developed identifying the type of culture organizations displayed. The material from the reports used in these chapters does not identify the site or any of the individuals involved in the assessments.

What the assessors found at these prisons across the United States were cultures that were highly fragmented and in which staff at all levels reported enormous distress, frustration, and resentment. Many of the issues they raised in interviews or focus groups echoed those you might hear about in most organizations. Race and ethnicity, gender, generational issues and conflicts, labor-management relations, and the day-to-day demands of the job were all mentioned. More often, however, the focus was on problems common in correctional workplaces. Conflicts, misunderstandings, and poor, even toxic, relationships between custody and non-custody staff, between line and support staff, or among and between staff, supervisors, managers, and executive staff were nearly universally uncovered in the assessment. Fragmentation was so pervasive that even the inmates at several prisons complained about it.

I doubt this comes as a surprise to anyone who has spent time around correctional institutions or agencies. Most of the places I have been, including prisons, jails, and parole agencies, have faced these same issues. In a large urban jail that I once worked with there was a program in which inmates who had been given a "ticket" for a disciplinary violation, but also had a mental illness designation, were placed in a special housing unit for mental health disciplinary cases. There, mental health services were delivered by clinicians from the local department of mental health in small-group and one-on-one sessions. Both the clinicians and the jail staff believed that due to confidentiality rules they could have only very limited communication about any individual inmate. A clinician would see his or her *patients* in the unit for a ninety-minute group or half-hour individual session but would tell the custody staff next to nothing about what was going on.

Meanwhile, the custody staff were supervising *inmates* twenty-four hours a day but gave the clinicians only vague information about day-to-day life in the unit during an occasional brief, informal discussion with them. At the same time, the clinicians privately believed that the restrictive housing was by definition harmful to the well-being of their patients. The custody staff privately believed that the clinicians were naive, to say the least, and were being routinely manipulated by inmates pretending to be sick. This state of affairs was not working well. It usually does not, but that does not seem to stop the corrections field from allowing such divisions to continue while still complaining about turf, "silos" that isolate one unit from another, and lack of collaboration.

Another example of the fragmentation identified during the Prison Culture Project concerned the very different perspectives and attitudes among custody versus non-custody staff. The team often heard non-custody staff say they were not respected. In one focus group, a program staff member complained that custody staff "looks at me as if it's my job to entertain inmates. They don't see how my role helps them with security." This was a common refrain in a number of prisons and routinely produced strained relationships between the groups. This fragmentation, in turn, made them more distant from each other and produced a sense of isolation. They ended up struggling with each other in managing even basic tasks and in what should have been routine interactions. Instead of addressing the issues of fragmentation, both groups had shut down and focused on their own jobs—and complained about one another.

The assessment team also found a profound level of dissatisfaction in these prisons. One of the reports said, "Employees at all levels described the staff with such words as 'wounded' and 'scarred.'" At one prison, according to the team, "years of exposure to a negative work environment and a lack of resources has resulted in a wearing away at staff in all departments." The report went on to say, "Collectively, it is clear that [the prison's] staff still suffer from past events . . . As one staff member described the situation, 'it's a war.' Other comments pointed to the fracturing of staff relationships: 'if the inmates are no problem, staff turn on themselves,' and 'staff give you more trouble than inmates.'" Later the same report said, "Staff at all levels repeatedly referred to the large number of their co-workers who . . . have become the 'walking wounded,' as 'emotionally scarred and alienated' and now merely 'do their eight and hit the gate.'"

The Prison Culture Project assessment team almost always found a strong preference among corrections staff for a more supportive culture, in contrast to an existing culture that was too hierarchical. They saw the desire by staff for less emphasis on stability and control and more attention to flexibility and discretion as a cry for relief from the existing culture. According to one report, "The assessment team has come to understand this as a call for help, or a 'red flag,' from staff who want attention to be paid to their pain and needs. The specific frustrations and issues staff has vary among institutions, but the bottom-line message is that staff was strongly feeling in need of support and relief from distress in the workplace." At this prison, one focus group participant said, "I pulled over to the side of the road and puked on the way to work because I was so stressed out." Another focus group member said that the team "would be amazed at how many people are on pills here."

The individual discomfort staffers feel in unhealthy cultures clearly affects them and the organization as a whole. Healing the organization will help to heal them. But creating a healing environment is not a "hug-a-thug" program or training designed to convince staff members to become social workers. Accountability, of and by staff and inmates alike, is an essential principle of creating healing environments. A healing environment changes the way correctional cultures function and has a positive influence on people who are inmates or under community supervision. It does this by influencing how correctional staff interacts with them in ways that will support and reinforce existing programs, training, and treatment. In Virginia, some wardens reported that this had happened as a side effect of the staff-focused Healing Environment Initiative, and some data on assaults and other inmate misconduct supported their instincts. But those advocating a healing environment do not pretend that inmates who are otherwise incorrigible will be magically transformed by a kinder, gentler way of speaking to them.

Where This Book Came From

The immediate genesis of this book was the National Institute of Corrections Norval Morris Project, initiated in 2004 to honor and remember law professor and criminal justice reformer Norval Morris (1923–2004).[20] One of his students, NYU law professor James Jacobs, once summarized Morris's work by saying that his goal was always to create a criminal justice system "that was more just, effective and humane."[21] At the beginning of his article on Morris's role in the study of corrections, Jacobs quotes him as saying, "Decency, empathy, the ability to feel at least to a degree the lash on another's back, the removal occasionally of our customary blinkers to human suffering, a respect for each individual springing from religious or humanitarian beliefs—these have been the motive force of penal reform and not any validated knowledge concerning the better prevention of crime or recidivism."[22] It is not "what works?" that, in the end, fundamentally moves us to be a better people; it is "what's right?"

Much of this book has been inspired by two of Morris's books, both of them now forty years old but still timely: *The Honest Politician's Guide to Crime Control* (with Gordon Hawkins) and *The Future of Imprisonment*.[23] Morris and Hawkins begin *The Honest Politician's Guide* with a succulent critique of the underlying problem in our system: "The first principle of our cure for crime is this: we must strip off the moralistic excrescences on our criminal justice system so that it may concentrate on the essential. The prime function of the criminal law is to protect our persons and property; these purposes are now engulfed in a mass of other distracting, inefficiently performed, legislative duties." In other words (mine), our collective purpose is fundamentally broken, fragmented across different actors and interests. It does not make sense to us, and lacking a clear, coherent understanding of our purpose, we struggle with each other rather than work in concert toward shared goals.

The Morris Project sought to promote Morris's legacy by following his model of using collaboration, interdisciplinary insights, and research to bring about innovative change in correctional policy and practice. The project's planning and logistical support came through a number of cooperative agreements between the National Institute of Corrections and Justice Systems and Training (J-SAT) of Boulder, Colorado, under the leadership of Bradford Bogue.[24] The project developed a unique strategy for identifying knowledge relevant to the field of corrections by working with thought leaders across multiple disciplines to identify, distill, and disseminate new knowledge in the field. One of the questions that emerged was "How can we transform correctional leadership and the workforce in ways that empower staff to reduce recidivism and promote prevention?"

In September 2009, during a meeting of subject matter experts to explore this question, one participant introduced the idea of creating a healing environment in corrections settings. The participant was Harold Clarke, then the commissioner of the Massachusetts Department of Corrections. The idea spurred immediate interest, and immediate skepticism, but the group took to it. They developed an action plan for the implementation of a healing environment in a jurisdiction, if one could be found, willing to undertake such an initiative. As it happened, a jurisdiction was found about a year later; the Virginia Department of Corrections had a new director who was very interested in bringing the idea of healing environments to reality in the Commonwealth. The new director was Harold Clarke.

Clarke's record is among the most distinguished of anyone now active in the corrections field.[25] During my work with him over the years, he always impressed me, as he has many others in our profession, with his dedication to public service.[26] Clarke is the longest-serving correctional administrator in the country, having led four different state systems over twenty-five years. He also has a long string of leadership roles in national organizations such as the American Correctional Association and Association of State Correctional Administrators. Born in the Canal Zone of Panama to Jamaican parents, Clarke retains a Caribbean lilt in his speech. After finishing high school in the Canal Zone, he went to Doane, a private college in Crete, Nebraska, on a combined academic and athletic scholarship. He competed at Doane in track and field and still looks like the athlete he was then.

When he finished college with a B.A. in psychology and sociology, he had intended to return to Panama or to settle somewhere in the Caribbean Islands; his extended family (his father was one of seventeen children) was scattered across the Caribbean, mostly in Jamaica. He decided, however, that before leaving he should get some work experience in the United States. As an undergraduate studying sociology, he had visited the state penitentiary in Lincoln with his professor and class. The experience reminded him of a time when he was growing up in the Canal Zone and lived near a small correctional facility. Watching the goings-on there had sparked an early interest in corrections. He ended up working at the state penitentiary as a counselor, beginning in July 1974. Over the next fifteen years he held a dozen positions in the Nebraska system before becoming director of corrections in August 1990.

It was in the early years of his tenure as director of the Nebraska Department of Corrections that Clarke's vision of the future of corrections came together. His first insight came during a Future Search Conference in Nebraska that was organized with the help of NIC.[27] Clarke remembers very clearly one afternoon at the conference when his group was asked to envision the ideal future for the department. He recalled, "I thought about corrections benefiting the community as a whole by making those entrusted to our care better people as they left. So I came up with the idea of healing. I was envisioning a clean and pristine place when thinking of the institution—a place wherein people could go into and everybody understood their role and understands their mission and they are able to work in a clinical manner almost with the offenders to make those persons better—get rid of all their baggage and get them back out there." Clarke said with a laugh that when he shared this vision with the others in the group, one of his wardens was "looking at me kinda like 'What? What's he talking about?'" Despite the initial reaction, which was much like the one I had when I first heard of the idea almost six years later, the idea became one of the vision points that came out of that Future Search Conference in Nebraska. When the Virginia project began, a Future Search Conference was one of the first steps taken.

The next step in the development of Clarke's thinking came when he was introduced to Dialogue. He was invited to join a team of executive leaders from the Royal Dutch Shell Corporation for a weeklong training course in Woodlands, Texas. While he was there, it became clear to him that Dialogue could be the vehicle for achieving his vision of a healing environment in corrections. Clarke told me that he saw Dialogue as "the best approach that I knew to engage others, to explore the concept or the idea of a healing environment, just using dialoguing skills to appeal to the intellect of individuals and to sit down and to exchange and to work this idea of changing environments to its finest points, trying to equate the benefits of the healing environment to our mission which is to ultimately create lasting public safety."

Clarke was both impressed with his first experience with Dialogue and surprised to learn from Peter Garrett, one of the facilitators, that it was already being used in prisons. He decided that he and his staff should receive more training and eventually sent all of his executive team and wardens to a three-day training program called "The Art of Thinking Together" taught by Garrett and William Isaacs in Maine. Clarke himself undertook an extended course of developmental sessions in Dialogue, called "Leadership in Collective Intelligence," making bimonthly trips to Maine over a nine-month period.

When I first learned, late in 2010, that Clarke was going to Virginia, I called him to find out if he was still interested in the healing environment idea. Not only was he interested, but he told me his purpose in going to Virginia was to implement the approach there. Clarke immediately accepted an offer to form a partnership with NIC to provide financial and technical support for the initiative. Beginning two years before Clarke arrived, Virginia had undertaken the Adult Reentry Initiative, an ambitious effort to transform the way Virginia corrections helps people coming out of prisons to return to their families and communities.[28] As part of the initiative, the Department of Corrections implemented improved practices in such areas as the development of individualized case plans based on a standard assessment and evidence-based programs to prepare people for their transition to and stabilization in the community. Clarke planned to apply the experience he had gained during his tenure as director in three other states, Nebraska, Washington State, and Massachusetts, to his new position in order to help Virginia build on the work it had already begun.

To bring Dialogue to Virginia, Clarke turned again to two people with whom he already had worked. They were Peter Garrett and Jane Ball, Garrett's business partner. Garrett and Ball had long been active in working in prisons and in the private sector as consultants through their company, Dialogue Associates, and also a not-for-profit charity, Prison Dialogue, both based in the United Kingdom.[29] In Virginia, they worked with the whole department by coaching executive staff members, training the extended leadership team, and advising on implementation and support of Dialogue practices. They also worked to build internal capacity through their Dialogue Practitioner Program, training in the first two years of the project more than eighty staff members, who in turn trained others and provided local support for the project.

Evaluation of the Virginia Initiative

In addition to funding a new Future Search Conference, assistance in strategic planning, and leadership training, NIC also funded an evaluation of the project in Virginia. Led by Dr. Shelli Rossman and Dr. Janeen Buck Wilson of the Urban Institute in Washington, D.C., the evaluators repeatedly surveyed the staff of the Department of Corrections, once every year, to assess the impact of Clarke's Healing Environment Initiative on staff perceptions and attitudes. In addition to the Urban Institute's survey, I conducted a confidential survey of all wardens, superintendents, and community corrections district chiefs in early 2014, and I also received data from the department's Research and Management Services Unit and reviewed reports from its Research and Forecast Unit.

I review the preliminary findings from these sources in more detail in chapter 7, but overall they are very encouraging. According to the survey I conducted of wardens, superintendents, and community corrections district chiefs, the initiative enjoyed strong support. Nearly nine out of ten said that the Healing Environment Initiative had produced benefits for their facility or office. They also reported that they had seen changes in attitude and behavior among the mangers and staff in their unit as a result of the initiative. A sizable majority of these leaders also said that they had seen changes in the attitudes and even the behavior of inmates and among people under community supervision. They also reported that there was substantial support for and a high level of participation in the Healing Environment Initiative by their staff. In the Urban Institute's survey of staff, they found a high level of both knowledge of and support for the Healing Environment Initiative, which increased from the first wave, in 2012, to the second wave, in 2013. For example, 88 percent of second-wave respondents agreed or strongly agreed with the statement "I believe in the value of the Healing Environment initiative," compared with 77 percent in the first wave.

There is also evidence from the performance data available from the department that the system as a whole benefited from the initiative.[30] For example, the total number of institutional charges for infractions of facility rules by inmates fell from 2010 to 2012. There had been four serious assaults on staff in 2010 and six in 2011, but only three in 2012 and none in 2013. There also had been one or two escapes each year in 2008–2011, but there were none in 2012 or 2013. It wasn't just that inmates were doing better. There were fewer on-the-job injuries reported, and the total number and rate of disciplinary actions against staff declined steadily over the 2010–2013 period. And all of these results, it appears, ultimately sprang from the insights of David Bohm into the power of genuine dialogue between people.

David Bohm and Dialogue

In chapter 6, I review how Bohm's vision of Dialogue got translated by Garrett into a way to work with organizations, including many prisons. Bohm's own interest was in how the way people think about things usually creates a fragmented understanding of the world around them and leads them to see boundaries that are of their own making.[31] Bohm's solution to the problem of fragmentation is to use Dialogue. He said, "Dialogue is really aimed at going into the whole thought process and changing the way the thought process occurs collectively. We haven't really paid much attention to thought as a process. We have *engaged* in thoughts, but we have only paid attention to the content, not the process . . . If we ran machines without paying attention to them, they would break down" (emphasis in original).[32]

This insight applies equally to organizations. We have to be engaged with what is happening in them and pay attention to the way they run as a whole from one minute to the next. During a panel discussion in 1979, the moderator pressed Bohm by asking, "If you have coherence, what would be different?" Bohm replied, "Well, we will produce the result we intend, rather than the results we don't intend, that will be the first big change . . . the major source of unhappiness is that we are incoherent and are producing results we don't really want."[33] Later, Bohm wrote, "It is a matter of culture. In the overall culture there are a vast number of opinions and assumptions which help make up that culture. And there are also subcultures that are somewhat different from one another," and when people from different subcultures try to communicate, "they may not realize it, but they have some tendency to defend assumptions and opinion reactively . . . And we are often *unconsciously* defending our opinions."[34]

David Bohm's life was a remarkable journey from humble beginnings in the working-class, coal-mining town of Wilkes-Barre, Pennsylvania, to international renown as a physicist and professor at the University of London.[35]

Born in 1917, he was the son of a used-furniture dealer, and grew up living above his father's store. The Bohms were one of only a few Jewish families in a neighborhood of Polish miners and their families, who were the main customers of the furniture business. By the time he was ten years old, Bohm was already developing a fascination with science that was fueled by a steady diet of popular science fiction magazines. He went on to Pennsylvania State College, where he followed his deepening interest in quantum and sub-atomic physics. From there, he went to the University of California at Berkeley, worked at the Lawrence Radiation Laboratory, and earned a doctorate in 1943. While he was in California, he studied with J. Robert Oppenheimer and worked on some aspects of the Manhattan Project, which was responsible for building the first atomic bomb. He also dabbled in leftist politics. In 1947 he became an assistant professor at Princeton University, where he continued the research in physics that established his reputation as a scientist and innovative theorist.

In 1951, Bohm wrote what would become a classic textbook on quantum theory, in which he laid out the Copenhagen interpretation of quantum physics that had been developed in the 1920s.[36] He gave a copy of the book to Albert Einstein, who was also at Princeton, and began an extended series of conversations with him. Einstein was very enthusiastic about Bohm's work, but both men were already questioning the orthodoxy of quantum theory. Bohm began to articulate what later came to be called the "causal interpretation of quantum theory," on which he worked for the rest of his life.[37] His views were at first dismissed or sometimes met with hostility, but in later years his work was reassessed and is now treated more seriously.

Part of the problem with the early acceptance of Bohm's theories was that he had come to the attention of the u.s. House Un-American Activities Committee. The committee was searching for hidden Communists, who they thought had given Russia the "secret formula" for building their own bomb. When Bohm would not testify against his colleagues and associates, his academic career in the United States was destroyed. Princeton refused to renew his contract, and he was unable to get a job at any American college. He finally found one in Brazil; from there he moved to Israel, and then to Britain in 1957. He worked first at Bristol University and later became a professor of theoretical physics at Birkbeck College at the University of London, where he continued to work until the day of his death. By all accounts, Bohm was a socially awkward but remarkably generous and kindhearted soul. He was described by colleagues and students alike as unselfish, generous, open-minded, and passionately devoted to the search for knowledge. One of his former students said, "He can only be characterized as a secular saint."[38]

Theories similar to Bohm's analysis of how our own thinking can cause us problems have been proposed by others.[39] But what is unusual is how Dialogue has been used and how its practices and principles were developed after Bohm died. Through a happenstance of history, the development of Dialogue was strongly influenced by its use in prisons. In the late 1980s Bohm actively promoted Dialogue in the United Kingdom as an approach to addressing social problems.[40] Peter Garrett, a businessman with an interest in improving communication, invited Bohm to one of his seminars. Garrett was so impressed by Bohm's talk on fragmentation and Dialogue that he developed a close association with him.

Bohm and Garrett continued to meet over an eight-year period, until Bohm's death in 1992. During this time Garrett organized a series of private Dialogues in England, Israel, Norway, Sweden, and Switzerland. In 1991, Garrett coauthored a paper with Bohm and Donald Factor titled "Dialogue: A Proposal."[41] As an indirect result of that article, Garrett was invited by Dave Parsons, a probation officer, to help start a Dialogue group in Whitemore Prison, a high- and maximum-security facility in Cambridgeshire, the United Kingdom, in 1993.[42] While Parsons later left, Garrett went on to run weekly Dialogue groups for seven more years.

While Garrett was working in prisons, he met Peter Senge, who had established the Center for Organizational Learning at the Massachusetts Institute of Technology, which ran the MIT Dialogue Project (Senge included a version of Dialogue in his best-selling book *The Fifth Discipline*).[43] The principles and practices of Dialogue were developed and refined as Garrett worked with others associated with the project, most notably William Isaacs, an MIT lecturer. As the approach was being tried out with corporate clients, Garrett tested the ideas against what he was learning from the use of Dialogue with staff and inmates in correctional facilities.[44] The result was a system of practices and principles that worked in both settings. Garrett, later joined by Jane Ball, continued to work in prisons in the United Kingdom as well as in the United States with Harold Clarke.

Dialogue and Fragmentation

Like a smashed watch, organizations become dysfunctional in the sense that the goals of the system are not served by the unified functioning of its parts. In a smashed organization, even conversation is difficult, because the people involved often do not have a shared understanding of what they are supposed to be doing together. Even the words they use are interpreted differently. Too often, when we tell people what we think works, we have fallen into the box of telling them what we think they should want. A good sign that a debate is going nowhere is that we start telling each other we need to think outside the box—again.

My experience has been that whenever you try to think outside the box, you end up mostly thinking about the box. What we really need to do is to think *inside* the box, to unpack it as if it were a never-ending series of nested boxes. Whether you call the box a mental model, a paradigm, or the culture, the point should not be thinking inside or outside of it; it should be to forget the box altogether. We can do this by dismantling the tacit understandings and meanings that keep the box in place.

This is what Dialogue does. It helps people unpack the boxes of their own culture and discover together what it is that they share and what holds them together. A basic premise of Dialogue as it was developed by Garrett is that everyone, at least potentially, wants to be constructively engaged, can act intelligently, and will do so ethically. If that is not the case, there must be a reason for it that can be understood and addressed through a process of inquiry. This is not our usual approach. Usually we debate the issues in an effort to convince each other that we are right and that others are confused, willfully fail to understand the obvious, or are just wrong.

If our organizations are fragmented, we adapt to that reality. Under these circumstances, everything seems too hard. Our aspirations shrink and we focus on simpler plans with more immediate results rather than on more complex, long-range efforts. Our goal becomes dealing with the current crisis, and anything beyond that seems like too much effort to waste on too uncertain an outcome. We are exhausted, frustrated, and tired of being tired of it all. Because what we do and what we get back are psychologically and emotional disconnected from us, we rob Peter today even though we know we will have to pay Paul later. At work, our goal becomes to do our own job in our own unit and measure our own performance against our own past. The effects of what we do on the larger mission of the organization and its contribution to the world are not meaningful to us because they seem so distant from our actions.

In Virginia, the Council for the Healing Environment was created to promote understanding, coordination, and communication and to lend energy to the creation and implementation of a healing environment. The council developed this description of a healing environment: "The Healing Environment is purposefully created by the way we work together and treat each other, encouraging all to use their initiative to make positive, progressive changes to improve lives. It is safe, respectful, and ethical—where people are both supported and challenged to be accountable for their actions." While the text may bear the imprint of a committee-written document, the council members clearly recognized that the Virginia Department of Corrections was able to create a new environment because of its success in maintaining a safe and secure workplace.

During the course of my work with Harold Clarke, Peter Garrett, and Jane Ball, I was introduced to the practices and principles of Dialogue. During the first two years of the partnership with Virginia, I took part in Dialogue training several times with different groups of executive staff, unit heads, and other staff seeking to become trainers and resource people for problem solving. My involvement in the project led me to study Bohm's work and his analysis of the way things can go wrong when we try to understand our physical and social environment and to work together for a common goal.

Implementation

In chapter 7, I describe how change in the Virginia correctional system was implemented through Dialogue and how the same process can be applied elsewhere. In an age of evidence-based practice, implementation itself has developed into an evidence-based process. Dean Fixsen and his colleagues at the National Implementation Research Network have led the way in synthesizing the existing knowledge on implementation. In their view, implementation is the art and science of incorporating into the routine practice of an organization an innovative policy, practice, or program. They write, "According to this definition, implementation processes are purposeful and are described in sufficient detail such that an independent observer can detect the presence and strength of the 'specific set of activities' related to implementation."[45] Cameron and Quinn also proposed a six-step process for change that is essentially an expansion of the first step of the Fixsen model. The implementation process they describe focuses on developing a shared agreement among key staff members about what the organization's current culture is and what the future culture should look like. They stress that this process be inclusive and that all of the important subgroups within the organization that are essential to success be involved.

The problem with step-by-step, linear implementation approaches, however, is that they usually do not work. Simply moving from one step to the next often means that as new challenges appear, as they always do, it is already too late to easily go back and fix what should have been dealt with earlier. Over the years, Garrett and Ball have developed a model for adaptive change in organizations that they call the "Implicate Change Model." The model and its application are examined in greater detail in chapter 7.

Garrett and Ball contrast their model with the more typical experience of organizations trying to change. In the usual sequence, a new leader announces a reorganization, the new approach is rolled out, people pretend to go along while they decide whether they like it, questions and complaints start to take the wind out of the sails, various forms of resistance result in delays, leaders push harder to get cooperation, and people begin to question if the whole thing is worth it. At this point, with the change process stalled, a new leader is appointed. This is essentially what happened repeatedly when the NIC Culture Project attempted to facilitate cultural change.

It is not what happened in Virginia. With Harold Clarke and his senior staff leading the effort, the Virginia Department of Corrections was able to incorporate the practices and principles of Dialogue. They did it with the help of Garrett and Ball, who demonstrated how their Implicate Change Model could be taken to scale in a large department of corrections. In chapter 7, I review in detail how they did it.

In the end, however, whatever success Virginia has had in creating a healing environment, it is only one jurisdiction. It may be able to demonstrate that the approach can work there, but the sort of transformation I hope its example will spark will depend on others believing that it can work elsewhere. For that to happen, we need a national dialogue about what we think we are doing when we punish people and how, as a society, we can do something different. But this requires Dialogue, not an endless stream of reports, speeches, or more initiatives. In chapter 8, I return to these issues when I discuss the future of imprisonment. And the question remains: How many tragic ironies are too many?

CHAPTER TWO

The Big Squeeze in American Corrections

Abraham Lincoln, in his famous "house divided" speech, said, "If we could know *where* we are, and *whither* we are tending, we could then better judge *what* to do, and *how* to do it."[1] My experience working with corrections leaders and organizations has convinced me that the profession needs to understand and honestly acknowledge exactly what we have done and are doing before we can know how we could do better in the future. It is the "where we are" and especially the "whither we are going" that lead me to believe that we ought to transform the culture of corrections from the inside out, not wait for external forces to change it from the outside in. The phrase "the new normal" has gained currency in recent years to describe many things, among them the state of corrections and corrections budgets. Aside from the fact that the phrase has rapidly become more annoying than informative, the "new" normal is not so new. A more accurate description of the recent state of corrections is "the big squeeze."

The big squeeze is the experience of being up a creek at the same time you are between a rock and a hard place. It is something like being stuck in a narrow canyon and trying to paddle upstream against high water. Ongoing prison population pressures, a product of the changes in sentencing policies and practices that began in the 1970s, push us back. On the one side is the rock in the form of continuing budget constraints on corrections that have been a constant feature of the landscape for several years. And the hard place is the fact that, on issues of crime and justice, America remains a house divided. It, too, is fragmented, with many competing actors working at cross-purposes. The continuing cultural gridlock and polarized political environment at all levels of government have blocked, watered down, derailed, or blunted nearly every effort to institute meaningful changes in the basic structure of our justice policy and practice.

This has played out in the recent history of corrections through three broad, long-range trends that have interacted with one another in complex and confounding ways.[2] The first trend has to do with crime rates, which began to rise in the 1960s, then started to fall dramatically after the mid-1990s, and have continued to fall. The second trend is the trajectory of incarceration rates, which began to rise in the early 1970s and continued to rise until very recently. The last trend concerns money. Economic booms and busts have driven revenues at all levels of government, with some unexpected effects on corrections spending. A robust economy in the 1980s and 1990s made increased spending on corrections possible, but since 2001 state and local government expenditures on corrections have fluctuated. The 2008 recession produced short-term effects (and may have altered the longer-range fiscal prospects of state and local governments) but did not have much effect on incarceration.[3]

The surprising thing about trends in national incarceration rates is that they have changed very little in the past fifteen years, despite the fact that crime is down and most state budgets have been on an economic roller coaster. Each time a recession produces a budget crunch, observers of the system argue, or at least hope, that it is "not sustainable" due to the huge direct and indirect social and financial costs. Two waves of economic recession, however, have demonstrated that most states can and will find a way to sustain their corrections systems even if deep cuts are required in other areas. The resiliency of the incarceration rate, even under historically severe economic conditions, speaks volumes about how the system as a whole has come to operate.

The sentenced state prison incarceration rate, the rate per 100,000 of sentenced prisoners under state jurisdiction, for example, has shown three distinct phases in recent history.[4] For several decades, it remained more or less stable, at around 110 prisoners per 100,000 in the u.s. population. In the mid-1970s it rose for the first time above 120 per 100,000 and continued to rise to a peak of 506 per 100,000 in 2007. In the past few years, the rate of growth in the sentenced state incarceration rate began to slow, and by the end of 2012, when there were more than 1.5 million prisoners, the rate had declined to 480 per 100,000 in the population.[5]

Keep in mind that the statistical incarceration *rate* (which is based on the total number of people in the general population) can be flat even when the total *number* of people being incarcerated is still growing. For example, in 2008 the incarceration rate was 506 per 100,000 and the number of prisoners was 1,547,742. In 2009 the rate had fallen to 504 per 100,000, but the number of prisoners was up, to 1,553,547. By the end of 2012, there were 1,571,013 prisoners, but the rate was 480 per 100,000. And by the end of 2013, the rate had dropped to 478 per 100,000 even though there were 4,300 *more* sentenced inmates in prisons than twelve months earlier. For a declining rate to lead to a declining prison population, it must drop faster than the general population grows. This is another part of the big squeeze. Even when incarceration rates are flat, total prison populations can still increase.

One fact many people find surprising is that crime rates and incarceration rates have not closely paralleled one another and recently have gone their separate ways. While the incarceration rate began to rise from the 1970s on, crime rates in the United States had begun to go up more than ten years earlier.[6] For example, the rate of violent crime in 1960 was 160.9 crimes per 100,000 in the population. It peaked in 1994 at 713.6. Like the rates for other types of crime, however, the violent crime rate has fallen since the mid-1990s; in 2012 it was 386.9, about what it had been in the early 1970s. How and why the u.s. crime rate fell has been a subject of much debate, but no clear explanation has been generally accepted.[7] How and why the crime rate, but not the incarceration rate, could fall has received less scholarly attention and is even less clear.

During the economic boom in the 1990s, corrections budgets benefited along with other government agencies from increasing revenues. In March 2000, the National Conference of State Legislators (NCSL) reported that "FY 1999 was the fifth straight year for excellent state finances." It also reported that every state had ended the year with a balanced budget and that more than two-thirds had reserve balances over 5 percent, the usual measure of a strong fiscal position. In 1999, general fund revenue grew 5.9 percent, and state general fund spending growth was 6.7 percent above 1998 levels.[8] Almost a year later, in January 2001, the NCSL wrote, "State finances continued to be remarkably healthy in FY 2000," when, for the sixth consecutive year, aggregate state general fund balances were over 5 percent of general fund spending, and "states are in their best financial condition in decades."[9]

By May 2002, the tone of the NCSL reports had changed: "The strong fiscal conditions of a year ago have been replaced by anemic revenue growth and expanding budget gaps." The NCSL reported that the first signs of an economic slowdown had become apparent by the fall of 2000 and that by February 2001 state revenue collections "were in a slide—the higher-than-expected revenue growth that had become almost routine turned painfully to lower-than-expected growth." According to the report, state officials initially thought the lackluster revenue performance might be short-lived, but "eventually, most officials conceded that the robust economy of recent years had ended." In fiscal year 2001, aggregate state balances fell 24 percent and nineteen states were already dealing with budget gaps.[10]

During fiscal years 2002 and 2003, the states' fiscal problems became more widespread and severe. The NCSL said of conditions in 2002, "By practically any measure, the states faced their worst financial conditions in a decade." As these problems wore on, states began taking measures to deal with them, and these actions were reflected in their financial health. As states tapped their reserves to close budget gaps, their year-end balances fell, dropping 28 percent from 2002 to 2003. The number of states with reserve balances above 5 percent fell significantly. Only nine states ended FY 2003 with a balance above 5 percent, compared with twenty-eight states in 2002.

By 2004, however, the fiscal conditions of states started to improve. Federal assistance and higher tax revenues led to a 55 percent increase from 2003 to 2004 in year-end balances. The fiscal health of states continued to improve after 2004. No state ended fiscal year 2005 with a deficit (although Arkansas and Michigan ended with zero balances). According to the NCSL, "The state fiscal recovery that began late in FY 2005 grew stronger in FY 2006. Robust revenue growth that vastly exceeded projections boosted year-end balances and supported spending above originally budgeted levels," and "State fiscal conditions were solid in FY 2007."

During these years, as crime rates were falling and incarceration rates were continuing to move up, state correctional expenditures did not keep up.[11] After the period of rapid growth during the 1990s, state expenditures on corrections slowed during the recession in the early 2000s.[12] In 2000, total state expenditures on corrections were $36.1 billion. Expenditures flattened in 2001–2003, but they began to rise by 2004 and reached $52.3 billion by 2009, only to fall again in 2010. By 2012 funding on corrections was beginning to rebound. The trend actually looks better than it was, since these numbers represent growth in the nominal amounts for each year, not real growth. In constant dollars, the corrections expenditures appear to have risen steadily after 2002, but in real dollars they actually declined by 2 percent from 2002 to 2007.[13]

This is one part of the big squeeze. The effects of the recession that began in 2008 came after an eight-year period of budget upheavals going back to early 2001. Many states and localities, in fact, never fully recovered from the last big recession. Cost cutting and cost containment were therefore an on-going theme throughout those years, and most of what could be done had already been done when the recession of 2008 rolled over state and local budgets. (One state senator complained, "All the low-hanging fruit has been eaten" when faced with the few options still available after more than a decade of austerity budgets.) But even these four years of relative prosperity after the distress of the 2000–2003 period ended abruptly with the onset of a new and more severe recession in late 2007.

State fiscal conditions began deteriorating in fiscal year 2008, in stark contrast to the outlook only a year before. Not every state experienced the immediate impact, but it quickly became clear that the effects on the state's fiscal health would be substantial. In April 2009, the NCSL wrote, "We now know that the nation entered a recession in December 2007 . . . Although the full brunt of the recession was not immediately obvious, evidence of an economic downturn was present: Aggregate balances continued to decline from their high point in FY 2006; revenue growth was sluggish; and nearly half the states faced mid-year budget gaps."

Despite all of this, it appears that the level of corrections spending in many states is locked in. By late 2013, the National Association of State Budget Officers reported that state spending on corrections in fiscal year 2012 had been $52.4 billion.[14] The association noted that corrections spending had risen steadily over the past three decades, outpacing growth in total state budgets. This had caused states to "direct more resources for prisons and incarceration, sometimes at the expense of other priorities. Corrections now comprises a larger share of general fund budgets than it did in prior decades" and represented more than 7 percent of general fund expenditures since 2008. The report acknowledged that policy makers had expanded programs to reduce recidivism, provided more alternatives to incarceration, and increased drug treatment programs, but that "state spending for corrections has yet to exhibit any meaningful slowdown in corrections and incarceration costs continue to rise." The state expenditures do not include the costs incurred by local governments for jails and juvenile facilities, which totaled another $26.6 billion in 2011.[15]

How We Got Here

The big squeeze is the product of a decades-long chain of events that began with the massive global wave of social, economic, and political changes that followed World War II and continues to this day. Each step in the process made some sense at the time and seemed both a reasonable and a necessary response to the pressing challenges that had arisen from the preceding step. Change means disorder, and the United States experienced its share of disorder, including rising rates of crime and violence as well as social and political unrest. The initial response, beginning in the mid-1970s, was an attempt to institute reform throughout the justice system, driven primarily by a justice model that stressed such values as consistency, transparency, proportionality, and accountability.[16] By the mid-1980s, as crime rates continued to rise, a reaction set in that was fueled as much by fear of what was happening to the country and a loss of faith in the ability of our institutions to cope with it as by the need to respond to the disorder itself. This helped produce the "tough on crime" era in sentencing that emphasized a more punitive approach.[17]

Before the punitive turn, there was an essentially uniform system of sentencing across all the states, in the District of Columbia, and at the federal level. This system had emerged during the Progressive Era in the years around World War I.[18] The approach is usually referred to as "indeterminate sentencing," but a more accurate term would be "discretionary sentencing," since its hallmark was the distribution of discretionary authority across several parts of the criminal justice system. Under discretionary sentencing systems, judges had broad latitude in setting sentences, corrections authorities could use good time as a basis for significantly shortening the time an inmate served, and parole boards could decide to release inmates or keep them in custody. The approach produced such a stable pattern over the years that many believed it was self-regulating in the sense that it adjusted for variations in the crime rate, allowing the system to respond to changes in the incarceration rate by exercising its discretion.[19] The system, then, was coherent, but it soon began to fragment.

The wave of sentencing reforms that got under way in the mid-1970s and accelerated through the 1980s and into the 1990s ended the discretionary system. The result was the fragmentation of sentencing, in which the state and federal governments adopted more structured sentencing, eliminated parole, and/or enacted mandatory minimums, truth-in-sentencing policies, "three-strikes" laws, or other habitual offender statutes.[20] By 1996, when crime rates peaked, states varied enormously from one another in their sentencing practices.[21] Looking back, we can understand what we did and see that it was the wrong response. When systems are under pressure they become fragmented, and when that happens there is very strong pressure to impose order, which actually increases fragmentation.

After the reforms, states ended up with different combinations of discretionary versus structured sentencing (and if structured, of different types: determinate, voluntary/advisory, or presumptive). They also differed in the way they carried out post-release supervision (whether or not parole had been "abolished"); what type of mandatory minimums they had, for whom, for which offenses; and, if they had a "strike" system, how many strikes and of what type. In the discussion about changes in the past three decades, sentencing, structured sentencing, mandatory sentences, and strike systems are often pointed to as the explanation for higher rates of incarceration. This is only partly true; most states in theory actually retained discretionary structures, but in practice much of the discretion drained out of them, as judicial decision making was limited, truth-in-sentencing constrained corrections officials, and the remaining parole boards became more conservative.

How and to what degree did these changes affect the state prison population? Alfred Blumstein of Carnegie-Mellon University and Allen Beck of the Bureau of Justice Statistics analyzed what drove the growth in the state prison population from 1980 to 1996.[22] It turns out that the growth in the crime rate and in the number of arrests per known offense accounted for only about 12 percent of the growth during that period. What really drove the growth was an increasing likelihood that judges would sentence people convicted of a crime to incarceration (half of the growth) and that these people would stay in prison longer (one-third the growth).

This same period, however, saw the war on drugs, and its effects have overshadowed underlying trends. So Blumstein and Beck also looked at the growth of the non-drug offender prison population. In their analysis, changes in the crime rate do not account for *any* of the increase in the non-drug offender population. For these offenses, including violence, the higher commitment rate has a lower effect on population growth, but the role of longer time served is much higher. The increases in the u.s. incarceration rate were, therefore, driven primarily by changes in the policies and practices of the criminal justice system, especially longer time served, not by changes in crime or arrest rates.

The current state of affairs has clearly not occurred overnight. It is something like waking up to find that the bathtub is overflowing because the faucet has been left running and a washcloth is stuck in the drain. A long list of sentencing laws and policy decisions over the years increased the flow into the American correctional system and reduced the rate at which people "drain out." In an overflowing tub, the key factors that regulate the level of water are how quickly water flows in (the position of the faucet handle) and the rate at which water drains out (whether or not the drain is obstructed). By analogy, the presence of forces that have increased the flow of people into the criminal justice system and those that have slowed their exit explains how and why so many people are in the system today. Beginning in the 1970s our society opened the faucet and stuffed a washcloth in the drain.

In 2008 Alfred Blumstein and James Wilson, then the Ronald Reagan Professor of Public Policy at Pepperdine University, weighed in on the issue of the impact of incarceration on crime.[23] Wilson was, as always, clear on his views. "Deterrence works, though not perfectly . . . What counts is whether among all would-be criminals (or all people) we find that bad behavior lessens as the costs rise and the benefits fall. They do." Wilson referred to the work by William Spelman, a University of Texas economist, and concluded that "the combined deterrence and incapacitation effect of prison alone is responsible for about 25 percent of the decline in crime."[24] Blumstein agreed, citing the same research and the same estimate, 25 percent. This seems a low bar to set for the effectiveness of imprisonment, and it is not even a direct measure of deterrence. Since the effects of specific deterrence and incapacitation (and rehabilitation and post-release supervision) cannot be separated empirically from general deterrence effects, all we are left with is the global influence of prisons. And there is still this question: If this is the full effect of imprisonment, what might account for the *other* 75 percent of the change in crime rates?

Crime is believed to arise from many things, but the fact is that corrections is only indirectly related to crime rates. Corrections does not control crime. What corrections *does* do is try to control known (or at least suspected) criminals. It gets involved only after a person has been arrested for a crime. The best available research and most scholars, including those who support deterrence, recognize that corrections has a marginal and indirect influence on crime. At the risk of being repetitive, I want to emphasize that, overall, incarceration (including incapacitation, specific deterrence, general deterrence, and rehabilitation, both during incarceration and under community supervision) accounts for about a quarter of changes in crime rates. You cannot raise or lower the crime rate simply by adjusting the incarceration rate up or down like you do the thermostat in your house.

None of this implies a resurrection of the "nothing works" school of thought. About half of the people who leave prison never come back. And that really means *never*; a person's risk of reoffending falls quickly to a baseline based on the person's age in a few years.[25] Many of those who do return are recommitted for violating the conditions of their post-release supervision (i.e., parole), like curfew violations or repeatedly missed appointments. Many are sent back for failing drug tests. We know that programs designed to reduce recidivism work when they are properly implemented and effective post-release support and programs are in place. But these effects are already baked into the cake of incarceration and community supervision and are part of the 25 percent impact on crime rates. Historical trends in recidivism and revocation rates have not changed as the medical model, "nothing works," and the return of rehabilitation and reentry have come and gone.

Being the Problem

Patricia Caruso, a former director of the Michigan Department of Corrections, sometimes tells people that her life mirrors the transition from the military-industrial complex to the prison-industrial complex. She moved to Michigan at age fourteen when her father was transferred to an air force base in the Upper Peninsula. Eventually, she worked in the same place, but by then a prison complex was standing where the base had been. Caruso worked her way up through the department, serving in a variety of roles, and was director for eight years, from 2003 to 2010. During her tenure as director, she made significant progress in changing the department's approach while at the same time reducing its prison population. If there is one point that Caruso is emphatic about, it is the need for corrections to "stop being the problem" and become part of the solution.[26]

Nearly all of the host of changes in sentencing laws, policies, and practices instituted in recent decades remain in force and continue to drive high incarceration rates through higher commitment rates and longer times served (both in prison and under community supervision). All of these reforms were designed to enhance the level of punishment, but in fact there is no evidence that enhancement did anything to reduce crime.[27] What it did do was drive a huge expansion of the criminal justice system's capacities. Once created, those greater capacities, from law enforcement, prosecution, the operation of the courts, and prison and jail beds, remained. When crime rates began to fall in the mid-1990s, the system's capacities allowed it to become self-sustaining and increasingly disconnected from external checks. The system now seems unable to save itself from itself.

This is what researcher Diana Gordon once called the "justice juggernaut," the self-perpetuating system that continues to arrest, prosecute, and incarcerate people in nearly the same number as it did when crime was much higher.[28] Although the number and rates of crime in the United States are a fraction of what they were fifteen years ago, the number of arrests is still about what it was a decade before. According to the FBI's Uniform Crime Reports, an estimated 12,408,899 people were arrested in 2011. In 2000, the estimated number of arrests was 13,985,979.[29] John Pfaff, a Fordham University law professor and researcher, has argued that most of the growth in prison population in recent years is traceable directly to prosecutors. He writes: "The criminal justice system is not a coherent 'system' of actors but a sprawling web of competing institutions: police, prosecutors, judges, legislators, governors, and parole boards, all of whom respond to different constituencies and have different incentives. It is thus important to ask which actors are driving prison populations upwards . . . data indicate that at least since 1994, prison growth has been driven primarily by prosecutors increasing the rate at which they file charges against arrestees."[30] Meanwhile, the total number of admissions to prisons in the United States went from 654,534 in 2000 to 609,800 in 2012.[31] The fragmented system is being maintained by the actions of myriad actors within the system itself, not by outside forces such as crime rates.

The Tippers versus the Wisers

Although the decline in the incarceration rate in recent years has been very modest, given the worst economic conditions since the Great Depression, many observers have hailed it as a turning point in the way the criminal justice system works, just as they did in the earlier recession. Even Norval Morris, a true professional skeptic of the system, found hope in the possibility that fiscal constraints would force states to reduce their use of incarceration. He wrote in 1995 that incarceration had become "the plaything of politics" and that "I shall not hazard a guess as to when our political masters will acknowledge that vote gathering by these mendacious means is a sin against the future . . . it is political irresponsibility that has generated the cancerous growth of imprisonment." Morris continued, "The one potential break in this depressing pattern is at the state level, where an increasing number of governors and legislators face daunting financial dilemmas . . . Perhaps the choice between schools and prisons will force a break in the political rhetoric favoring incarceration."[32] But it was not to be.

Those I call "Tippers," however, repeatedly argue that some recently observed change is clear evidence that, as Todd Clear, dean of the School of Criminal Justice at Rutgers University, wrote in 2013, we have arrived at the "beginning of the end of the great punishment experiment."[33] Others, however, are not so sure. They are the (Sadder-but-)Wisers, who have seen before what they hoped was the dawn of a new era, only to find that the new day was pretty much like the old ones.

Dr. Clear has a distinguished record of scholarship and engagement in national policy discussions and enjoys a well-deserved reputation among criminologists and policy makers alike. In a review of the dramatic changes in incarceration since the 1970s, he writes that "prison expansion happened as a consequence of intentional policy: over time, the cumulative effect of many sentencing reforms meant that the imprisonment rate of people convicted of felonies tripled and the time they served in prison doubled. By 2010, the number of prisoners in the United States had increased six-fold, and the incarceration rate had grown by 500 percent. No other democratic nation had anything approaching our numbers—it was a uniquely American social experiment in a penal policy centered on prisons."[34]

The use of the past tense was intentional, since Clear goes on to say, "But this is now changing . . . the last two years have seen a national *decline* in the number of prisoners—small, but after 38 years of unrelenting growth, remarkable. In fact, every sector of corrections is now losing numbers: probation and parole; jails; and prisons" (emphasis in original). (For the record, the total u.s. correctional population peaked at 7.3 million in 2007 and by the beginning of 2013 had dropped to 6.9 million.)[35] Clear allows that one of the reasons for this population decline is the fiscal crisis in the United States over the past few years. He goes on, however, to cite a long list of events that are among "the many bellwethers that the great prison experiment of the twentieth century may be slowly ending." Clear is not alone. Other writers and organizations active in the public policy debates on incarceration in this country routinely decry the past, but find recent proof that the beginning of the end has arrived.

Although the decline in the incarceration rate in recent years has been, as Clear notes, "small," many other observers hailed it as a turning point in the way the criminal justice system works. A decade ago, when the previous recession resulted in a depressed state prison population rate, they made the same claim.[36] More recently, the Vera Institute of Justice, a New York think tank, closely examined the apparent impact on correctional populations of the budget changes from 2006 to 2010.[37] According to Vera's report, "States have begun to reexamine their sentencing and correctional policies as a way to decrease prison costs immediately and over the long-term." Vera points to two broad strategies it says show promise: making more offenses eligible for "non-prison sentences or sanctions" and reducing the length of time people serve in prison. The goal is to reduce costs by shifting more people to supervision in the community, which is much cheaper than keeping them in custody.

But Vera also found relatively modest changes in a few states. Expenditures clearly dropped during the period, but there was no discernible relation between the size of the drop and the percent change in the sentenced prison population. Similarly, in two related reports Vera provided a long list of legislative changes that had occurred over the preceding decade, which, the Vera authors believed, showed that important changes were taking place in how states approached sentencing policies.[38] The Pew Charitable Trusts, another longtime skeptic of the u.s. level of incarceration, also lauded the decline. Pew noted, however, that states varied widely in their trends, with twenty-seven showing a drop but twenty-three reporting an increase.[39] The Sentencing Project, a Washington, D.C., advocacy group, issues a "Chopping Block" report that lists states that have closed, or are contemplating closing, institutions; in 2013 they identified only 11,370 prison beds (out of a prison population of nearly 1.6 million) that could potentially be eliminated.[40]

The Wisers Speak

Then there are the voices in these policy debates of the Wisers. Joan Petersilia, for example, gave a remarkably candid keynote speech at the June 2012 annual conference on criminal justice research sponsored by the National Institute of Justice, one of the main research funders in the U.S. Department of Justice.[41] Petersilia, a professor of law at Stanford University, prolific researcher and writer, and veteran of many efforts over the past thirty or more years to translate research into policy, had been deeply involved in the huge changes occurring in the state of California. In her speech, "Looking Back to See the Future of Prison Downsizing in America," she noted, "We have been here before." In the 1980s the intermediate sanctions movement tried to reduce incarceration and was built "on the backs of community-based alternatives that turned out not to work in the long run." The result was that "prison downsizing then fueled a resurgence . . . [of more imprisonment] . . . when the alternatives [were] found to be wanting."

Petersilia added, "After all, people said in those days, 'We have tried community sanctions and they haven't worked. We've given them their try and now our only choice is basically to build prisons.'" She admitted that she was not happy being the bearer of this message, saying, "It's funny for me to be now giving you a talk which is kind of a downer, which basically says, you know, we really need to rethink this. But it's the truth, and we've got to be honest about this." She went on to refer to the work of two other well-known researchers with policy credentials to match her own, Franklin Zimring and Michael Tonry, in giving several reasons that the task of reducing prison populations permanently might be even harder than in the past.[42]

The first reason she cited is that the sheer scale of imprisonment is so much larger than it was before. As Todd Clear pointed out, there are a lot more people in prisons today than there were thirty years ago. Petersilia said that the "power of the opposition at downsizing prisons will be incredibly huge . . . There are vested interests that, in fact, have now grown" and include unions and communities (with elected representatives) that want to keep prison jobs. The second reason is that the one big "easy fix" that existed before is gone; most states have eliminated parole board discretion, so they cannot simply lower the threshold for parole release. A third reason has to do with the surveillance technology industry. Things like GPS and electronic monitoring are made and marketed by people who have an interest in making sure their products are bought and used. Petersilia noted that surveillance strategies often compete with treatment, such as substance abuse programs and vocational education, for resources, and when they do, "I think surveillance wins." "We need to be honest," she said. "We don't have a lot of good solutions." Petersilia's last reason is about money: "It's going to all be about funding. It's going to all be about the money. This could not be happening at a worse time."

To be fair, I should note that Petersilia is not entirely pessimistic about current efforts and sees several factors that might contribute to success. She notes, "I think the science is much better than when we did this in the intermediate sanctions movement and certainly much better than in the 1970s. We have gotten better." She also believes that practitioners and researchers are in much closer alignment and are working together more. In addition, there are more stakeholders involved now than in the past, including law enforcement agencies, members of the judiciary, and prosecutors.

And while Petersilia sees promise in a greater focus on performance measures, she believes there is a danger in focusing too much on a simple-minded notion of recidivism as the penultimate measure of success. She says she is sometimes asked by policy makers, "Can you guarantee me if I go out on a limb and fund this program, recidivism rates will be reduced?" "I always look at them and say, 'Yes, I can guarantee it because by policy I can reduce your recidivism rates.' We just decided to revoke people under different things. We all know that game. That's just a shell game. Okay. Let's don't violate technical violations. I can get that down. Okay. Let's just decide we are going to let people fail three or four times and not violate them. I can get your arrest rates down. I can get a lot of things down. But have we really changed behavior? And so that's a much different thing." She concludes that, when talking about performance indicators, we need to be "putting more on the table than just recidivism. Because recidivism, as we all know, is a combination of the offender's behavior and agency discretion about what we're going to record."

Finally, Petersilia notes that some prisons at least are being closed and that once prison capacity has been reduced it will be difficult to increase it again. "We're not going to have prisons open at a level that is going to allow us to simply expand the prison population in the way that we did . . . to open up a prison, it takes 4 to 7 years, it's going to be just as hard once we close those prisons to open them up." She adds that public opinion has shifted. "The scale of the problem has now influenced public opinion at so many different levels . . . you know that commercial, . . . 'what goes on in Vegas stays in Vegas'? I think what we've showed the American public is that what goes on in criminal justice does not stay in criminal justice. It bleeds to communities." When intermediate sanctions were attempted, the public was "never with us. The public opinion was tough on crime when we tried to implement alternatives. And I think now for this period of time, we are going to see a much, much different end game." And this, ultimately, may be the key question that divides the Tippers from the Wisers: "This time, will there be a much different end game?" Todd Clear believes there will be, and Joan Petersilia (and I) hope he's right but fear it will be otherwise.

Justice Reinvestment

Another ongoing debate between the Tippers and Wisers is centered on an ambitious, nationwide initiative known as the Justice Reinvestment Initiative (or JRI), which is in many ways a direct descendant of the intermediate sanctions movement. JRI was begun in 2007 by the Justice Center, a part of the Council of State Governments, and was eventually funded by the Pew Charitable Trusts and later by the U.S. Department of Justice's Bureau of Justice Assistance. JRI actually starts with the logic of the big squeeze, although the phrase is not used. A 2013 report by the Council of State Governments noted, "Over the past 20 years, state spending on corrections has skyrocketed—from $12 billion in 1988 to more than $52 billion in 2011. Declining state revenues and other fiscal factors are putting a serious strain on many states' criminal justice systems, often putting concerns about the bottom line in competition with public safety."[43] But the report then shifted to classic Tipper language: "Strategies tested in numerous states and local jurisdictions, however, show that there are effective ways to address the challenge of containing rising corrections costs while also increasing public safety." According to the report, the initiative has been applied in seventeen states to "develop justice reinvestment strategies," and four of those states have recently adopted policies that are "projected to generate more than $1 billion in savings over five years."

The report lists six lessons that "have emerged from these experiences that inform the work of other states tackling rising corrections costs and public safety challenges." These lessons form the basis of JRI's six-step strategy. The first step is to analyze the available data from the jurisdiction to determine what is driving increases in correctional populations and costs. The second step is to engage a wide range of stakeholders in the process of defining the problem and suggesting solutions. The next step, which makes clear that the main thrust of the effort is controlling recidivism, is to use risk assessments in order to keep the focus of proposed policies and practices on people who are "most likely to reoffend." The next three steps include investing in "high-performing programs," strengthening community supervision, and "incentivizing performance." JRI has been among the most well financed and heavily promoted interventions at the level of criminal justice systems in recent memory. The Vera Institute and the Urban Institute, in Washington D.C., have shared the work and the funding of the Justice Center.[44]

The most careful recent attempt to assess the impact of JRI was made by researchers at the Urban Institute. Its 2014 report repeats many of the generally laudatory claims for the impact of the initiative on prison populations and corrections budgets. However, the remarks about the actual evidence supporting these claims are much more tentative. According to the report, "It is too early to assess the impact of justice reinvestment policies in a majority of JRI states, as many have only begun to implement JRI legislation. In eight states, at least one year has passed since JRI legislation has been in effect, enabling an early exploration of impact. These eight states—Arkansas, Hawaii, Kentucky, Louisiana, New Hampshire, North Carolina, Ohio, and South Carolina—are all still engaged in the implementation phase. None of the JRI states have reached the end of their projection years, so the full impact of JRI has yet to be realized . . . Comparing projected population changes and cost savings with actual population changes and cost savings is a delicate task. Multiple factors can affect prison population levels, such as changes in policy and practice outside JRI and changes in crime rates. These factors are difficult to foresee at the time a projection is created. One cannot attribute all population changes, or lack thereof, to JRI."[45]

In 2013, the American Civil Liberties Union (ACLU) issued a report, written by a who's who of researchers and advocates, that took exception to JRI as it was then being carried out.[46] These included James Austin, a well-regarded consultant, advocate, and researcher; Todd Clear of Rutgers University; Kara Dansky and Vanita Gupta of the ACLU; Marc Mauer and Nicole Porter of the Sentencing Project; Susan Tucker, former director of the After Prison Initiative at the Open Society Foundations; Eric Cadora of the Justice Mapping Center; Judith Greene of Justice Strategies; and Malcolm C. Young of Northwestern University Law School.

The authors reviewed the work done in connection with JRI in twenty-seven states over the span of a decade. They noted that under the initiative, eighteen states passed legislation designed to control correctional populations and contain costs. The authors, however, were at pains to draw a distinction between Justice Reinvestment as it was originally conceived and the Justice Reinvestment Initiative (a.k.a. JRI), which refers specifically to the program by the Council of State Governments with funding from the Pew Charitable Trusts and the U.S. Department of Justice's Bureau of Justice Assistance. They said that the latter had "played a major role in educating state legislators and public officials about the bloated and expensive correctional system, persuading them to undertake reforms not previously on the table. Considering the country's four-decade addiction to mass incarceration and harsh punishment, the general refusal to acknowledge its failures and the monumental resistance to change, JRI's most enduring contribution to date may be its having created a space and a mindset among state officials to seriously entertain the possibility of lowering prison populations . . . [our analysis] . . . leads us to the conclusion that while JRI has played a significant role in softening the ground and moving the dial on mass incarceration reform, it is not an unmitigated success story; the picture is complex and nuanced. The Justice Reinvestment Initiative, as it has come to operate, runs the danger of institutionalizing mass incarceration at current levels."

According to the ACLU report, the original intent of the Justice Reinvestment movement, as opposed to JRI, was to address the disproportionate impact of sentencing policies and incarceration on people of color and their communities.[47] The intent was to reduce the cost of corrections and use the savings for the "purpose of reinvesting in high incarceration communities to make them safer, stronger, more prosperous and equitable." The report said that, instead, JRI generally failed to reduce incarceration rates, focusing simply on controlling the rate of growth of the prison population and reprogramming any projected savings achieved in the form of avoided costs to balance general fund budgets or increase funding for law enforcement and community corrections. The report continued, "Some have argued that compromise necessitated by politics and the need to reach stakeholder consensus has meant that avoiding projected prison growth has become more feasible than achieving substantial reductions in actual prison populations . . . By focusing on state-level political and administrative policymakers, the JRI process has too often marginalized well-established local advocates and justice reformers who bring knowledge of local conditions and politics to the table, and who have a vested interest in providing long-term implementation oversight and ensuring sustainability of reforms. We believe this is an important moment to take stock of JRI, especially within the context of an unusually favorable climate to challenge mass incarceration, and assess how to get a more ambitious Justice Reinvestment movement back on track. We believe that a revived, reoriented Justice Reinvestment effort could significantly reduce U.S. corrections populations and costs; and through smart, targeted and locally determined reinvestments, could aid substantially in repairing the destructive impact of high levels of concentrated incarceration on poor communities of color. Achieving this goal will require meaningful, multi-year support for a range of coalitions and networks to pursue strategic goals consistent with the principles of Justice Reinvestment aimed at reducing admissions to corrections systems and lengths of stay, changing incentives for systems players, and reinvesting in public safety by strengthening community institutions. We are not naive to the challenges associated with long-term corrections reform, but we believe it would be irresponsible not to seize today's opportunity for change with a much more substantial impact in mind."

JRI in Oklahoma

One place where JRI did not turn out well was Oklahoma. From 2000 to 2010, Oklahoma's prison population grew by double digits and its spending on corrections increased by more than 40 percent. During the same ten-year period, the state's violent crime rate increased slightly, while nationally it dropped by 15 percent. This led Governor Mary Fallin, with the support of legislative leaders and judges, to propose a Justice Reinvestment Initiative project. With technical assistance provided by the Justice Center of the Council of State Governments and with funding from the Bureau of Justice Assistance and the Pew Center on the States, the project began in early 2011.[48]

First, state officials established a bipartisan, interagency working group that, with the help of the Justice Center, collected and analyzed data from across the criminal justice system to identify the drivers of Oklahoma's high incarceration rate. By the beginning of 2012, the working group had developed a set of recommendations, and in May, Oklahoma House Bill 3052 was signed into law by Governor Fallin. It required at least nine months of post-release supervision, created "halfway back" houses with substance abuse treatment for probationers and parolees who had violated the terms of their supervision, required that risk and needs assessments be done before sentencing for felonies, established a grant program for local law enforcement, and allowed judges to change sentences for up to two years post-conviction under certain conditions. Among the working group recommendations not included in the bill were modifications to drug offense sentences and changes in good-time calculations. A recommended program for establishing crisis stabilization centers to divert people with mental illnesses from the system was also not included but was later funded separately through the state's mental health department. After HB 3052 passed, an implementation working group was formed to help put in place the provisions of the bill. In February 2013, two years after the project started, Governor Fallin declined further funding for implementation, and the implementation group stopped meeting in March 2013.[49]

Following the unceremonious end of the Justice Reinvestment Initiative, various departments continued to work on implementing pieces of the bill on their own. Staff in seventeen counties were trained in conducting risk and needs assessments. The attorney general's office released a request for proposals and awarded grants in August 2013 to local law enforcement agencies. The Department of Corrections designated beds in some facilities for people whose community supervision had been revoked, but the beds were being used less than had been expected. The mandatory post-release supervision was included in only a small percentage of sentences. According to the 2014

Urban Institute report, "Although it is too early to assess the impact of HB 3052, preliminary discussions with Oklahoma stakeholders suggest that the utilization rate of JRI policies has been much lower than expected. Stakeholders believe more training and information sessions for key decision makers across the state are needed to fully implement HB 3052."[50]

Although not much actually happened in Oklahoma, the "projected savings" to the state was still being advertised in 2014 as one of the successes of JRI. The Justice Center's website notes the provisions of the 2012 Oklahoma bill, mentioning the state-funded grant program for local law enforcement agencies, the pre-sentence risk and needs screening process, the mandated post-release supervision, and the creation of "more cost-efficient and meaningful responses to supervision violations." It also says, "These policies mitigated the state's growth in prison population by 1,759 and are projected to save up to $120 million over 10 years."[51]

This claim was based on the original projections, in which the initiative's planners had assumed that the state's prison population would grow by 9 percent from 2013 to 2021 and that this would lead to a projected increase of $259 million in corrections spending. HB 3052 was supposed to reduce the prison population growth to only 2 percent, thus saving the state up to $120 million. According to the annual report of the Oklahoma Department of Corrections, however, the sentenced prison population increased 4 percent during the two years of JRI.[52] In 2011, there were 25,458 sentenced inmates in Oklahoma prisons. By 2013, there were 26,553.[53]

Justin Jones had already been director of the Oklahoma Department of Corrections for seven years when I began talking with him in 2012 about the fragmentation of the criminal justice system.[54] Jones had worked in corrections in Oklahoma for thirty-six years at that point, having begun as a parole officer shortly after graduating from college. He said that he stumbled into the work but quickly discovered that the field was a fascinating one. "The fact that you're dealing with humanity, whether you're religious or not, you'd have to agree that the human being is the most complex creature on earth . . . So when you incarcerate an individual or have them under supervision, you have a lot of responsibility." Jones, with obvious frustration, added, "You don't want to apply common sense to the criminal justice system when it comes to research. It will drive you insane. Research is not applicable because most sentences are based on anecdotal cases . . . We have a saying in my state: 'In

Oklahoma, everyone has the right to go to prison.' Oklahoma makes it very easy to go to prison. It is one of the few states were a person can be incarcerated in a state prison for a day or two on a nonviolent offense."

Jones has worked extensively with two of the ACLU report's authors, Todd Clear and James Austin, hiring each of them under various contracts "off and on for decades," and respects them both. But he said he must respectfully disagree with their thesis that JRI could be revitalized by involving more outside groups, especially advocacy and reform groups. Jones added that "the political environment is so charged and so polarized that if you look at their paper and if you look at them talking about the failure of Justice Reinvestment to engage these other organizations and groups, that's true." However, Jones also said that, on the basis of his experience in Oklahoma with JRI, an effort to engage those groups "would have been just dead on arrival." What he saw in Oklahoma and has seen with the initiatives around the county is that "every Justice Reinvestment process has been watered down through the political process from beginning to end . . . So what I would say is that . . . you need to cultivate these groups, get some type of systemic process in place, years before you ever come in and start trying to look at really applying science and data analysis to sentencing practices and things of that sort."

Jones said of the report's authors, "I think they underestimate the power of current and future politics, and I think they overestimate the ability of these other organizations, associations, and groups to have an impact unless you're willing to stay in a state for a decade . . . You really have to have a paradigm shift between cultures . . . So it's really a revolution by the people being affected by crime; it's that group speaking in unison that will make a change, as opposed to anybody coming in and allowing them to come to the table." That, however, would be "a metamorphosis that hasn't occurred yet." The bottom line, according to Jones, is that "what everybody is underestimating—*absolutely underestimating*—is the influence of not only private prisons, but the machine itself—all those collateral vendors and businesses, whether it's food service, medical services, canteen services, public safety equipment services. Everybody wants to be Wal-Mart, but they can't all be Wal-Mart." In other words (mine again), communities, too, need to be healed. They are also fragmented. And Dialogue may be just as useful in communities as it is in organizations seeking to create a different future.

The healing, when it comes, will have to reach into the politics of crime and justice. Max Williams served as director of the Oregon Department of Corrections for eight years before leaving in 2012 to become president of the Oregon Community Foundation.[55] He has one of the most unique professional backgrounds among his peers. Williams began his career practicing civil and commercial law and came to corrections via the Oregon legislature; he was elected to the Oregon House of Representatives three times. His work as chair of the House Judiciary Committee and legislation that he sponsored to encourage the use of evidence-based practice in the state eventually led to his appointment as Department of Corrections director. Williams has seen firsthand how even modest proposals can "crash on the rocks politically."[56] Asked how this happens, Williams said, "No one wants to look like they're soft on crime . . . the smart, no-risk-to-public-safety, cost-effective strategies still run the risk of having a campaign ad or mail piece that says, 'Bill Smith voted to let criminals out early' or 'reduced sentences for violent offenders' . . . I and others urge legislators to use data, and so on, but that doesn't overcome the fear of what might happen or how an opponent could use the issue." Still, he does not see the problem as partisanship with a capital "P" so much as it is the product of the mix of different interest groups, advocates, and the appeal to the public of "an anger- and punishment-based, retributive approach."

In such an environment, Williams said, the ability to rein in the system becomes especially difficult, because the different parts of the system tend to work to their existing capacity and under local authority. According to Williams, "In many states, including Oregon, there is a disconnect between the use of prison resources and the local decision making around it—choices by local law enforcement about who they're going to arrest, the district attorneys about who they're going to prosecute, and the judges on who they're going to sentence to prison versus who they're not going to sentence . . . All those decisions that drive the prison population in a state like mine are locally based decisions, out of a completely separate funding stream . . . they're not tied in any way to the costs of the things being done on the state level."

Williams gives the example of year-and-a-day sentences. A sentence of one year or less is usually served in the county jail (and paid for by the county). But a sentence of more than a year (even one day more) is served in state prison. Williams asks, "If I can push somebody into a prison bed and it's not going to cost me any money and it's not affecting county resources, why wouldn't I?" This is obviously the logic of a fragmented system. In this case, local officials are acting rationally, but only insofar as the immediate effects are local. The global impact on any larger system does not drive the decision. They know that, of course, but they have their own jobs to do, budgets to balance, and voters to serve.

Wither We Are Going?

Some readers may be surprised to learn that this chapter is not intended to discourage or depress you. Well, not too much anyway. I hope the Tippers are right and the social, economic, and fiscal stars are aligned in such a way that the trajectories of recent trends will be fundamentally altered. This is not that tall an order. James Austin has shown that even marginal changes in the rates of admission to and length of stay in u.s. prisons would produce large reductions in the prison population in just a few years.[57] Unfortunately, social scientists are particularly bad at making long-range predictions about such things, so hedging our bets might be prudent. And, as I've already argued, a smaller inmate population will not make the job of corrections professionals easier; it will make it harder. For corrections professionals, what matters has less to do with how many people are under correctional supervision than about the practical question of what to do with the ones we have.

The criminal justice system is caught in a self-perpetuating cycle that has become disconnected from our purported mission of public safety. Being at the end of the line in the system, corrections suffers the accumulated results of the system's dysfunctions. People in corrections think of themselves as being downstream in the flow of case processing and must supervise in a safe and secure manner the people sent into their care and custody. But what if corrections can reverse the flow of the stream on a cultural level?

I know the notion that changing correctional cultures by working with staff within correctional systems will spur a broader transformation might be seen by some as overly optimistic. I do not think so. One reason I believe this is that the entire criminal justice system and our society's view of crime and justice have already changed, dramatically, over the past thirty years. Is it so farfetched to expect that the pace of change could continue and that in the next thirty years the changes we experience will be just as dramatic? The system we have today arose within very recent history. The future will be different; it always is. I believe, however, that we should talk about what we are doing and how we are doing it more deeply than we did the last time.

Earlier, I used the analogy of being stuck in a narrow canyon and trying to paddle upstream against population pressures while being hemmed in by declining budgets on the one side and politics on the other. It seems to me that since going forward, backward, or to either side is proving so difficult, the only way to get out of this canyon is to climb *up*. The factors that continue to drive high incarceration rates and limit the effectiveness of corrections have their roots in the cultural functions and symbolism of punishment. Altering this dynamic, therefore, will require a change in the cultural orientation of the criminal justice system and ultimately in American society and culture as well. If political and legal institutions in the United States cannot accomplish this and if other parts of the criminal justice system seem reluctant to take up the challenge, why should not corrections try?

CHAPTER THREE

Cultural Styles

In the preceding chapters, I said that achieving the goal of healing corrections and thereby re-creating it as a healing profession will require transforming correctional cultures from the inside out. This sounds good, but it leaves un-answered the question of what a culture is, much less how it changes. I define culture as fundamentally about communication between people acting and reacting to each other as they live and work together; it is the whole network of interactions between and among the people participating in that culture. What we see, hear, and feel in a living culture are the expressions of this net-work of interactions. This approach to culture is rooted in the interactionalist perspective and has a long history.[1] The perspective assumes that cultures are a product of collective learning, are adaptive, and change in response to internal or external challenges or conflicts. It sees a culture as something people do together and that has its own style and tempo, much like a musical performance. Like a piece of music, a culture is both fluid and repetitive, con-stantly changing but with identifiable tempos, rhythms, and styles. Changing cultures is no easy task, because what you hear and see is only the surface, not the substance, of what makes cultures work.

Ultimately, cultures have the practical function of helping people survive and thrive in their physical or social environment. Cultures tell (or show) people how things are done by teaching them the roles and rules concern-ing what is expected of them and what they can expect of others. It is be-cause cultures are learned and taught that they are grounded in patterns of communication. People participating in a culture, whether they are at work or elsewhere, first learn and then maintain their culture as they collectively manage the challenges of daily life.

Out of this process a cultural framework emerges that finds its expres-sion in the distinctive style of a given culture. The world changes constantly, and a functioning culture adapts to new circumstances. Edgar Schein, a pi-oneer in the study of organizational culture, described culture as something that "was learned by a group as it solved its problems of external adaptation and internal integration, that has worked well enough to be considered valid and, therefore, to be taught to new members as the correct way you perceive, think, and feel in relation to those problems."[2] At any given point in time, organizations and their cultures are adapting or failing, growing or waning, surviving or dying. In the process, the level of coherence varies; sometimes cultures become more fragmented as things stop working and, in turn, more cohesive as they pull back together.

This chapter was difficult for me to write, and getting through it is going to be hard on you. The problem is that cultures are more easily done than said; we live in cultures by participating in them, not by writing (or reading) about them. People in a culture develop shared understandings as they experience living and working with each other.[3] Many of the most important understandings are intuitively felt rather than articulated, but we use language with all its symbols, ideas, and associations to talk about this shared experience. But as Bohm pointed out, because of the way our minds work we talk as though we were referring to things and ignore how they were created as social constructions.[4] To communicate with you about the processes of cultures, I talk about cultural things like roles, expectations, assumptions, values, beliefs, attitudes, and cultural styles. But you should keep in mind that they are all really expressions of underlying processes of interaction and communication that are constantly changing.

Bohm traced our difficulty in solving our practical, day-to-day problems to the way we think about them and our habit of analyzing the world around us by dissecting it. "The thing we use to solve our problems is the thing that causes our problems . . . thought is breaking things up into bits that shouldn't be broken up." Bohm went on to say, "What we are doing is establishing boundaries where there is really a close connection, that's what's wrong with fragmentation . . . we experience these things as different because we think they are different." He related fragmentation to incoherence and said that a major sign of incoherence is when "you want to do something but it doesn't come out that way . . . that's a sign you have wrong information somewhere." He contrasted simple incoherence with sustained incoherence, when we persist in a situation where our conscious intention does not produce the intended result.[5]

This is important because the reason most organizations fail when they try to bring about cultural change is that they forget this and focus too much on things (like our assumptions, values, beliefs, norms, paradigms, and mental models). Most writers who prescribe the change-the-culture cure skip over this problem of describing cultures. Instead, they offer a quick definition that usually refers to things shared by the people belonging to an organization or group. This is not helpful because we do not have any clearer notion of exactly what assumptions, beliefs, or attitudes are than we did of what a culture is. This has not stopped a great many people from talking a lot about culture and arguing that we can somehow change organizations' cultures by addressing false assumptions, distorted beliefs, and resistant attitudes, as though it were obvious what these things are and how they can be changed. The problem is that things do not change; the processes that create those things, when altered, produce different things.

An attitude, to give one example, is a complex cognitive construction that has been learned.[6] It is, first, an expression of feeling—you love (or like), are indifferent to, or hate (or dislike) something or someone. The object of your love or hate can be anything or anyone you have feelings for or against, including people (even yourself), things, places (like your workplace), events, activities (like your job), or ideas. Many attitudes are explicit; we know that we like or dislike something and we know why. I do not like sardines because I believe that I hate the way they taste. Or attitudes can be implicit. I may like an old sweater because it is a particular shade of green, and without my being aware of it, that color reminds me of the grass in Michigan during the summers when I was growing up (even now, I can feel the sun on my face and the warm buzz of a hot afternoon). You might be able to get me to change my attitude toward sardines by getting me to eat some, but how likely is it that you will be able to persuade me that I really do not like my old sweater and should stop wearing it? (Hint: Ask my wife; she knows.)

In the classic definition, attitudes have this feeling component, but they also have associated beliefs and behavioral components (not only do I dislike sardines, I also believe they are nasty little things and will not eat them). Attitudes serve a variety of functions for individuals.[7] Many are simple guides to making decisions or taking actions (no sardine sandwiches for me) and are usually explicit. Many are implicit and serve functions such as psychological comfort and defense or as expressions of self-image.[8] Changing an attitude, therefore, requires addressing the function it has for a person. If the attitude is both implicit and part of a person's identity, trying to persuade the person he or she wrong is equivalent to saying there is something wrong with the person. And trying to change an organization's culture by telling people there is something wrong with them is unlikely to work. This is why I consider it a very poor strategy to try to change a culture by trying to change the culture, if what you mean by culture is a set of values, beliefs, attitudes, and so on.

We usually do not spend much time examining how our attitudes (or our assumptions, values, beliefs, norms, paradigms, mental models, etc.) emerge out of the pattern of interactions within our own organizational culture. Generally, this is a good thing. Cultures exist to maintain an organization's functioning. They structure how people solve problems together, and under normal circumstances it is far more efficient to have all those involved understand and perform their expected roles without much fuss. When food services in a prison needs to feed more than a thousand people in three hours, that is not the best time to unpack the contents of our consciousness or debate the nature of cognitive constructions. If a fight starts in the dining hall, there is no time for reflection. A set of shared and accepted understandings allows us to both act quickly and understand what is happening because we know what to expect from others. Things feel right and what to do next seems obvious. Culture becomes habitual because we need to have habits of thought and action.

By way of illustration, Bohm occasionally referred to the philosopher Michael Polanyi's idea of tacit knowledge and the example of riding a bicycle. Polanyi pointed out that the physics of bicycle riding can be expressed precisely with mathematical formulas. Knowing these formulas is, however, of no use to you in actually riding a bike somewhere. Riding a bike is an entirely different kind of activity, involving balance, muscle control, and a well-functioning nervous system. About this distinction, Polanyi said, "We know more than we can tell."[9] Bohm concluded that "this may be regarded as a kind of implicate order which unfolds into an explicate order of the motion of the bicycle . . . In fact, without tacit knowledge ordinary knowledge would have no meaning . . . when we talk most of the meaning is implicit or tacit . . . the action which flows from it is implicit or tacit."[10] Once a person or organization has learned to do something reasonably well, there is not much reason to change it.

After all, if a way of doing things is working well enough, people are quite reasonably reluctant to open a new can of worms. When an effort to initiate change starts to encounter resistance, it is usually because some people feel uncomfortable about what is happening. They may simply not be convinced that it is in their own best interest. Often, they do not even know what is going on in the first place because they were not engaged in the planning. The planners, who may have been deeply engaged for a long time, can very easily assume that because "everyone" has been talking about it for a long time, everyone must know and understand the plan. But people do not learn by osmosis; they have to be engaged in a process. Sending them emails does not count, nor does a PowerPoint presentation at a staff recall.

There are also many implicit attitudes that we do not want to talk about simply because they are unflattering. For example, the idea that an organization is at the mercy of outside forces and has little control over its own future is something we sometimes believe but seldom talk about. Orders from central office, for example, often seem to fall from the heavens and commonly reinforce the feeling that local management and staff are powerless. Other cultural beliefs, such as whether people can be trusted to do the right thing without being closely watched, whether they will always resist change, or whether they usually act selfishly rather than for the common good, concern human nature. To complicate matters, organizations often declare a set of *ideals* that flatly contradict the *reals* of daily behavior. An organization may have a values statement such as "We value open and honest communication throughout the agency," when the real value, as expressed in day-to-day behavior, may be closer to "We value telling others only as much as we have to." Ironically, moving toward the ideal in this case would actually require open and honest communication, not a values statement pretending the fact. The issue of communication, usually how poor it is, is a constant theme in the Prison Culture Project's reports.

One of the problems with fragmentation that is seldom discussed but is important to keep in mind is that the fragments of a system that have not been integrated into the working whole do not simply disappear of their own accord. Those fragments that do not fit in must somehow be dealt with; they have to go "somewhere." Usually they get buried, with a potent emotional charge attached to them. These suppressed thoughts or feelings take the form of the many elephants in the room that affect decision making as we ignore or minimize the voices of one or another group or when people pretend to be happy when they are actually seething with anger and suspicion, much to the befuddlement of management, which routinely misreads its staff members' states of mind. If our own mind is fragmented, such that there are ideas or feelings that do not fit in with the consistent structure we need to maintain, it will cause us problems. We may try to ignore them, but they will still have an unconscious influence on us. Very often they are projected onto something or someone. Organizations do the same thing. Projection takes place in an organization when one group blames another one for a problem that the whole organization has had a hand in creating or when the organization finds some external group, such as interfering headquarters, opportunistic politicians, exposé-seeking reporters, or crusading advocacy groups, to explain its failures. At every level, including correctional facilities or systems, the justice system, and legal and political cultures, fragmentation has been an ever-present influence.

Sometimes, fragmentation and the misunderstandings and mistrust it can generate become comical. At one prison visited by the Culture Project assessment team, a staff member told a story about a former warden. On a hot summer day, the story went, the warden, as a gesture of goodwill, went to a local supermarket, bought every bottle of water in stock, and distributed it to the staff. The staff, who did not like the warden, did not take the gesture as it was intended. They decided it meant there was something wrong with the prison's water supply. They in turn told this to the inmates, who refused to bathe or eat. When the warden found out what had happened, he became so upset he promised never to do anything like it again. It apparently did not occur to him to wonder why the staff assumed his act of generosity was really a cover-up.

Cultures in Action

Every organism, and every *organization* of organisms, must deal with two fundamental issues to survive within its environment. This is true for all organizations, whether formal or informal, public or private, temporary or permanent. An army has a culture and so does a bowling league. So does a multinational corporation, religion, or government department, including a department of corrections or probation and parole agency. First, each organization must first work out the value it will place on an internal focus to maintain its day-to-day processes, as opposed to the value it will place on an external focus to monitor and respond to its environment. Second, like a society or group, it has to choose how much it will value stability and control to maintain its identity and structure, as opposed to valuing flexibility and agility in order to adjust to changing demands. The choice people make determines how well they will succeed in whatever mission or purpose they have chosen or been assigned.

A culture in action is something like a symphonic performance. All of the instruments have a very specific sound, but out of their individual sounds emerge the characteristics and qualities of the music as a whole. The tempo of a composition is the speed at which it is played, and it often determines the mood of the piece. Tempo is usually indicated by an Italian term, because so many of the great composers in the seventeenth century (when tempo indications were introduced) were Italian. The second movement of Beethoven's Seventh Symphony has been a favorite of audiences since it premiered and is called *allegretto,* a reference to its tempo and meaning (in Italian, of course), "a little lively." Other tempos are *presto* and *allegro*, which both indicate faster playing (*presto* is faster, but *allegro* is supposed to sound more joyful). The terms can be mixed to indicate a more complex speed and mood. *Agitato* indicates "agitated," so an *allegro agitato* tempo would dictate a jumpy, faster way of playing the music. This is the tempo George Gershwin used for the last movement of his Concerto in F Major for piano and orchestra.

Beethoven and Gershwin were not seventeenth-century Italian composers. The musicians who play their compositions today are not seventeenth-century Italians. But they know what the terms *allegretto* and *allegro agitato* mean because they were trained in the classical music tradition. They know what tempo feels like because they played pieces with different tempos as they were initiated into the world of music. It is part of their culture. If a conductor in rehearsal shouts, "Make it more *allegro!*" the orchestra members know what that means. There is a world of difference between the pieces of Beethoven and Gershwin, but both are examples of musical styles. And everyone involved in performing their works knows that they are making music.

It may seem a bit poetic to say that organizational culture is like a musical performance, but the analogy is a good one. Just as a symphony is made up of the sounds of all the instruments, a culture is made up of the voices of all those participating in it. The tone and tempo of the interactions between people are part of what determines the style of a culture. To make this example more true to life, think about what it would mean if the orchestra members were playing without a conductor, by ear without sheet music. Depending on a musician's location, his or her perception of the performance would differ from that of the musicians in other sections. For example, a violinist in the string section would be too busy focusing on the violin part to pay full attention to what was going on elsewhere in the orchestra. In most organizations, which are fragmented, everyone is playing by ear all the time.

The characteristics of the music, like its tempo, emerge during the performance. They are in the ears of the performers and the audience. If we wanted to change the tempo of a song, we could not do so by trying to convince the tempo to change. We would have to persuade the musicians to change it. Organizations adopt their own tempo according to how quickly things happen. We see this when one organizational unit that has a can-do attitude encounters another that insists on a slower, more deliberative style of decision making. When the custody or program staff in a prison work with the support staff in human resources or the business office, for example, there is often friction that originates in the clash of differing tempos; "right now" means different things to different people.

None of the differing styles of doing things a particular organization adopts is necessarily wrong for that organization. Some organizations thrive in a competitive culture based on self-interest, while others survive in a culture based on a sense of duty and self-sacrifice. Which sort of culture the people in an organization adopt and keep over time depends on the purpose of the organization and how well its cultural framework works in achieving its goals.

The Layers of a Culture

Culture is layered. An individual violinist, the string section, and the orchestra coexist as parts of a whole, but conceptually they are separable for the purpose of thinking and talking. Schein, for example, identified three levels of organizational culture. The first level is what is seen in an organization—its formal structure and chain of command, the titles, policies, procedures, and its public image.[11] The second level is what an organization says, such as its stated mission and values, its codes of conduct, and even its name. The third level deals with tacit assumptions in the organization requiring in-depth analysis. Change is easier to bring about at the first two levels. Organizations often do a paper implementation by making changes such as renaming a program, adopting a new mission and values statement, or rewriting policies or procedures.[12] The majority of efforts to change organizations fail because they are limited to the first two levels of organizational culture; they never reach beyond the ideals to confront the realities. A more serious approach may focus on assumptions (or attitudes, values, etc.), but this still does not go deep enough to reach the patterns of interaction that are creating these cultural things in the first place.

Culture and cultural change are also about more than the climate of the organization or the staff's morale. The difference is often confused, in part, because the literature about climate or morale has not made the difference between them clear.[13] Climate and morale are more superficial and easier to change than culture. They are strongly influenced by temporary changes or random events. People in an organization may be unhappy or frustrated with how things are going at any one time, but that may not have anything to do with the fundamental organizational culture. Like other organizations, many prisons manage to run very well even though everybody seems to be mad, sad, or just lost. Since dysfunctional cultures usually breed poor organizational climates, however, a first step in cultural change is often to fix something particularly irritating or frustrating for staff. Still, it is unclear if an organization needs to have a positive climate to do cultural work or whether a negative one is more motivating.[14] The important point is that the organizational climate, whether positive or negative, can be improved far more easily than the culture can be changed.

I know of one case where the staff at an institution with a history of problems had a long-standing pet peeve about parking. At this facility, the parking area for visitors was paved and close to the front entrance. The staff parking lot was unpaved and farther away. Whenever it got wet, the staff parking lot got muddy, and this irritated the staff. This was especially true of those staffers who were not on the day shift and had to walk across the paved and empty visitor's lot in the dark to wade through the mud or snow to get to their cars. A new warden somehow contrived to get the staff parking lot paved, which won him much appreciation from the staff. Some years later, I did a cultural assessment at the same institution, and it still had many serious problems. But everyone remembered fondly the warden who had paved the parking lot.

The Push-Me / Pull-Me of Cultures

The push and pull that the different forces at work exert on the people participating in a culture's social space influence whether the cultural style will "move." The idea of forces of attraction and repulsion operating in a social space can be traced directly to Kurt Lewin, the modern founder of group dynamics.[15] According to Alfred Marrow, his biographer, Lewin "postulated a theory of psychological tensions in which tensions function as forms of energies . . . tensions arise when there is a need or want. It is their striving for discharge that supplies the energy for, and is consequently the cause of, all mental activity."[16] Lewin did not see these tensions as all bad; they also motivate people to achieve goals by bridging the gap between the ideals and the reals, to use my terminology. This way of looking at things allows us to visualize social spaces as something like physical spaces in which we can move around, getting closer or farther apart, moving toward different positions relative to each other, and adjusting to different conditions in the field. For example, think about how the members of a baseball team arrange themselves on the field, sometimes "playing back" (for a strong hitter) and other times "close in" (with runners on base and expecting a bunt).

Beethoven at the Ballpark

I will now bring back our orchestra, but I will get the musicians on their feet and let them move around. Say that a new artistic director has decided to bring classical music to the masses by giving a concert at the local baseball stadium. The plan is to play a selection from each of Beethoven's nine symphonies before each inning in the game. This will require the entire orchestra to assemble on the field, play a selection, and then leave, until all nine innings have been "played." (This is the kind of thing artistic directors are paid to dream up.) During rehearsals, the musicians arrange themselves around the infield, as shown in figure 3.1, both because it is closer to where they come onto the field through the dugouts and so the conductor can stand on the pitcher's mound. The exception is the percussion players, who will wait with

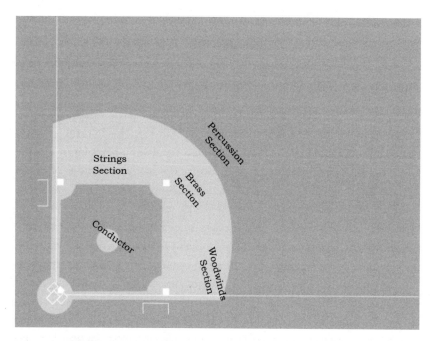

Strings
Section

Percussion
Section

Brass
Section

Conductor

Woodwinds
Section

FIGURE 3.1: The Orchestra in Rehearsals

their bulkier instruments in the pitcher's bullpen area between innings. Their position during rehearsals is on the grass in center field.

On the day of the concert/game, the orchestra members take their positions before each inning. As the game progresses, however, the day grows warmer and the sun casts a shadow across the infield. Increasingly hot and tired, the different sections start to shift to take advantage of the shade. They also cluster together to be closer to the conductor and hear each other better as the crowd gets louder. Except for the percussionists. Caught in the hot sun, they become less willing to haul their instruments all the way to the infield. Always a more independent lot, the percussionists start to take their position closer to the bullpen and farther from rest the musicians, who are now clustering around home plate. Finally, the conductor has to turn her back on the percussion section to lead the rest of the orchestra (figure 3.2). By the time of the famous opening cords of Beethoven's Ninth Symphony, the new artistic director has been fired.

The experience of feeling your unit has drifted into deep left field while

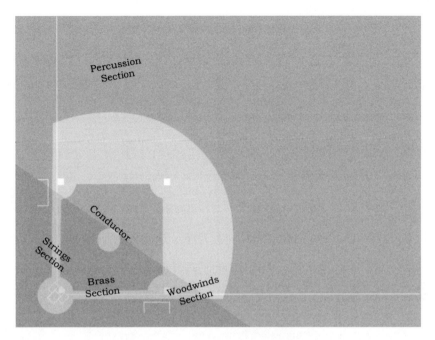

FIGURE 3.2: The Orchestra by the Ninth Inning/Symphony

the rest of the organization is clustered in the shadows far, far away is a common one. From day to day, month to month, and year to year, organizations adjust to changing circumstances. They may do this together in a coordinated way, but very often each section pursues the more immediate demands of getting its own work done. When that happens, the organization can look a lot like our orchestra wandering across a baseball field.

Competing Values Framework

Here is where we need to talk more about the "things" of culture, but keep in mind that we are referring to the processes that are embodied in its core. The Competing Values Framework provides a vocabulary for talking about different styles of organizational culture that lends itself well to the idea of social spaces. It is also the framework the National Institute of Corrections used in working with correctional agencies across the country on cultural issues. NIC adopted the Competing Values Framework after a review of the

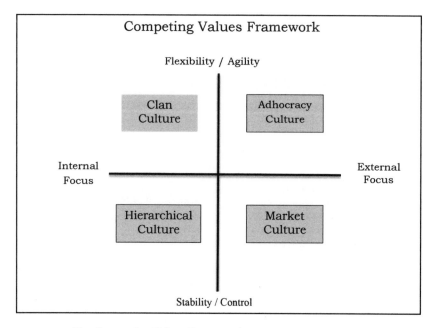

FIGURE 3.3: The Competing Values Framework

literature.[17] It turned out to be an excellent choice. Over the next few years the project conducted dozens of cultural assessments that included interviews, focus groups, observations, and the use of the Organizational Culture Assessment Instrument—Prisons. The latter was based on the original assessment instrument developed as part of the Competing Values Framework, which was modified with the permission and support of the authors and provided at no charge.

The Competing Values Framework assumes that every organization must balance the emphasis it places on the competing values of an internal versus external focus, on the one hand, and structure and control versus flexibility and agility, on the other.[18] The framework is illustrated with a chart showing these two value dimensions placed across one another to form the grid in figure 3.3. The grid also shows the four styles of culture that are created in their purest form, depending on where they are placed along the competing values dimensions (the names of the styles also come from Cameron and Quinn). The framework is not about competition within or between organizations. It is about the push and pull of the internal/external and the structure/flexibility dimensions, the tension between them, and the influences they have on the culture.

An organization that places a high value on the effective integration and seamless unity of processes (internal focus) and also highly values reliability and clearly defined structures and roles (stability and control) is labeled *hierarchical* in this framework. This type of culture is typically found in correctional organizations because of the nature of their mission.

Correctional agencies have, for good reason, adopted a style that encourages people to respect authority and closely follow established procedures rather than routinely exercise individual discretion and decision making. In corrections, it is a very sensible thing to want people to follow procedures and obey orders. This bit of wisdom has usually been learned the hard way. Every correctional agency I know of has at some time in its history experienced something traumatic like a riot, escape, hostage situation, homicide or suicide of an inmate or staff member, indictments against staff, or a shocking crime by an inmate, probationer, or parolee. An organization's experiences mixes with its existing culture in ways that have a powerful and lasting effect on how people perceive and respond to the challenges represented by external or internal pressures. This is not, as is sometimes assumed, the collective expression of authoritarian personalities at work or other collective pathologies. It is a reasonable adaptation to a tough working environment.

A culture with a hierarchical style is focused on rules, specialization, and accountability to produce an organization that functions smoothly and reliably. The type of leader you would expect to find in a hierarchical organization would focus on directing operations, coordinating and monitoring activity, and maintaining discipline. Such organizations define success in terms of efficiency, timeliness, consistency, and stability. "A good day is when nothing happens" is a common observation in the corrections business. For many, the worst thing that *can* happen is that you get in the newspapers (because something bad has happened). The ideal image of a hierarchical organization is one that runs smoothly through well-defined operational processes and controls. The staff who run this operational utopia so smoothly are process-oriented, highly competent specialists who pay attention to details and strive to maintain and improve their skills.

A very different type of culture exists when an organization places the same high value on integration and unity (internal focus) but also highly values individuality, discretion, flexibility, and agility. In the Competing Values Framework this type of culture is labeled *clan* to capture the more familial and collaborative feel of organizations with this kind of culture. One way to contrast these two is to say that in a hierarchical culture there is a strong emphasis on doing things right, while in a clan culture the emphasis is on doing things together. A ubiquitous perception in the Prison Culture Project assessment reports is that the organization is too hierarchical and people want it to become more clan-like in the way it operates. Calls for more teamwork, building trust, or eliminating silos are usually demands for the organization to move toward a more flexible, individualized cultural style.

The Prison Culture Project assessment team repeatedly found a nearly identical pattern in the perceived existing and preferred cultures at the dozens of prisons that were visited across the country over several years. The culture in these prisons was routinely found to be hierarchical, focusing on stability and control, standard procedures, adherence to structure, and consistency of operations. According to one assessment report, "This finding is expected, given both the basic public safety and security mission as well as the nature of prison work." Just as frequently, the team found an almost universal preference among staff for a shift toward a clan culture. In the assessment reports, clan culture was variously defined as one that "places a greater emphasis on teamwork, internal focus, and attention to the needs of staff" or as "being more focused on their needs, by valuing their hard work, including them in decision-making, and by fostering a more cohesive workplace."

These were not calls by staff to *replace* their hierarchical culture; they were almost always "pleas," to use the words of the assessment team, to mitigate what staff saw as an overly rigid structure. Staff members who were unhappy (and most seemed to be) with their workplace environment wanted the organization to be more people-oriented. In one early assessment, the team found the staff's view of their prison's existing organizational culture profile was nearly identical to the pattern that had already been seen in previous assessments and that they described as "consistent with the correctional industry norm," that is, a preference for less hierarchy and a more clan-like environment.

A clan culture is internally focused, but it is much more individualized in the way it operates than a hierarchical culture would be. It values flexibility, decentralization, shared goals, participation, and inclusiveness. In this type of culture, leaders are expected to serve as facilitators and mentors, be supportive, and work to encourage inclusiveness and collaboration. A clan organization defines success in terms of individual development and the degree to which people working there feel a sense that what they do is meaningful and fulfilling for everyone. An ideal clan organization has a supportive work environment, high levels of engagement, and commitment to the organizational mission. In corrections, the push/pull of the competing values between orderly control and operational agility is felt, often painfully, in day-to-day work life.

While hierarchical and clan cultures have an internal focus in common, the two other cultural types, market and adhocracy, have an external focus. They place a high value on interacting with and/or competing against those outside the organization, such as customers, market competitors, and stakeholders. These two cultures match more closely our images of companies in the private sector. They differ from one another in the value they place on stability and control versus flexibility and agility. An organization with an external focus, which also highly values stability and control, is labeled a *market culture* on the grid in figure 3.3. By contrast, an organization with an external focus that also highly values flexibility and agility is labeled an *adhocracy*. This label comes from the term "ad hoc" and implies an organization that values a dynamic approach with specialized, often temporary ways of organizing its work. While a market culture might emphasize "doing it fast," an adhocracy might emphasize "doing it first." The two cultural types on the external side of the internal/external dimension lend themselves to different leadership styles.

Successful leaders in a market culture are themselves focused, competitive, and goal-oriented. Market cultures, as the name implies, define success in terms of market share, profitability achieved by competition, and focus on external stakeholders and customers. In an ideal market organization, employees are energetic partners in the business, are adept at applying business, marketing, and strategic analysis skills to the solution of problems, and have a high achievement orientation.

An adhocracy culture, like a market culture, is externally focused but places a higher value on flexibility and decentralized decision making. The goal is to have an organization that is agile, innovative, responsive, and constantly reinventing itself. The leaders are expected to be innovative, entrepreneurial, and visionary. Adhocracies define success by whether they are leading their field in producing innovations and are continually fostering change, encouraging transformational and systems thinking, and stressing collaboration. The leadership style that works within an adhocracy is characterized by a stress on constant innovation and an entrepreneurial approach that promotes experimentation, risk taking, organizational agility, and continual reinvention. Such an organization would recruit, develop, and promote a workforce that thrives in an ever-changing workplace.

A correctional agency, on the other hand, would not last long if it adopted the same style. This does not mean that even the most hierarchical organization will not benefit from a little experimental risk taking. In fact, borrowing an element from a different cultural style and experimenting with it is the basic strategy for changing an organization's culture. Focusing externally on results, for example, enables an internally focused organization to move on the grid in an externally focused direction.[19] At the same time, a focus on developing the corrections workforce could move the same organization toward a more clan-like cultural style.

Many consultants and best-selling authors on leadership extol the qualities of visionary and transformative leaders in market and adhocracy cultures. In the case studies I present in the next two chapters from the Prison Culture Project, wardens with market or adhocracy philosophies of leadership usually found themselves running afoul of the hierarchical cultures in the prisons they sought to lead. This was because the people participating in those cultures were not organizational theorists. From inside their own organizational culture, they had a ground-level, not a bird's-eye, view. They interpreted their situation and expressed their preferences in the context of their own cultural framework. They saw whatever plans senior management cooked up for them from a local perspective. Since the managers in these cases tended to assume that they knew what the staff thought and what they would want (once they understood what it was), the process was frustrating for everyone.

The "pure" styles in the framework are still abstractions, a quick way to summarize the dominant characteristics of different types of organizational cultures. They are useful in helping us to talk about cultures and understand how they work. But they should not be taken too seriously. If something an organization is doing or wants to do does not fit into the framework, it is time to let go of the framework; it has become another box. The purpose of looking at the main style of a culture and its associated definitions of success is to give us a sense of how working within that culture feels, so we can move on to a deeper understanding of how it works.[20]

The four types of culture in the framework should not be treated as though they were real organizations that could reasonably be described as a single type. Living cultures are more complex than that. In approaches to organizational culture, they have often been assumed to be one or another of these ideal types and to be integrated wholes, but more often they have been recognized as more complex.[21] Organizations can be collections of subcultures, coexisting more or less peacefully and having enough shared goals and mutual interdependence to operate well enough. In other circumstances, the subcultures can be so alienated from one another that the culture is fragmented and the organization's ability to act collaboratively is seriously impaired. One of the downsides of a preoccupation with organizational performance is that it tends to focus each unit's attention on its own performance, not that of the organization as a whole (like the orchestra's percussion section).

Subcultures can also become countercultures in that they develop an adversarial relationship with the dominant culture and its presumed goals. When management and the union are routinely at each other's throats, that is probably an indication that the organization's culture is not functioning holistically. Subcultures, even ones that are at odds with the dominant culture, may be a good thing. When any part of an organization mobilizes in an effort to change the organization, it is essentially forming a subculture. Any group of self-identified change leaders are organizing with the conscious intention of moving the organization to a new position in the cultural space. For example, if they believe that an organization has become too hierarchical, they may undertake to move it toward a more clan-like culture. How can they do this? By altering the patterns of interaction within the organization to infuse the dominant culture with some elements more typical of a clan culture. Such a subculture can emerge from the grass roots of the organization as an act of bureaucratic insurgency by middle management or as an initiative from the chief executive.

A Fresh Look at Correctional Cultures

Most correctional agencies, because of their public safety mission and their chain-of-command rank structure, display a hierarchical cultural style. Hierarchical cultures have usually been presented in negative terms, in reaction to what have been perceived as the stifling cultures of rigid bureaucracies and the authoritarian leadership styles they employ. For example, in a typology of leadership styles published in 1961, Rensis Likert argued that the leadership and cultures characteristic of hierarchical organizations were to be avoided.[22] In their 1964 book, *The Managerial Grid,* academic researchers and business consultants Robert Blake and Jane Mouton developed a model similar to the Competing Values Framework, but their dimensions were "concern for people" and "concern for production." They concluded that hierarchical cultures, which they saw as focused on production with little concern for people, exhibited an "impoverished style" of management.[23] While these and other theorists focused on corporate cultures, the tone they set in describing hierarchical organizations has had a strong influence on the way many view such organizations, including those in corrections. (The "paramilitary" label that is often used here has a pejorative tone that is as much about not liking the military as it is about prisons.)

A better way of using the Competing Values Framework to describe correctional culture is to look at the mission of corrections and how it has molded its culture. In a 2010 article, Bradford Bogue reviewed the literature on high-reliability organizations and identified several key characteristics such organizations have in common with corrections.[24] Other organizations that require high-reliability cultures are air traffic control, nuclear power plants, air and rail transportations systems, aircraft carrier deck operations, combat operations units in general, and firefighting units. These seemingly different types of organizations in fact share certain cultural characteristics. All of them are also alike in that they are involved in businesses where very bad things can happen suddenly and mushroom quickly into very, very bad things.

These organizations have adapted to their missions by incorporating specific characteristics as they have responded to the challenges of their operational environment. Foremost among them is a *preoccupation with failure,* meaning that they strive to be constantly aware that any incident can become a major crisis and that organizational readiness is essential.[25] This readiness involves close, ongoing monitoring of operations to identify potential risks and respond to them quickly. In addition, a *reluctance to simplify* and *sensitivity to operations* are parts of the culture of a high-reliability organization. These organizations resist oversimplification of practices or processes by relying on redundancy, multiple levels of review, and close coordination across operational units to avoid gaps in the system. Sensitivity to operations refers to the close monitoring of operation details, frequent program reviews or audits, and a preoccupation with adherence to operating procedures. Anyone familiar with corrections operations should find this familiar ground.

Two other characteristics of high-reliability organizations are familiar to anyone working in correctional organizations. They are *deference to expertise* and a *commitment to resilience.* High-reliability organizations place a high value on expertise and skill, especially when these have been gained through years of hands-on experience. During critical incidents, agencies must have the capacity and the confidence in staff to shift decision making to the front lines where instant responses are necessary. A commitment to resilience means displaying a high level of organizational pride in meeting challenges and overcoming adversity. The camaraderie and morale, often called esprit de corps, commonly observed in high-reliability organizations like correctional agencies are a fundamental expression of their cultural style. Like deference to expertise, commitment to resilience adds to the dynamic qualities of organizations and works to counterbalance the rigidity that a preoccupation with failure, reluctance to simplify, and sensitivity to operations can create.

From the perspective of the Competing Values Framework, high-reliability organizations can be seen as hierarchical organizations with some clan-like elements. This mix of styles keeps such organizations from becoming too rigid in their operational posture and allows them to pivot rapidly in a crisis. The unique mix of styles has been learned by corrections organizations and professionals as they deal with the challenges of their work. The push and pull of structure and flexibility that often generates tensions between staff in prisons is not accidental. It is a product of the complex mission and challenging environment that have created correctional cultures over time.

One of the beauties of the Prison Culture reports is that they describe, from the perspective of the participants, the culture in each prison. A unique aspect of the assessment was the team's use of the Organizational Culture

Assessment Instrument—Prisons (OCAI-P). Most questionnaires used in re-search on organizational cultures are intentionally opaque. They are usually a set of Likert-style questions (with the familiar responses "strongly agree," "agree," "somewhat agree," and so on, to "strongly disagree"). The questions are intended to yield a number of theory-based scales that can be used for statistical analysis. For example, the theoretical construct of "organizational commitment" is constructed mathematically from the responses to a num-ber of statements. Someone who responds "strongly agree" to statements like "The mission of this organization is personally important to me" and "I feel proud of what this organization does" and other statements like it will score high on "commitment." The statements about commitment are interspersed with others that are used to construct other scales like "job satisfaction" or "organizational cynicism." The respondent is not supposed to know what these scales are because, according to the logic of organizational research, that would bias the results.

The OCAI-P, however, is refreshingly transparent. It lists six sets of state-ments that require the respondent to strike a balance between the competing values of internal/external and structure/flexibility by allocating 100 points among four options. The six sets of statements refer to six different domains of organizational culture that play an important role in Cameron and Quinn's framework: dominant culture, leadership, management of employees, orga-nizational glue, strategic emphasis, and criteria of success. The OCAI-P is ac-tually concerned with two things. The first is what the organization is like now, and the second is what the respondent would *prefer* it to be like. It can be filled out in a few minutes and scored immediately. The scores for any one person or group can then be plotted onto the Competing Values Framework grid. This produces a kite-like pattern in which the tail of the kite points to the dominant culture. Cameron and Quinn did exactly this for more than a thousand organizations and produced an average culture plot for them, as shown in figure 3.4.[26]

The majority of the organizations that Cameron and Quinn studied were in the private sector. These included companies in finance, insurance, real estate, mining, manufacturing, construction, retail and wholesale trade, transportation, communications, and gas and electric. In other words, they were market organizations. Cameron and Quinn also studied and plotted forty-three public-sector organizations, mainly in public administration.

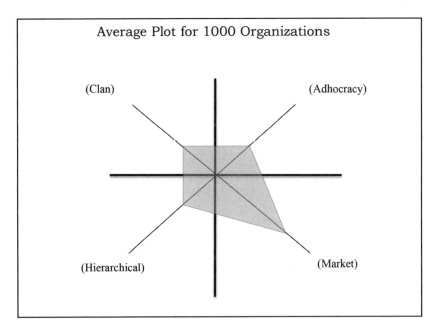

FIGURE 3.4: Average Plot for 1000 Organization

Those organizations, not unexpectedly, proved to be more hierarchical and internally focused. They were plotted on the grid (figure 3.5) and, as we might expect, look like government bureaucracies.[27]

In 2009, the Criminal Justice Institute, in an unpublished report, presented an overview of the culture work it had performed during the previous nine years, mostly with federal funding but also with some state support. The CJI plotted OCAI-P data for about two dozen prisons on the same grid Cameron and Quinn had used. The culture plot for these prisons, drawn from assessments across the country over several years, looks very much like the one Cameron and Quinn found for other government agencies. The tail of the kite points strongly toward a hierarchical culture (figure 3.6).

This, however, is not the cultural type that correctional staffers typically have a preference for. As discussed in chapter 4, line-level staffers in particular routinely say they want the culture of their organization to be more like a family or "clan." In figure 3.7, the preferred culture plot is superimposed on the existing one, as shown in figure 3.6.

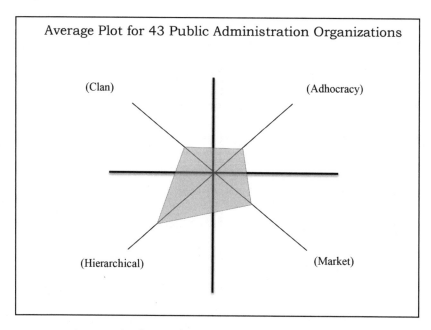

FIGURE 3.5: Average Plot for 43 Administrative Organizations

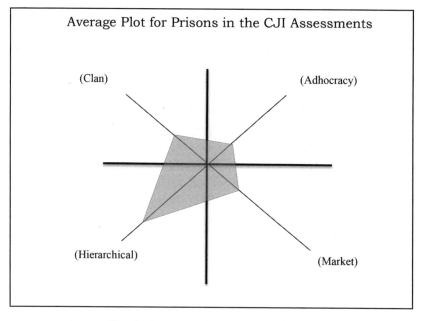

FIGURE 3.6: Average Plot for Prisons in the CJI Assessments

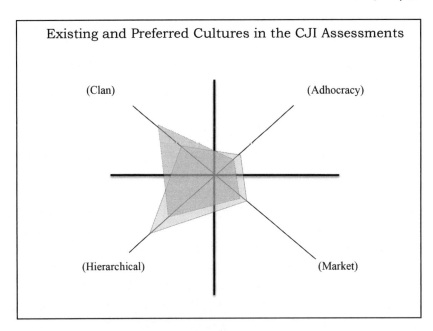

Existing and Preferred Cultures in the CJI Assessments

(Clan)   (Adhocracy)

(Hierarchical)   (Market)

FIGURE 3.7: Average Plot for Existing and Preferred Cultures in the CJI Assessments

There is good news and there is bad news in the match between these prison plots and the ones for other private- and public-sector organizations. The good news is that there are clearly features of the typical cultures in these prisons that track well with other government agencies, and this implies that many of the strategies or tactics that have been used in other types of public agencies could be applied to prisons. The bad news is that much of the leadership and management literature that exists and was developed for private-sector, market culture organizations will not translate well into prison cultures. But Dialogue has been used extensively in prisons, in both the United Kingdom and the United States, as well as by the Virginia Department of Corrections in connection with the Healing Environment Initiative.

Is There an Inmate Culture?

One tradition in the research on prisons, institutional misconduct, and recidivism has focused on the existence of an inmate culture that supposedly develops in the peculiar environment of prisons. The premise that inmates have their own culture is one of the bases for the argument that prisons are criminogenic by nature. The argument has two variants. The first is *prisonization,* the view that inmates are socialized into the unique culture of prisons, which essentially serve as "schools for crime."

The second variant is *deprivation,* the idea that the conditions of incarceration lead to the development of antisocial attitudes and behavior.[28] In the research literature on inmate violence and other misconduct, these arguments are often contrasted with *importation,* according to which people are in prison in the first place because they have committed crimes, so it is not much of a mystery why they continue to commit crimes once they are locked up.[29] I used this contrast myself in a 1997 article on misconduct in federal prisons, where I said that "the 'importation' view tends to characterize inmates as already criminal in their orientation or antisocial in their outlook when they arrive in prison, which is why they are there. In this view, misconduct in prison is not unexpected, inasmuch as it is a simple continuation of the criminal career that the person began long before arriving there."[30]

At the time I wrote this, I also argued that one of the problems with the concept of inmate culture was that it required us to claim that the causes of harmful behavior within prisons was different from the causes of essentially the same behavior outside prisons. In fact, I found, just as did many others who had and have since studied violence and misconduct in prisons, that you do not need inmate culture to explain inmate behavior. The same set of factors, such as demographics, criminal history, and seriousness of past offenses, explain most of the differences between those who cause trouble in prison or on the streets and those who do not. These days, I would go further and say that the concept of a distinct inmate culture is a myth.[31] The "culture" of inmates is really the culture of street life in America that inmates bring with them. A great many people who go to prison have a long experience in the "code of the streets," to use the phrase of Elijah Anderson.[32]

I am prepared to say that, at least as I define culture, inmates do not have one. Or, to be more precise, what they have is so fragmented and incoherent that it really does not qualify as a culture. The notion of an inmate culture emerged from the early ethnographic studies by some of the pioneers in criminology. These included the classic works by Donald Clemmer in the 1930s and, following him in the tradition, by researchers like Leo Carroll and Mark Fleisher.[33] These studies, based on direct observation of life in prisons, treated violence and other misconduct as a given, but did not focus on them. The focus was on the values or attitudes of inmates and whether and how they changed while people were incarcerated. Even if there was once a distinct inmate culture, I believe it was a casualty of mass incarceration. Prisons are no longer the "total institutions" they might once have been when the experience of incarceration was limited to a relative few.[34] Today, with hundreds of thousands of people circulating between prisons, jails, and the streets and with correctional institutions so permeable (allowing visiting, frequent telephone contacts, and nearly constant access to television, popular movies, newspapers, books, magazines, etc.), the idea that prison culture is an island unto itself is not plausible.[35]

This is not to say that people living in prison do not adapt to the unique conditions of incarceration by coping as best they can. Unfortunately, the ways they learned to cope in the past are often what got them incarcerated. The explanation of why people get themselves into trouble could be as simple as the fact that they do not know what else to do. Most people who get involved in the criminal justice system live extraordinarily fragmented lives. They usually lack the psychological, human, and social capital to navigate society. They become loose cannons on the deck of life, and they inflict an incredible amount of harm on others, their communities, and themselves. They are by no means blameless, and society rightfully holds them accountable for what they have done. But it seems to be a good idea that, while they are incarcerated, we do something to break the cycle of their lives.

As inmates, however, many of them will carry on as they did on the streets, if the staff will allow them. When this happens, inmates and staff alike suffer. In one prison assessed by the Prison Culture Project, a balance of power had emerged that had a profound effect on the staff's perception of who was really running the prison. The assessment report said, "Remarkably, at all levels and in all departments, employees almost universally expressed feelings of powerlessness. They also perceived other staff as being powerless—all the way up to the Warden. When asked who was not powerless, the only response received was 'the inmates.' There are many sources of this sense of powerlessness, including some that are very profound and real, aside from the natural frustrations of prison work and State bureaucracy. When we inquired about how significant changes get made and by whom, we repeatedly heard 'it's whoever gets to the legislators first—the inmates or the union.' And, the inmates more often prevailed."

As a remarkable example of the reach that inmates can sometimes have, inmates at one prison thwarted an attempt by a new warden to take control over the amount of personal property the inmates could have. The inmates could choose to wear street clothing on the yard and many wore "dressy or fashionable outfits at times." In an attempt to eliminate contraband and excessive amounts of personal property, the warden began to limit inmates' property to that allowed by policy. Almost immediately, he received orders from headquarters placing an immediate, ninety-day moratorium on enforcing the policy. The enforcement of the personal property policy was apparently blocked by the long-term inmates who garnered support from external community members, legislators, and activist organizations. The moratorium was still in place three years later when the assessment team arrived. During the assessment, staff continued to complain about the moratorium, which prevented the banning of such possessions as spiked heels and crotchless panties. Inmates at this prison had also become proficient at manipulating medical services by "doctor shopping" to get prescriptions and approval for things like heating pads and special pillows that would otherwise be considered contraband.

CHAPTER FOUR

Correctional Cultures: Reals and Ideals

The geoscientific community has generally accepted the once (fifty years ago) controversial notion that the earth's crust is a giant jigsaw puzzle made of huge tectonic plates. These plates crush against, grind along, or overlap one another to create continents and oceans, build mountain ranges, dig deep-sea trenches, and set the stage for life on earth. The plates, eight continent-sized ones and many smaller ones, hundreds of kilometers thick in some places, float across the surface at speeds of up to 100 mm a year, about as fast as your hair grows.[1] That might not sound very fast, but keep in mind this is what generates volcanic eruptions, earthquakes, and tsunamis that every once in a while wipe out a civilization. Just as our physical world is fragmented, so does our cultural world have its own upheavals, some of which have wiped out whole cultures or civilizations. In prisons, the fault lines can give rise to riots or other disturbances, work and hunger strikes, homicides, suicides, and escapes. And that is just what the inmates can do—the divisions among the staff at all levels can, in the long run, be even more destructive to operations and security, health and safety, well-being and healing.

Although it did not start out looking for fragmentation, the Criminal Justice Institute assessment team arrived at a similar view of cultures early in the NIC Prison Culture Project. The idea became part of the boilerplate inserted into the reports. These reports said, "One way to conceptualize institutional culture is as clusters of small, overlapping circles. A common institutional culture can be found at the intersections of the organization's subcultures and consists of what is common among them. Thus, institutions can be placed along a continuum according to the relative degree of unity-fragmentation among their subcultures. Where there is tight clustering and much overlap, there may be a unitary institutional culture, but where the area of overlap is small there is little justification for attribution of an institutional culture." The assessment team eventually started using "culturegrams" to create a visual representation of the organization (in a footnote, the team cites the work

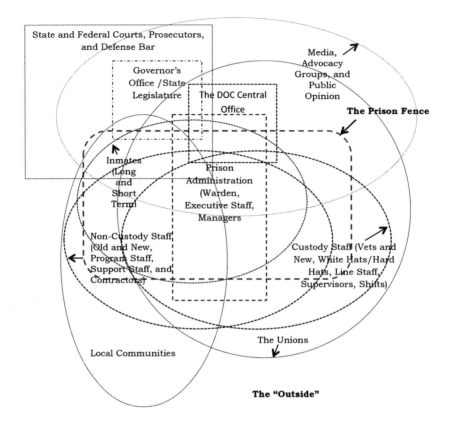

State and Federal Courts, Prosecutors, and Defense Bar

Media, Advocacy Groups, and Public Opinion

Governor's Office /State Legislature

The DOC Central Office

The Prison Fence

Inmates (Long and Short Term)

Prison Administration (Warden, Executive Staff, Managers)

Non-Custody Staff (Old and New, Program Staff, Support Staff, and Contractors)

Custody Staff (Vets and New, White Hats/Hard Hats, Line Staff, Supervisors, Shifts)

Local Communities

The Unions

The "Outside"

FIGURE 4.1: Example of a Culturegram

of the organizational theorist John van Maanen as the inspiration for this idea).[2] I was not involved in the project when these reports were written (nor had I heard of David Bohm, fragmentation, or Dialogue), but I was happy to discover that the assessment team had already found the idea of fragmentation and coherence useful, even if it did not use the terms.

The culturegrams developed by the assessment team in the later years of the Culture Project where often extraordinarily elaborate but were very effective in capturing the complexity of the cultures in prisons. In figure 4.1, I have taken elements from these culturegrams to illustrate how many moving parts the culture in a single prison can have.

Division between groups seems to be epidemic in prison cultures and can form along almost any gap in space, time, or function. Once it emerges, it is magnified into different views of what the purpose of each group's work should be and who is to blame for why things are not working. In many cases, those differing views evolve into suspicion, resentment, mistrust, animosity, and even insubordination or sabotage of efforts to fix the problems. The list identified by the cultural assessment team seemed to multiply with each new assessment, and every prison has at least a half dozen different groups. Often these groups actually become visible. In prisons and community corrections offices, it is common to see people arrange themselves into separate areas at roll call or staff recalls, in break rooms or dining halls, training programs (sometimes beginning at the academy), and even social events.

Many of the divisions in prisons are the same ones that appear in all sorts of organizations. Race and ethnicity, color and creed, gender, politics or ideology, education and social status, language and dialect, religion, and lifestyle are all possible sources of division. People bring these with them when they go through the sally port, just as they do when they pass the factory gate, take the elevator to their office, punch in at the clock, or sit down in the boardroom. Many of the groups the Culture Project team identified are also among the usual suspects in correctional fragmentation; the day versus night versus midnight shifts; custody versus non-custody staff; correctional "traditionalists" versus "hug-a-thugs" (in one prison they were known as the "hard hats" and the "white hats," respectively); institution staff versus administrative and support staff; longtime staff versus short-timers; union versus non-union members; local staff versus those who transferred in; and so on. Then there are the "white shirts" (majors, captains, lieutenants, and sergeants, whether one group or different ones—i.e., lieutenants and sergeants in one boat and majors and captains in another) and the "blue shirt" correctional officers. This is just the short list of staff-versus-staff fragmentation (management vs. everybody else is the subject of the next chapter).

Given what prisons are, most of this should not be much of a surprise. By design, they are organized with a formally defined command and control structure. So they all have the usual hierarchy of front office, department heads, middle managers, line supervisors, and line staff (plus, of course, inmates). But because of the nature of their operations, the work includes more than the typical business administrative functions, like human resources, budgeting, public information, and legal applications. They are also

full-service hotels of a sort, with food service, laundry, maintenance, custo-
dial and grounds keeping, and even retail operations (like the commissary
and telephone services). They are medical and mental health care providers, dealing with urgent care, running a pharmacy, an infirmary, and "out-
patient" services, and offering dental care, treatment for every type of acute
and chronic medical or psychiatric condition, infectious disease control,
and even hospice and wellness programs. They have schools for basic and
secondary educational programs and vocational training. They have chapels
for religious services, gyms and playing fields for recreation, plus a law and
general library. Most have factories or workshops as part of prison industries
programs. Some have their own waste management systems. They are essentially small towns, except that instead of being towns with a jail in it, they are
big jails with a town in it.

Assessing Correctional Cultures

When the NIC Prison Culture Project began in 2000, the idea that organizational cultures strongly influenced performance and that organizations could
address their own operational issues through cultural change was a hot topic.
A common theme at the time, repeated in many business advice books, was
that the great successes of the Japanese were the product of their national and
corporate culture. The main point of these books was that organizational cultures could drive performance and that they could be deliberately managed
by the organization's leaders to improve productivity and competitiveness.[3]
The reality turned out to be a bit more complicated, with organizational cultures proving to be more like a mass of tectonic plates pushing and grinding
against each other than a huge chessboard for visionary leaders.

Under Susan Hunter's direction, NIC laid out a multistage plan that began
with developing an assessment protocol, pilot-testing it at facilities, and
training consultants to do cultural assessments.[4] The protocol called for the
use of institution records, individual interviews, focus groups, and observations of daily operations. The assessment team also used the OCAI-P from
Cameron and Quinn's Competing Values Framework, which it administered
to focus groups and those the team interviewed individually, then employed
to analyze organizational cultures.[5]

Starting in 2002, the project conducted assessments at dozens of correctional facilities across the United States. Each assessment was conducted by a team of three to five assessors, who spent up to a week at the site and made observations during all shifts. During the assessments, individual, semistructured interviews were conducted with senior staff members and key department heads or others, such as union leaders, who were seen as influential. Several focus groups were also conducted with line staff on different shifts, line supervisors, support staff, and usually one or two focus groups with inmates.

The prisons NIC chose for an assessment were largely self-nominated. The director of a state correctional system or the warden of a particular prison requested the assessment in response to an announcement by NIC inviting participation in the project.[6] The selected prisons, therefore, were all ones where someone thought something was wrong or the culture was dysfunctional, so there may have been some bias toward more problematic institutions. The prisons were not a representative sample, but on another level they serve my purposes well since they were institutions where someone in authority believed that something was fundamentally wrong and needed to get fixed. What was unusual about the assessed prisons, however, was that they often had new leadership that was attempting to implement changes. Staff resistance to the new regime was often one of the issues raised by the department director or the warden in requesting the assessment. The reports the assessors compiled were written for the wardens and the prison's executive staff to assist them in understanding the culture of their own prison.

The reports are also instructive in that they essentially are reflections of the standard-issue theory of organizational cultures being applied to prisons. In one of the first assessment reports, the team summarized its view of organizational culture: "Culture is herein defined as a system of values, beliefs and norms held in common by a group of people and by which they interpret and give meaning to their experience. In the course of adapting to problems inherent in any physical or social environment, culture is reflected in the 'persistent and patterned way of thinking about the central tasks of, and human relationships within, an organization' (Wilson, 1989). As such, culture serves as a set of rules that guide prescriptively and proscriptively the behavior of members of the organization." (The reference is to James Q. Wilson's book on government bureaucracies.)[7]

The CJI team report went on to say that all organizations have both a formal and an informal culture. The formal culture, according to the report, "is codified in their mission statements, policies and procedures and embodied in the rules, roles, and operational routines of the institutions." The report pointed out that the staff become acculturated during their training at the academy and subsequent on-the-job experiences. In addition, "cultural values are frequently communicated and affirmed through symbols and ceremonies, such as staff awards and recognition ceremonies."

The standard-issue model of organizational culture, however, quickly began to evolve as the assessment team discovered deeper layers to the cultures found in real prisons. For one thing, the team began to recognize that formal culture (the usual locus of change efforts) can go only so far in guiding a prison because it cannot anticipate everything that might come up in the day-to-day operations. Said the report, "Informal cultures develop that stand beside and juxtaposed to the formal cultural system. Staff must adapt and develop ways to respond to the physical and social environments and realities of the institution. Over time, informal ideas, notions, and values come to be persistent and patterned from these adaptive practices. These ideas are transmitted among organizational members and to new members through informal communication and relationships. Cultural elements, such as cohesion, trust, stress, support, and pride, are defined and embodied within the informal culture. Informally, culture is reflected in the stories that staff tell."

The report continued, "Operational practices are accomplished within the domains of both the formal and informal cultures that define the 'texture' of institutional life and depend on the unique and interpersonal styles that members come to use in relating to one another. When the formal and informal cultures are aligned, they support accomplishment of the organization's mission. However, when the two are not aligned, staff solidarity declines and performance suffers. Staff may experience anxiety and alienation. Trust may be lacking. Important information may not be shared vertically and horizontally throughout the organization. Fragmentation is likely. Such disconnection may occur between management and line staff, among functional disciplines, between labor and management or among specific individuals or groups."

This is one of the original reports in which the term "fragmentation" appears. However, the formal/informal dichotomy referred to is itself a form of fragmented thinking and an example of failing to see organizations holistically. The report concluded, "Focusing on organizational culture alerts us to the fact that within rationally designed organizations there may exist a variety of unplanned, organically developed and shared designs for living; and that these may facilitate or impede the attainment of organizational goals. In prisons, it would seem that the capacity for sub-cultural development is perhaps greater than in other organizations of comparable size and complexity." Whether it is more or less likely in corrections than other organizations is unknown, but "sub-cultural development," that is, fragmentation, was common in the prisons the team visited.

The assessment team's reports on the culture of these prisons were guided by an understanding of what culture is and what it ought to be. Mainly the team believed that organizational cultures ought to work to achieve the goals of effective and efficient operation. This is not a criticism of them; improving prisons was the whole point of the exercise and the reason NIC was funding the work. Still, the particular cultural lens the assessors brought to their work did influence how they saw the differing perspectives of the people being assessed. One thing the team tended to assume was that the mission and purpose of the organization, as defined by management, could be understood and shared through a constructive, problem-solving approach organized and led from the top.

The team produced extensive reports summarizing the results for the warden of each prison. According to one of these reports: "Following descriptions of the team's activities while on-site, both qualitative and quantitative results of the assessment are presented in detail. These include assessments of the distinctive cultural characteristics and determinants of the institution and its various subculture groups, the degree of congruence between the formal and informal aspects of the organizational culture and between the perceived 'current' and 'preferred' organizational cultures, and the extent to which staff components differ in their values and points of view . . . The result is a descriptive 'picture' of the culture and an elaboration—mostly in staff's own language—of how they would like it to be. Rather than concluding with a list of specific recommendations or areas that need to be 'fixed,' the assessment is designed to inform leadership regarding the perceptions of staff about the quality of work-life, their values and beliefs, and their feelings about what they believe contribute to both negative and positive aspects of the organizational culture.

"The intent of this report is to raise leadership's awareness of how staff perceive the workplace, and to ultimately inform all staff so that culture change can be initiated from both the top-down (e.g., led by the warden and executive team) and the bottom-up (through a representative, democratic process that includes primarily rank-and-file participants) in order to gain the buy-in from staff at all levels and functional areas of the prison. In the end, it is anticipated that follow-through culture change activities will occur and that any necessary resources (e.g., training, technical assistance) will be requested of, and made available by, the department and—to the extent possible—the National Institute of Corrections. As the sponsoring agency, NIC holds the expectation that this assessment is only the beginning of a multi-year process of culture change aimed toward improving the quality of work-life for staff and subsequently the quality of correctional services and outcomes for inmates."

The Organizational Culture Assessment Instrument—Prisons

One of the particularly important aspects of the Prison Culture Project is that during the early assessments the team routinely used Cameron and Quinn's Competing Values Framework and the results of the OCAI-P to organize and analyze the information it had compiled. In the preceding chapter, I described the four types of cultures that make up the Competing Values Framework: the hierarchical, clan, adhocracy, and market styles. The descriptions and the graphic displays illustrating the types, however, were all bird's-eye views of the culture types. The example of the orchestra in a baseball stadium was shown from the angle of someone looking down, as if from a blimp floating overhead. People living in a culture do not see their own culture from above. They see it from the particular angle defined by their own position within that culture.

Members of the assessment team were outsiders and they tended to think about the prison cultures they were visiting from "above" them. The reports themselves are cultural artifacts because they reflect the assumptions of the team and the team's understanding of the purpose of the visits to diagnose a prison's "presenting problems" as part of an information-gathering effort to help the executive-level management of the prison develop a strategy. The assessment team was essentially a group of correctional subject matter experts who were being paid by a federal agency to provide advice on how to solve technical problems faced by correctional managers.

This means that the OCAI-P statements, written from the perspective of the observing outsider, take on different, culturally informed meanings that are extraordinarily revealing in terms of how they are interpreted by the respondents. We know what they mean because the team presented them in focus groups and interviews. The OCAI-P statements are reproduced in what follows, but they are clustered by the type of culture they describe rather than by the dimension (dominant culture, leadership, etc.). For the culture of an organization to be considered hierarchical, the people working there would have to give the greatest weight (allocate the most points out of the 100 they are allowed) to the following six statements):

The Department is a very controlled and **structured** place. Formal procedures guide what people do.

The leadership in the Department generally seems to be coordinated, **organized**, or smooth-operating and efficient.

The management style in the Department emphasizes job security, conformity, predictability, and **stability** in relationships.

The glue that holds the Department together is formal **rules** and policies. Maintaining a smooth-running institution is key.

The Department emphasizes keeping things the same from day to day. Keeping operations simple, **controlled**, and smooth is important.

The Department defines success as efficiency. **Dependable service**, smooth scheduling, and low-cost operations are critical.

Some people might cringe at the prospect of working in an environment that places such a strong emphasis on structure, control, stability, rules, and dependable operations. But this is often exactly what people working in high-reliability organizations endorse. In one assessment, a line correctional officer said, "Structure is a comfort zone . . . it tells me what I should be doing."

The team also used the OCAI-P to find out from respondents at each of the prisons (all of which were thought to be troubled or dysfunctional) what type of organization they would prefer to work in. In figure 3.7, the *preferred* culture plot, pointing to a clan culture, is compared with the current culture plot, pointing to a hierarchical culture, taken from figure 3.6. The interesting thing is that the staff at these prisons did not want much less structure or internal focus. What they wanted was the structure to be maintained with less emphasis on hierarchy and more emphasis on clan culture. To get a clearer idea of what they meant by a more clan-like culture, it is useful to look at what statements they endorsed. For people working in a prison to endorse a more clan-like emphasis in their organizational culture they would have to give the greatest weight to the following six statements:

The Department is a very **personal** place. It is like one big family. People seem to share a lot of themselves.
The leadership in the Department generally seems to coach, support, and help **people** grow.
The management style in the Department emphasizes **teamwork**, agreement, and participation.
The glue that holds the Department together is loyalty and mutual **trust**. Commitment to this institution runs high.
The Department emphasizes **human needs**. High trust, openness, and participation are important.
The Department defines success as helping staff grow, teamwork, employee commitment, and **concern for people**.

As a group, these statements seem to describe an organizational culture that is oriented toward human relations to the point of being touchy-feely. How can staff who say their organization does and should emphasize structure, control, stability, rules, and so on *also* want a personal, nurturing, and supportive environment? I believe that, because they are in high-reliability organizations, they endorse structure but sense that the organization has gone off track. What is wrong is that their organizations do not honor deference to expertise and a commitment to resilience. As noted in the preceding chapter, deference to expertise and commitment to resilience counterbalance the rigidity that a preoccupation with failure, reluctance to simplify, and sensitivity to operations can create in high-reliability organizations. The balance between these two has to be worked out, adjusted, and readjusted day by day. That does not happen when the flow of interactions and communication is disrupted. It is the dynamic factor of ongoing interactions that preserves these organizations' agility in responding to challenges or threats. When the culture of a prison becomes fragmented, it loses this vital dimension. The responses to the clan statements just listed are informed by and in part are a reaction to the fragmentation staff are experiencing in the hierarchical culture that they endorse but that is not working for them.

When the same correctional staff read the OPAI-P statements describing adhocracy or market cultures, they also respond from where they are in a living culture. Here are the six statements that describe an adhocracy culture:

The Department is always changing and trying new things. People are willing to stick their necks out and take **risks**.

The leadership in the Department generally seems to take chances, do things new ways, or take **risks**.

The management style in the Department emphasizes individual risk-taking, doing things **new ways**, freedom, and uniqueness.

The glue that holds the Department together is commitment to **new ideas** and ways of doing things. There is an emphasis on being on the cutting edge.

The Department emphasizes growth and creating **new challenges**. Trying new things and looking for opportunities are valued.

The Department defines success as having the most **unique or newest** ways of doing things. It is a leader and an innovator.

If you were running a high-tech startup company, you could not wish for more (besides additional capital) than having employees who are risk takers, love innovation and new challenges, and want to be the first and the best at everything.

Here are the six statements that describe a market culture:

The Department is very **results**-oriented. A major concern is with getting the job done. People are very competitive and achievement oriented.

The leadership in the Department generally seems to be no-nonsense, **aggressive**, or results-oriented.

The management style in the Department emphasizes hard-driving **competitiveness**, high demands, and success.

The glue that holds the Department together is the emphasis on meeting **goals**. Aggressiveness and winning are common themes.

The Department emphasizes competitive actions and **achievement**. Being the best prison around is important.

The Department defines success as **beating the competition**. Being the best prison around is key.

If you were running a market-culture-style corporation, you would be over-joyed to find your staff endorsing statements describing your operation as results-oriented, hard-charging, and focused on achieving goals and being competitive. If your employees said that was both the way the organization ran and just the way they wanted it to run, that would be great.

If you were a warden, however, you might be a little worried. You would be right to be concerned. The cultural assessments done in prisons found time and again that when staff say a prison is operating like a market or ad-hocracy they almost never mean that as praise. From their perspective, these types of cultures are too externally oriented, too reactive to outside pressures, too experimental, and too focused on results or goals that will appeal to out-siders such as central office, politicians and media, or even the inmates and their advocates. Repeatedly in interviews and focus groups, correctional staff bemoaned the lack of clear structures and rules, while complaining that their work was not valued and their efforts were not appreciated.

As the preceding chapter showed, these competing values are intrinsic to any organization and can, in many instances, give an organization a basis for healthy, creative tension. In a fragmented organization, the competing values become conflicting ones and the fault lines become obstacles to com-munication. And if staff members cannot work together as a whole, there is always the possibility that inmates will find ways to turn those fault lines into opportunities. Headquarters cannot fire the inmates, but they can and do fire the managers and staff.

Fragmentation of Staff

The assessment team was not looking for fragmentation when it started the culture work, and it only occasionally used the term in its reports. But every-where the team went, that is what it found. The reports regularly reflect on the evidence of polarization, differing or conflicting views, mistrust and re-sentment, or the lack of effective communication. In many cases these factors very clearly make prisons a less safe place to work and live in. It often seems that if there are any differences between groups that can be seen or imagined, and there are always some, they can become the fault line along which frag-mentation can take place.

Among the most common examples of fragmentation in prisons are divisions between shifts, which reflect the differing roles and experiences of staff serving at different times of the day or night. One assessment report noted that "as is true in most correctional institutions and especially in those that are unionized, there were distinct differences among shifts in relation to their beliefs and attitudes." The report explained that the typical day of first-shift officers tended to be structured by the prison's master schedule, while the second-shift officers were more involved with inmates one on one (and, they believed, finishing up the work left over from the first shift). The third-shift (midnight) officers mainly took care of the duties assigned to them in the post orders. The report quoted a second-shift officer who summed it all up by saying, "If you want to work less and push things off, go to first. If you want to work hard, go to the '2 to 10.' If you want to sit around and gossip, go to third."

The officers on the first shift in this prison tended to be the most dissatisfied with the administration and their supervisors. They were generally more critical of and angry about favoritism they believed was common in the prison. Many said they had become disillusioned by the lack of recognition, absence of support from co-workers, and harassment by supervisors. It was in the first-shift officers' focus group that the oft-repeated expression of correctional disenchantment was voiced by those who said they just wanted "to do their eight and hit the gate." In contrast, the second-shift officers considered themselves "the meat in the sandwich," "a tight-knit, hard-working, and professional group." According to the report, the second-shift officers "took pride in their camaraderie and commitment to each other both on and off the job. One officer noted that he had stayed on second shift rather than go to first shift because he saw mentoring new officers as a way of 'giving back to the community.'" In this case, the speaker was referring to giving back to the community *inside* the prison; there was no recognition that there was a community outside to give anything to.

The report went on to say, "As the counselors generally leave work at 4:00 PM, officers on the second shift fill this role in the evening hours, and take pride in their responsiveness to inmate needs." Unlike the first-shift officers, they focused their criticism on the failure of their supervisors to support their decisions, take suggestions from them, and hold accountable those officers who jeopardized security by "playing on the job" and being too friendly with inmates. Comparing the two descriptions of work life in that prison, it is difficult to imagine how both groups of officers could be working in the same prison, but such radically different viewpoints are commonplace in correctional organizations.

Many prisons are burdened by a physical plant that is ill suited for use as a contemporary prison or is in need of serious repairs, but a fragmented culture can develop even in well-designed facilities. And it can be helped along by policies that tend to reinforce divisions among staff. One assessment took place at a state-of-the-art maximum-security prison with about twelve hundred inmates, most of whom had histories of violence, chronic misconduct, or gang involvement. All of them occupied single cells in a prison that was high-tech and climate-controlled and where "graphic user interface (GUI) computer terminals operate a virtually keyless security system. An integral part of the security system is a matrix with hundreds of cameras that record activities throughout the facility 24 hours per day. The successful use of these technologies has enabled the staff to effectively manage the inmate population." The report said, "The atmosphere was exceedingly calm for a maximum security facility. Staff were professional, cooperative and well spoken. The inmates interviewed were open, orderly and willing to participate in the assessment team's activities."

For a maximum-security prison, the facility was unique in the number of programs available to inmates and the significant amount of inmate movement allowed. The prison had been designed to allow a higher level of movement while still maintaining security. But this, according to the report, "created issues for many custody staff who felt that [a maximum-level] facility should not have programs and inmate movement should be at a minimum. This was a major issue of contention that permeated the institution, was raised in focus groups, individual interviews and in briefings." The first (day) shift and the second (evening) shift had come to view the mission of the prison in very different ways. While staff interactions were described as "amicable," the focus groups revealed a division among staff to the point where "it felt as though there were two different institutions contained within the walls on first and second shifts. Once the second shift was on duty, the facility felt more closed and security seemed to be emphasized more than it was on first shift."

The schism between the day shift and the evening shift was the product of both the lack of a clearly articulated mission and the way posts were assigned in the prison. The facility followed the practice of "bidding" shifts by seniority, so that the first shift was made up of older, veteran staff who had a more relaxed attitude toward departmental rules and regulations, as well as a more informal relationship with management. These officers also had more direct experience with the programming taking place, since it occurred during the day. The second-shift officers, however, were younger and had shorter tenures on the job. They were also more likely to have been recruited locally and to have been told they would be assigned to a "super-max" that would be a tough, no-nonsense, end-of-the line institution with zero tolerance for disruptive behavior by inmates who were the "baddest of the bad." (The prison, in fact, was operating as a step-down facility from an even higher security prison in the system, so the inmates were really the "second-most baddest" in the system.)

In the first-shift focus group, one officer admitted, to the laughter of the others, that he was a "white hat" (e.g., he granted inmates requests as long as they were technically within the rules and reasonable) rather than a "hard hat." Since these officers worked at the busiest times in the institution, they felt overburdened compared with second-shift officers, who they saw as largely "pumped-up, macho types." The second-shift officers saw the inmates being pampered by the white hats. Said one in their focus group, "All you should have to do for inmates is count, feed and medicate them. Everything else is a bonus . . . They get six movies a week and dessert with every meal. They have the movie schedule in the cell and yell if it's a few minutes late or if they don't get their pudding."

The second-shift officers also believed that their jobs were made harder by the leniency displayed by the first-shift white hats. The inmates, too, were aware of the division. One told the team that the second shift was made up of "young 'cats' with all of this power over people—they are full of testosterone, too." He added, "When they encounter someone who's doing time, it's their will that has to be done—and there's no reasoning with these young officers. They lack the experience to know how to reason with an inmate." He continued, "I prefer dealing with a seasoned, experienced [first-shift] officer."

Other Lines of Fragmentation

While the division of shifts into day and night might produce different outlooks, the assessment team found that almost any division of time, space, or function could have an effect. Even the physical layout of a facility can become a fragmenting line around which a host of misunderstandings, mistrust, and conflicting views can grow up. One of the prisons assessed was on hundreds of acres; less than a fifth of the prison was inside the fence. A power plant, the maintenance shop, warehouse, laundry, kitchen, and training buildings were outside. In addition, the prison inside the fence was divided into two compounds. Compound A contained general population living areas plus the disciplinary and administrative segregation units. Compound B, in addition to general population housing, had an administrative segregation unit for inmates serving less than a month. Otherwise the two compounds were configured alike. Still they operated very differently. An attempt had been made to bring the two compounds together with an administrative fix—instead of each compound having an assistant warden for custody and one for programs, the oversight for custody and programs for both compounds was consolidated so that one assistant warden for custody and one for programs had responsibility for both compounds within their respective areas.

According to the assessment team, however, the two compounds still operated differently. Said the report, "There was still significant fragmentation between the staff that worked in each compound. There were differences of management style between these two compounds due to the security chiefs, majors and captains who managed the operations of the two compounds." Compound A was said to be less strict than Compound B, and the inmates claimed that Compound A officers "treated them with more respect, that there were fewer incidents and 'less drama,'" and that it was a "better place to do time.'" One manager at this prison said that the management styles were so different that when staff was assigned to one or the other compound they had to figure out if they should do their job the A way or the B way. The assessment report noted, "Most staff confirmed the belief that there were significant philosophical differences between the two compounds. Staff did not feel that the differences actually interfered with their day-to-day activities but they did." The staff said they feared "being transferred to the 'other' compound where they might lose their days off or be assigned to a supervisor who they didn't like or know well." In focus groups, the line staff from both compounds were convinced that the staff at the other compound had better staff levels and an easier job. One focus group participant said there had always been conflict between the compounds because "the security chiefs are territorial. A little competition is good but too much is destructive."

In this prison there was actually a third, even more isolated unit. The complex had a therapeutic community for substance abuse treatment that was located on the prison grounds but operated more or less independently of the rest of the institution. The team report said, "Historically, changes in policies and practices that affect them have not been communicated well." As an example, the team reported that, after an escape, the inmate count was rescheduled to take place every two hours. The therapeutic community unit never got the message and continued to do its count every four hours. According to the report, "This discrepancy went on for some time before it was noticed." The report did not explain how the administration reconciled the counts when they were getting no report from one of the units half of the time.

Custody and Non-Custody

In most prisons the line staff is divided between custody and non-custody even when they want to work together. In one prison, the assessment team reported that both custody and non-custody staff expressed a clear desire in focus groups to interact and work together, but both groups more or less operated in a vacuum and were largely unaware of each other's work. In addition, there was a considerable degree of tension between the groups and distrust of non-custody staff by the custody staff. This was a product of "first, the perceived disparity of disciplinary action between the two, and second, the lack of communication." On the issue of disparate treatment, this was one case where the two groups agreed; the non-custody staff said the custody staff were treated worse.

This prison had a continuing problem of contraband, especially drugs, circulating in the institution. The custody staff was clearly the main target of interdiction efforts and was routinely subjected to more invasive screening when they came to work, which included the use of dogs and more thorough pat-down searches. One corrections officer said, "I don't understand why they treat officers differently except they may have had an officer in the past who was bringing stuff in. So now they think that we are more inclined to do that but non-custody staff could do it too and they'd never know" (because they were not being searched as often). When the team asked non-custody staff about custody staff's perception that they are held to a different standard, one staffer said, "They are . . . They get it more than support staff. I've even escaped discipline by saying, 'I'm not custody; how was I supposed to know that?'"

In this same prison, management's suspicion of custody staff was communicated every day in another way. The non-custody staff were allowed to punch in at the administration building, but custody staff were required to punch in inside the fence. The policy was designed to keep the custody staff from punching in for their shift but then going back to their cars or having a smoke before going to their posts. The officers complained that the policy meant they had to report about ten minutes earlier for work than non-custody staff. One said, "Officers are forced to punch in late due to backup in passing through security. The officers get 'gigged' and written up for being late when it isn't their fault . . . We're told not to worry about those write-ups—that they don't mean anything. But officers know that they could prevent them from getting a promotion. Non-uniformed staff can clock in the administrative area and they don't have to deal with this problem."

An interesting thing the assessment team found in this prison was that despite the poor relationship between the custody and non-custody staff, they respected each other more than they knew. For example, the team often heard from non-custody staff that they felt safe working at the prison because the custody staff knew their business. But according to the team report, when these remarks were repeated to the officers, "their facial expressions were shocked and they were left speechless. It was as if they had never heard such a comment from a non-custody staff member." Since they seldom talked to one another, except to complain, they probably had never heard anything positive.

At the root of this disjointed culture was the lack of ongoing interaction between these two groups that is ordinarily needed to maintain their cohesion in the organization. The assessment team reported, "Lack of communication was a significant factor in this strained relationship, and contributed to the sense of separation and isolation that both groups felt. When asked about how communication flowed throughout the institution, one officer laughed and said, 'It doesn't.' As a result of not having effective channels for communication—and the basic differences in their respective job functions—custody and non-custody personnel continued to struggle with each other over the most basic of tasks and interactions. To deal with this, it appeared to the assessment team that both groups had 'shut down' and focused solely on their own responsibilities." Fragmented organizations devolve into disconnected pieces instead of parts of a whole when they abandon a shared sense of what they are doing and confine themselves to what they think is good for their own unit or group.

A nearly universal finding of the assessments was that prison staff felt unappreciated. According to one summary report, "This is believed by the assessment team to be indicative of the cultural characteristics of the prisons as a whole. Staff, at institutions across the country, frequently express that they are rarely given positive feedback on their job performance from day to day, and only hear from their supervisors when they do something wrong." At one prison, the line staff members were almost unanimous in their perception that they got little recognition for their work, describing the prison as "a nice friendly place for inmates but not for us." Dissatisfied correctional officers often compare themselves unfavorably with inmates and argue that their situation is worse. Comments during one assessment included "I'm an inmate too," "Inmates have more rights than we do," "I get less respect than the inmates," and "Officers get more punishment than the inmates" (meaning they are disciplined more often than the inmates are).

In one prison, this finding was sometimes backed up by information from collateral sources. In focus groups and interviews, the team heard comments such as "Management doesn't care about you," "The administration doesn't show its face on the unit," and the staff have "no voice" in running the prison. The staff's attitude was captured perfectly by one staff member, who carried a large coffee mug that read, "F- Everything." During the same assessment, the team discovered that a staff survey had recently been conducted. In that survey, staff members often responded to questions about the administration's treatment of security staff with single-word responses, including "indifferent," "insignificant," "sucks," "unsupportive," "unfair," and "disrespectful."

At the same prison, the team reviewed comments made on exit interview forms completed during the six months prior to the assessment. The most common reasons listed for leaving were, in order, dissatisfaction with management, pay or benefits, location of the prison, security/safety, and morale. Comments included "Supervisors don't listen to us and we know what is going on," "People who make policy and benefits decisions need to spend time here," "It's sad when you trust inmates more than the people you work with," and "Hated not being listened to; we would give suggestions on how to do things better and nothing would be done about it." (When asked what they liked best about working at the prison, they most commonly answered, "My co-workers.") Despite having done a staff survey and seen the results of exit interviews, this prison's administration requested a cultural assessment by an outside team, which found exactly the same thing the staff survey and exit interviews had found.

Staff Appreciation

The usual response to staffers who say they feel unappreciated is to create a staff appreciation program. Such programs have to be seen against the cultural background of the organization. In one case, an institution with serious morale problems got a new warden who was determined to take direct actions to improve staff attitudes. The warden did such things as expand the correctional officer memorial by adding a memorial garden and initiate a staff newsletter (named through an employee contest) that recognized employee- and officer-of-the-quarter awards, staff achievements, and service time awards. He introduced innovations like a "Circle of Merit" to honor employees for charitable activities in the community, started a unit-of-the-year award, and set up an employee appreciation committee. In interviews conducted during a cultural assessment, however, not one staff member mentioned any of these initiatives and instead continued to complain about not being appreciated. The push by the warden to improve morale could not overcome the pull of the staff's insistence that they were not appreciated.

Staff are often unimpressed by management's attempts at recognition simply because they are so transparently ritualistic. Recognition programs in some prisons were seen as administration appreciation days because events were held in the administration offices outside the fence, where it was difficult for other staff members to attend, so many of those honored seemed to work in administration itself, and even the plaques with the "employee of the month" (quarter, year, etc.) were displayed in the executive suite, where few staffers ever saw them. In more than one case, the assessment team found these plaques still lining the walls even though no awards had been made in years. There were also complaints about cheap-looking "cookie cutter certificates" passed out at hastily organized and sparsely attended events with refreshments that consisted of the usual punch and cookies from food service.

At another prison, staff in focus groups laughed when asked about staff recognition and said that "the people who deserve the awards never get them." They believed that only those who were favored by certain supervisors or administrators got any formal recognition. They saw such programs as counterproductive because they reinforced the impression that personal relationships were more important than actual performance. While administrators said they thought programs were important in improving staff morale, their own staff were cynical about the administrators' real interest or intentions. The bottom line is that any recognition program is symbolic, but how different members of a culture interpret that symbolism is a function of their own cultural context.

At still another prison, the staff's sense that they were unappreciated was so pervasive that it produced an outright rejection of efforts by the administration to provide staff recognition; staff even picketed a staff recognition event and called those who did participate scabs. Said the assessment team report, "It is, perhaps, reflective also of the management/labor dichotomy that line staff had rejected efforts to offer them recognition out of concern that they might be viewed as being supportive of 'the other side.'" This seems to me an understatement. Just the same, despite this finding in the assessment reports, in the change initiatives that followed the assessment in some prisons staff recognition programs were nearly always part of the effort.

At another prison, a line staff member said, "I get kicked when I screw up, but nobody ever tells me I'm doing a good job." At still another, a correctional officer said, "If they say two words to pat you on the back, then five more are coming to kick you in your ass." At another, a focus group participant said, "You could have fifty good behaviors [documented] in your file, but you get one [negative] log entry and it almost cancels out the positives." The assessment report concluded that at that prison "the negative feedback [staff] received far outweighed the few positive accolades they were given." Often, even positive recognition of work performance is seen as a double-edged sword or a setup. At one prison, a correctional officer who was asked about receiving any recognition or acknowledgement said, "I'd think something was wrong." Another said, "Sometimes we're told 'great, you made it work' when we do something without sufficient staff," but added that "if we make it work, we'll always have to make it work," without additional staff.

Inmates Are Always There

One of the ever-present problems of running a prison is the ever-present inmate population, some of whom would like to run the prison themselves. Fragmentation, it turns out, can be very helpful to at least one group inside a prison—the people who live there. Inmates are always there, for every shift, day and night, and are always paying close attention to what is happening. Too often, inmates gain leverage over the staff by exploiting the sense that the staff need them to maintain order, by strategically using information in prisons where communications among staff are poor, by exploiting divisions among staff, using to their advantage the lack of clear boundaries between inmates and staff, and even by taking advantage of the prison's own policies or practices to game the system. A prison with a coherent culture is much less vulnerable to any of these possible avenues of influence.

At one prison, the line staff complained they had little control over inmates because the inmates routinely went directly to their supervisors, who often overruled them. The staff claimed that the supervisors never discussed the issue with them before giving in to the inmates and that, afterward, "the inmates would gloat when the officer returned to duty." The report said, "According to line staff, such practices by supervisors were common and undermined correctional staff by allowing inmates to create a split between officers and supervisors." How true this story may be is beside the point; the line staff, and probably the inmates, thought it was. At this same prison, the warden was not well liked by the staff, a fact that was noted by the inmates. One inmate said that the warden "ain't got no friend, that's what I like about him."

At another prison the assessment team concluded, "Inmates played a central role in defining the institutional culture . . . They wielded a great deal of power in many respects and gained more desirable circumstances insidiously over time." This occurred for several reasons; among them was the ability of inmates to intimidate staff by threatening to accuse them of misconduct. Due to a history of serious staff misconduct, the administration had instituted an aggressive and ongoing investigative process that, according to the staff, treated inmate accusations as a presumption of guilt. Investigators were so willing to accept and act upon inmate information that the usual practice of getting information from inmates about other inmates was turned around. According to the team report, "The snitch system was equally related to snitching on staff. It was reported that inmate snitches were 'protected' and often received special privileges," such as being allowed to keep more personal property. The system of rewarding and protecting inmate snitches was reinforced by the fact that there were no sanctions for false reporting by inmates. The report went on to say that the inmates "have become a silent but very influential subgroup within the facility. They have slowly and method- ically manipulated individuals and the facility as a whole to gain what they want. The inmates target staff who may be a bit less streetwise and shrewd than they are."

One team report, on a woman's facility that was dealing with ongoing problems with sexual misconduct, documented an extreme case of inmates running the prison. According to the report, "Much of the safety, com- fortability and equilibrium of [the prison] can be attributed to unspoken negotiation, compromise and mutual accommodation that while positive in many respects, lead to corruption of basic institutional principles and values such as professionalism and consistency." The team heard frequent accounts of inmates receiving preferential treatment or informal accommo- dations, "often as paybacks for favors given by inmates to staff including, in some cases, sexual favors." Long-term inmates—the "lifers"—had "managed to capitalize on the fact that the staff acknowledged that 'we need them' in order to get work done since they are understaffed, and security could not be achieved without cooperation" from inmates. Staff get the idea that they need inmates to run a prison when it is fragmented, and many inmates are more than happy to help them do it.

The team went on to say, with what sounds like grudging respect, "Like the numerous well-fed and cared-for feral cats that are allowed to thrive at [the prison] through accommodations, the lifers keep reasonable control over their lives, yet maintain aloofness. They remain comfortably close while eliciting—and to the new visitor, seducing—interest and affection, while not allowing others to achieve full control over them." This state of affairs had produced an organizational culture characterized by pervasive fraternization and a sexualized atmosphere. The assessment report quoted a staff member who explained to the team that men "tend to turn to women when they need emotional support, and the male officers who have these ties look to inmates who are often all too happy to give them what they are looking for and more."

This was in a state where any sexual contact between an inmate and a staff member was a felony.

One telling sign that communication among staffers is a problem is that the inmates know more about what is happening than the staff do. For example, in one case, the assessment team was told by the warden upon its arrival that the staff knew about and understood the purpose of the cultural assessment. The team found out, however, that most of the staff either did not know about the visit or had drawn their own conclusions about its purpose. While the team had been assured that all shifts had been notified, many staff members had no idea why the assessment team was there. Many believed that the assessment was somehow related to an effort to privatize the prison.

By contrast, at one of the two inmate focus groups, the inmates arrived with a typewritten list of ten issues, including the lack of an inmate handbook spelling out the rules and regulations. In the document the inmates prepared, their frustration was evident. They wrote, "Rules that do exist are not followed consistently, new policies will be implemented and then two weeks later it's as if [they] had never existed until an incident occurs, then they go back and find all the policies that they haven't enforced. They enforce them for a couple of weeks and then return to their regular mode of operation." The inmates also saw an absence of teamwork or collaboration across all levels of institutional staff. They complained, "There is no camaraderie amongst staff members. It is an everyday common occurrence to see and hear staff members talking bad about another staff member, or talking about another staff member's personal life. This undermines the respect for the officers from the other officers and the inmates."

At a second prison, the assessment team again found that the staff were unaware of the visit or its purpose, but the inmates prepared for their focus group with a written statement. The team reported, "Like the officers, offenders complained that 'staff are not on the same page most of the time,' and that it seemed 'like the left hand does not know what the right hand is doing.'" At this prison, the inmates confirmed the complaint by some officers that the inmates often knew about changes in procedures before the staff did. The assessment report cited an incident in which inmates knew about new policies on pat-down searches before the custody staff had been informed. The observations by the inmates at both these prisons essentially summarized the findings of the assessment team after its weeklong visit.

Unfortunately, the assessment team often found that the leadership of the prison did much to exacerbate conditions that gave inmates the opportunity to exploit vulnerabilities. At one prison, the warden told the team that because of the instability in leadership, the tradition there was "to make it up as you go along." An example the assessment team cited concerned out-of-cell time for inmates. The report stated, "Despite asking numerous staff members, the team was unable to determine such seemingly simple matters as how many hours these prisoners were locked in, whether cell mates were given a few minutes of privacy to use the toilet in the cell, and whether the tiers were given indoor recreation in alternate hours during the day. The answers we received to these questions varied depending upon who was asked." This is a made-to-order situation in which inmates are in a position to exploit confusion among the staff concerning basic policy. In these situations, there will almost always be some inmate who knows or claims to know what the policy is in other units.

A similar dynamic was found at an entirely different prison. According to the assessment team report, "Communication is both ineffective and inefficient at [the prison]. Staff only communicate when necessary and do not work together as a cohesive team. While they will come to each other's assistance in an emergency, there was otherwise the sense of 'everyone for themselves.'" The report concluded that this "inhibits and distorts both lateral and vertical communication, thus impeding teamwork. Department heads complained that 'we meet to death but rarely communicate.' They explained this by reference to the number of meetings that are required by policy, but we suspect that it is, in no small measure, due to the knowledge that the management team is divided, with members holding sharply different views on issues that have become emotionally-charged and, therefore, dangerous to talk about. Similarly, differences in basic understandings lead to distortions of downward communication." This is reminiscent of George Bernard Shaw's well-known observation, "The single biggest problem in communication is the illusion that it has taken place." Maybe this should be stenciled on the walls of every conference room in every prison or community corrections office.

CHAPTER FIVE

Management versus Everyone Else

The problem with poor leaders is that they are not usually content to do nothing. I've worked with several prisons, and even some departments of corrections, that had essentially absentee leaders. Many times they adjust to their situation when middle and upper management assumes the executive functions, such as coordination and planning, that would usually be done by the CEO. Unfortunately, in most cases leaders who are simply not very good become truly bad because they try to *do things,* which, of course, they do very badly. I do not know if it is especially deplorable for corrections agencies to be led badly, but I do know that corrections staff at all levels hate bad leadership. In my experience, corrections professionals are not antiauthoritarian in their outlook. They respect the idea of leadership and are willing to be led by competent leaders. For obvious reasons, however, they are sensitive to the dangers of incompetent leaders.

The cultural assessment reports make clear that the reason correctional staff do not like bad leaders is that they think they are dangerous, not that they have authoritarian personalities or are wedded to a militaristic worldview. The assessment team occasionally referred to correctional organizations as having paramilitary cultures, but the references were always negative. In one prison, the team noted that the organization seemed to never give positive feedback and speculated, "It is perhaps reflective of the paramilitary corrections industry, as a whole, that staff are simply not recognized, listened to, encouraged, and treated with common respect by their superiors." It is unclear why the team thought that a tradition of disrespect was a particular part of military culture. In only one assessment report is there a clear statement of a desire for an autocratic leader, but in that instance the recommendation was seen as a temporary fix. One report said about a prison focus group, "One member of this group—to whom the others appeared deferential—expressed the sentiment that, while ultimately they would prefer a family-type culture with a good bit of flexibility, to get there, 'what we need right now is authoritarian leadership that will enforce the chain of command.' No one in this very outspoken group disagreed—indicating unanimity."

An assessment report for a different prison summarized a more typical staff response: "The staff's preference for change away from the hierarchy culture does not suggest that staff wanted less structure. In fact, the opposite was true. Universally, staff expressed the need for clear structure throughout the prison. What they intended in their responses on the questionnaire was that the work environment needed to become less rigid and 'militaristic.' When they make mistakes, they would prefer to be coached to learn the way things should be done rather than management 'using a sledgehammer to kill a gnat.' Staff wanted the bonding mechanism that holds [the prison] together to be one of camaraderie and teamwork, not fear and control." What they wanted, in my terminology, was a high-reliability organization with a coherent culture. Very often, staff do not get that, and many times it is because the department's administration or the prison's management does things to create fragmentation. The preference commonly voiced by correctional staff is simply for a clearly demarcated structure with well-articulated policies, practices, and system of accountability. What they do not want is an impersonal culture made up of rigid rules and arbitrary controls.

Leadership, Instability, and Communication

Most correctional systems have high turnover at the director level, the director usually being replaced about every four years. Corrections directors almost always serve at the pleasure of the state governor, and it is not unusual for a newly elected governor to install a new director as part of his or her administration. In contrast to states where the director is assumed to be a political appointee and works for the governor, some states view the position as better filled by a professional. The former situation is the more typical; after each election, a wave of new directors appears at the next meeting of the Association of State Correctional Administrators. At these semiannual meetings, there is always a chart taped to the wall that rank-orders the current directors by tenure. Everyone studies it closely—the average tenure reported at such a meeting in early 2014 was 3.8 years.

Four years is not much time for a new director to make a significant change. This reality has a huge impact on the director's choice of strategy. A leader who expects to serve for fewer than four years needs to aggressively push his or her agenda from the start to get anything done. Staff know this too, and if they do not care for the new director's plans they can easily become "Webees" (as in "We be here when you be gone," to use Harold Clarke's phrase). On the other hand, a leader who believes his or her tenure might stretch out a little further, maybe eight years, may have the time to build a longer-range effort. Of course, someone who has been appointed director after having come up through a system faces a learning curve that is much more manageable (unless there are a lot of people who came up at the same time and wonder why they are not the new director). Another important factor is the range of the director's authority. If prisons and community corrections are both under the Department of Corrections, there will be a much better chance that a change-oriented director can do something that will have a lasting effect. So being a new director who has been promoted from within in a system that defers to the professionals and has prisons and community corrections under one roof is the most favorable condition for changing a system.[1] But if you do not have all that, good luck anyway.

Most of the prisons that were assessed did not have bad leaders. What they often had were good leaders trying to recover from a history of bad leadership. Instability at the top of the organization, in the form of high turnover, frequent reorganization, or other forms of management-by-musical-chairs, is especially disruptive and unwelcome among corrections staffs. At one prison, the assessment team could not find anyone who knew how many wardens had served there since it opened ten years before; estimates ranged from only four up to seven or more. According to the team's report, "This instability in the top post manifests itself in every aspect of the institution's culture . . . As a result, the institution has tended to drift along, its staff 'going with the flow' and doing what is necessary to keep things together." The report went on to say, "Responsibility for operating the facility has fallen to the department heads and supervisors who have been inclined to view issues from the perspective of their particular departments as opposed to the requirements of the institution as a whole."

At one prison the team assessed, the upper management did not even agree on whether *security* was a concern at the facility. The warden believed that security at the facility was already good and wanted to emphasize other priorities such as unit management and building staff morale with positive feedback and training for supervisors. Other executive-level staff, however, thought that attempting to implement the changes diverted attention from more basic security issues. As a result of the disagreements, the executive team meetings had become less frequent, institutional paralysis had set in, and the move toward unit management was in limbo. Ironically, it appeared that those concerned about security were probably right. The team reported, "During our visit we observed obvious lapses in security (e.g., the officers working control did not understand the 'interlock/override' concept and one officer silenced the fence alarm system without checking the camera to view the alarm area nor informing his/her supervisor)."

Living in Different Cultures Under the Same Roof

Often management and line staff are essentially coexisting in two different cultures in the same facility. One of the valuable benefits of OCAI-P is the way it can reveal the fundamentally different views of different groups within an organization even when everyone denies there are any differences. One cultural assessment was done at a very large prison with medium- and high-security inmates. The request for the assessment came from the director of the Department of Corrections and cited problems such as a lack of experience among both staff and supervisors, poor leadership skills among supervisors, and "multiple disconnects" (i.e., fragmentation) among units. The team described the environment in the institution favorably: "The climate of the facility was generally calm, with little overt tension observed. Staff were professional, friendly, cooperative and well spoken. The inmates interviewed were open, orderly and willing to participate in the assessment team's activities. Staff-to-staff interactions appeared generally cordial and cooperative . . . Staff-to-inmate interactions appeared generally amicable and respectful . . . inmates generally indicated that they felt safe."

Despite this generally rosy picture, however, there was a striking inconsistency between the views of upper management and those of most lower-level staff concerning the organization's culture. According to the warden, the staff were hard-working, energized, and positive. The staff seemed to concur; the assessment team reported, "Much of what we were told and saw suggested that staff were content with their overall work environment and worked well together as a team." But the team concluded that this impression was really a product of the staff putting on a good face. According to the assessment report the positive views of the staff "may be an indication of the staff's desperation to keep their jobs given the local economy, their relative youth (in both age and longevity), and to some degree a lack of awareness by administrators of the line staff's high level of frustration."

The results of the OCAI-P and focus groups revealed a sort of unspoken conspiracy of silence at work in the prison. One corrections officer said the situation was like a "two-way Emperor's new clothes," in which the staff pretended to be satisfied and management pretended to believe they were. Another officer referred to the appearance of good teamwork as a "smoke job." Staff also said they were afraid to say how things really worked because they thought that management was actually "vindictive" and "only wanting to hear good things." Another asked, "Why be on a committee? They only want to hear things are okay, not what the real deal is." One corrections officer summarized the situation well when she said she was unwilling to be candid because "I'm not throwing me under the bus."

This institution was another one where communication problems were immediately apparent to the assessment team. The staff insisted they knew nothing about the team's visit or its purpose and had just been informed, in some cases only minutes before, that they would be participating in focus groups. The warden, on the other hand, insisted that notices had gone out with every employee's paycheck and that the visit was announced in the prison's newsletter. (This was also one of the prisons in which the inmates not only knew of the assessment, but arrived at their focus group with a written agenda in hand.)

The isolation, both physical and cultural, of the warden and executive staff from the rest of staff was sometimes extraordinary. In one prison, the administration building was routinely referred to as "the Castle" by the staff. Located outside the perimeter, the building housed personnel, finance, administration, and other support functions. Most of the staff who said they worked "inside" referred to the staff working "outside" as "those people in the Castle." According to the assessment report, the inside staff believed that those who worked in the Castle were happier and received more resources because they were "favored by the warden, as was reflected in comments such as 'People in the admin building are his babies.'" The inside staff complained that ceremonies, celebrations, and social events were held only during the day shift to accommodate administrative staff, who were allowed to spend hours at the events while inside staff were lucky to be relieved "long enough to eat a meal and go back to their posts."

The assessment team, in fact, noted that the outside staff *did* "seem less tense than did the staff working inside the facility" and spoke more positively about the warden.

When asked about the inside staff's complaints about them, one outside staffer described the relationship as "adversarial" and said that "half of them probably hate us because we're playing with people's lives in this building," apparently meaning they were making decisions that affected them, which they resented (and about which they were apparently never consulted). Another outside staff member dismissed the complaints from inside staff by saying, "Nobody comes to work happy every day." The warden in this case had been brought in to help an institution that had a long history of problems. His take on the perceptions of his own staff inside the facility was that they resisted his efforts because "I messed with people's comfort levels." It is hard to see how this warden and his administrative staff were going to address any issue when their prison was literally and figuratively fragmented into "inside" and "outside."

Management Does Not See What Staff See

The assessment team found that wardens often viewed their prison's culture as "far more oriented towards a cohesive, team-oriented, family environment than do the staff as a whole." The team noted, "This is consistent with how prison wardens view their current organizational cultures. They diverge from their staff's view, who perceive the culture to be far less supportive and collaborative . . . The warden views the environment as being less focused on structure and procedures than his staff does. This, too, is consistent with how top managers and leaders view their environment—as top decision-makers tend to perceive themselves as less rule-bound and far less constrained by the organizations governing structure."

As discussed in chapter 3, the assessment team found again and again that prison culture, as measured by the OCAI-P, was hierarchical but that the staff preferred a clan culture. Staff did not want to eliminate their hierarchical culture; they just wanted it to be more flexible, that is, "clannish" in its approach. Repeatedly, however, the assessment team found that the higher up in organizational structure you were, the more you diverged from this norm. Managers frequently saw the culture in their organizations as less hierarchal and more clan-like than the staff perceived it to be. In some cases, managers saw the *existing* culture as essentially identical to what the staff said was the culture they *wished* existed.

A characteristic of the OCAI-P that is not immediately obvious is that it forces respondents to choose among the cultural types, since scoring one type higher means they have to score others lower, because they have only 100 points to allocate across the four statements in each section. So when a respondent scores the OCAI-P's statements about the preferred culture, the response says as much about what the respondent does not want as it says about what he or she does want. In the focus groups and interviews, the assessors often found that when people said they wanted a more hierarchical or clan culture, they did so mainly because they did not like adhocracies or market cultures. Staff associated adhocracy culture (with its emphasis on risks or new and unique ways of doing things, ideas, or challenges) with uncertainty and confusion and market culture (with its externally focused emphasis on results, goals, and achievements) with vulnerability to outside pressures.

Some wardens, however, associated hierarchy with a hidebound reliance on rules and regulations or department-imposed policies that limited their flexibility and control over the prison. The report said of one prison that "management staff differed from line staff in their desire for greater flexibility . . . This is contrary to what is typically the case in prison organizations, as management typically has a tendency to view the institutional culture as being more the way they believe it should be because they generally have a more active role in defining that culture . . . At [the prison], this difference was more noticeable than at most institutions due largely to the fact that management viewed the current institutional culture in two strikingly different ways than line staff. First, they saw it as being much more oriented toward the hierarchy culture, suggesting that they felt there was a significant institutional focus on policies and procedures. Secondly, they saw the institutional culture as being much less oriented toward the 'dot com' culture, signifying a perceived decreased emphasis on creativity and an imposed inability to be flexible in their on-site decision-making." (The assessment team usually used the terms "family" and "dot com" because it felt they were more user-friendly than "clan" and "adhocracy").[2]

In this prison, the difference between management and staff was more about upper management's reaction to the policies of a new warden. Before his arrival, the prison had been run more or less informally by an inner circle of upper managers. Under the new regime, there had been a change. The report notes that "the warden had recently strengthened the chain of command structure within the institution, requiring all levels of staff to carry out their job responsibilities in accordance with the Department's written policies and protocol." The changes sent "managers and executive staff members back 'behind the gates' to do their jobs . . . This significant change was felt most by top level managers and executive staff members, and may account for their view of the current institutional culture being less aligned with how they would like it to be as compared to line staff." The middle managers apparently wanted more adhocracy because they felt it meant less interference from their warden and greater autonomy within their own departments, not because it would be good for the organization as a whole.

Meanwhile, the warden had his own vision of where the organization ought to go. According to the team's report, his OCAI-P profile differed from that of others working in the prison in two ways: "First, the warden disagreed with the staff's desire to maintain the current hierarchy culture, instead wanting a decrease in it. Second, he wanted slight—though not significant— increases in each of the other three quadrants (family culture, 'dot com' culture, and market culture). It is clear from the warden's culture profile that he would like to see a much more balanced culture across all four culture types, but with the largest degree of emphasis focused on the family culture." The team described the warden as having "significant insight into the institution's culture and how he might influence it in the future . . . [the warden] knew that he first had to understand the intricacies of the culture . . . He viewed the culture assessment process as a means of giving him increased insight into how the problems manifested themselves as well as how he could address them through positive culture change."

This warden, according to the assessment report, was also "confident in his ability to engage in positive culture change, expecting significant support and latitude from [the department] in order to make it happen . . . He had confidence that the professional relationships that he had developed with his supervisors would enable him to move [the prison] forward with the full support of Central Office." His confidence notwithstanding, his reading of his managers' and line staff's perceptions of and preference for the culture at the prison was flawed. In the next chapter, I discuss how this warden might have used Dialogue practices to both better understand his managers and staff and help them develop a shared understanding of what they had and what they wanted.

Conflicts Between the Warden and Upper Management

Wardens may be just as at odds with their own direct reports as they some-times are with middle managers or line staff. Referring to the upper manag-ers at one prison, the assessment report said, "Like the warden, they wanted to control inmates and operate a safe and secure facility but differed on the style of management and correctional practice to achieve that goal . . . They had been used to running the operation of the prison for many years and enjoyed much more authority and control under previous wardens." These upper managers did not care for the new warden's management style and "found his micromanaging insulting. The result has been resentment, resis-tance to the changes, and in some cases actively undermining the changes being made . . . Although they acknowledged that the warden has done many things that were necessary, they believe he does not respect their abilities, does not truly listen to them, and does not want their input and involvement in decision-making."

The assessment team report, never at a loss for understatement, goes on to say, "Despite the fact that the management group expressed a desire to be more cohesive and to work as a team, they appeared to operate in somewhat of a vacuum—seemingly estranged from the warden (e.g., the lack of partic-ipation at staff meetings described earlier). It was clear from both the focus group discussions and individual interviews that the schism between the management team and the warden was reflected in their skepticism, resent-ment, and occasional anger over changes introduced by the warden." Partic-ipants in the management team focus group, when asked to give a brief de-scription of the atmosphere in the prison, said, "It's a battle of wills," "People are miserable in meetings and it stands out like a sore thumb," and "He does not stand up for us as other warden's do at other facilities." The assessment team concluded, "Some managers reacted to these changes by attempting to retain some authority—either out of frustration or angry defiance—usually resulting in clashes with the warden when discovered. About all this, the warden said, 'Force of personality and style has often superseded management principles.'"

At another prison the problem hinged on the differences between old managers and new ones. The assessment team described the kickoff meeting with the executive management group as "brief and tense" and said that "prior to the meeting there was little banter among the group, and following our explanation of the project, no questions were asked. But throughout the meeting, it was clear from eye contact and body language that they were suspicious of the assessment team and not entirely comfortable with each other." The assessment team found a similar discomfort among nonuniformed managers below the executive management level. About their focus group, the report said, "Mistrust and fear of retaliation were more commonly expressed by this group than by any other. Participants complained that they never receive compliments, commenting that those above them are 'in your face the moment you screw up,' and 'quick to drop paper [i.e. written reprimands] on you.'" Nor did they trust their co-workers, saying that "things said in confidence somehow become known [to their superiors] and often result in retaliation of some sort. One person summarized the group's feelings, stating, 'no good deed goes unpunished.'"

Comparing Line Staff and Management Views

In one prison, the line staff and management shared a similar view of the *preferred* culture in their prison, but they had completely different views of what the *current* culture was like. They both wanted a greater emphasis on clan culture and a decreased emphasis on market culture, which they traced to central office interference and budget constraints. Management also wanted to reduce the hierarchal aspects of the prison's culture but keep the adhocracy emphasis they saw existing in the current culture. Meanwhile, the staff's preference was for less adhocracy but keeping hierarchy as it was (line supervisors, the sergeants and lieutenants, agreed with management in this prison). In focus group discussions, the middle managers said they were not given the authority to make decisions by upper management and that left them "feeling undervalued, underutilized and in a vulnerable position. One participant described the environment as everything 'being on Jell-O,' and being 'second-guessed' for their decisions . . . This group was under tremendous stress as a result, indicating that several of its members were on 'high stress pills.'"

In yet another prison, the warden's responses to the OCAI-P showed that he saw his prison's current culture not only as well balanced, but as more or less fine just the way it was; his preferred pattern closely matched his current one. The assessment team had a high opinion of this warden, describing him as "highly experienced, realistic and rational, and—while generally agreeing with the need for more family culture component—also understanding the need for balance." At the same time, the team took note of the high level of agreement between the real and the ideal in this warden's view and concluded, "While this may reflect a somewhat optimistic 'view from the top,' it may also be somewhat of a validation of staff's view that leadership was somewhat unaware of the degree of dissatisfaction or stress experienced by them, and that communication between administration and staff was ineffective . . . The result may be that, due to their perception, staff simply do not communicate their problems because they do not believe or trust they would be received and responded to."

When Cultures Are Fear-Based

In one prison, the team found, again, a general perception that the facility was and should be hierarchical, with an emphasis on stability, control, standard procedures, a clear structure, and consistency in operations. What was unusual about this prison, however, was that the staff, according to the report, "viewed this more in terms of an environment of fear." There had been a long history of control by a small inner circle made up of the executive team and its close supporters. The staff members in this case wanted greater structure as a way of protecting themselves. The assessment team concluded, on the basis of focus group discussions and informal conversations, that the staff had become resigned to the view that "they have little input in decisions and that they have no control over their fate—that the informal culture of those who are in the 'in' groups along with the strong controls exercised from central office . . . drive the organization."

The assessment report went on to say, "The distress that staff felt over being distant from administration was compounded by the perceived influence of favoritism and a 'buddy' system within the facility. Line staff from both the custody and non-custody ranks firmly believed that promotions and formal rewards were based not on fairness and equity, but rather on whether or not a particular staff member was favored by his/her supervisors and the administration. The issue of favoritism was much more pronounced, according to staff, when it took the form of retribution for 'stepping out of line.'" The report concluded that the staff were "clearly experiencing a high degree of pain and anguish . . . They have been able to find ways to hold their frustration inside and have learned to 'deal with it' and leave it 'at the gate' without taking it home."

There was, of course, a strong desire on the part of the staff to move away from this fear-based culture. The assessment team saw the prison as one in which the staff was, in the team's words, "waving a red flag for help" in wanting a clan culture that "values teamwork, open communication, staff recognition and fairness . . . They desired a working environment where they were valued as contributing team members who had good ideas, and where they were recognized for the important role they played as individuals." The staff were frustrated because they felt they were being unfairly treated and complained that "inmates have it better than us" and "we're just warm bodies." This level of dissatisfaction was, it turns out, not that unusual; the team reported, "This situation is very similar to what CJI has found to be the case at most other prisons assessed to date, and appears to be a cultural characteristic of the corrections profession in general."

In this prison, there was general agreement among management and line staff that the organization should move toward a more clan-like culture and away from an overemphasis on the values of both market and hierarchical cultures. They wanted a deemphasis on hierarchal culture, but it was because they associated it with favoritism, the use of informal relationships, and the use of retribution against staff members who were not part of the in-group they believed was running the facility.

The in-group, on the other hand, had their own perspective on the organization's culture. For one thing, they were quite content with the arrangement. The assessment report said that "the Executive Team had a very unique perspective about the culture at the institution. In particular, they believed that the current workplace was nearly entirely the way it should be." The report went on to say, "This unique perspective clearly reflected how they viewed their workplace—and, to some extent, how they believed their staff viewed it." The five members of the executive team said they were a "very close-knit and collegial group. They are supportive of one another and consider themselves to be a very effective team of professionals who work well together to meet the goals and objectives placed before them by central office." One of them said, "We've always strived to be the best. Anything that central office asks us to do, we've done it—and done it well." The report pointed out, however, that "this is strikingly different from what their staff reported they experienced . . . and validates the perceptions of many line staff that 'administration' is not aware of, or in touch with, their realities."

CJI's Leading and Sustaining Change Project in Collaboration with NIC

One of the components of NIC's Prison Culture Project, also carried out by the CJI through a series of cooperative agreements, was funding the Leading and Sustaining Change Project. It began in September 2003 and was designed to dovetail with the cultural assessments to provide consulting and technical assistance to prisons attempting to address the problems revealed by the assessments. According to an unpublished CJI report prepared in 2009, the goal was to "aide institutional leadership and staff to remedy severe and persistent problems that have become deeply imbedded in the fabric of the cultures of the prisons within which they work—to improve the organizational culture and, ultimately, the quality of life for staff and inmates." The report mentioned the Culture Project and related efforts by both organizations and said, "Based on the expertise gleaned from these inter-related projects, it became clear to both NIC and CJI that there are several elements of changing a prison's culture that are necessary in order to accomplish a true change in the culture, a change that goes beyond addressing the climate of the prison." Like the assessment project, the Leading and Sustaining Change Project drew its inspiration from Cameron and Quinn's Competing Values Framework.[3]

The ultimate goal of the project was to produce a transformational change in a prison's culture in the form of, according to the 2009 report, "a major and significant shift in both thinking and behavior . . . It is a more dynamic and fluid process because, while there may be interest in moving away from the current state, the parameters of the new state are far less clear to those in the organization, and they may often feel as if they are 'flying blind' unless they are guided and supported by a competent Change Advisor." The change effort, the report said, "must be led rather than managed." This transformation "involves both a shift in staff's values and beliefs while concurrently modifying the ways in which business is conducted in the institutions." The Leading and Sustaining Change Project, therefore, ended up being designed to change the culture by changing the culture (i.e., focusing on the values and beliefs of the staff and reforming operational policies and procedures) and doing it by advising the leadership on how they could spearhead the change.

The project was structured to provide advice and support to the prison's executive leadership. The three main participants in the project were (1) one or more consultants, who would serve as "change advisors" to help guide the warden through the process; (2) the warden, who would serve as a "change leader"; and (3) CJI and NIC, which were to oversee the project and advise both the change leaders and change advisors. An innovative aspect of the project was that CJI decided to hire consultants who usually worked with non-correctional organizations, including private-sector companies. The CJI and NIC staff involved in the project brought the necessary correctional background to support the consultants. According to the report, "With both NIC and CJI project staff having years of experience in the field of corrections and being intimately involved with the cultural assessment process, those involved in changing an institution's organizational culture (Change Advisor and Change Leader) are able to draw on a significant support network and request guidance as they engage in the change process."

The 2009 report bluntly describes why correctional leaders should be interested in the culture within their prisons: "Managerial interest in culture is largely because of its possibilities as a form of social control." It points out that where managers usually exercise control through rewards and sanctions, "such controls are frequently experienced as constraint that increases the probability of resistance, which usually then produces greater constraint." By contrast, "cultural control promises to overcome these problems by emphasizing intrinsic rewards, the internalization of corporate values and norms, and enforcement of these by peer pressure. In effect all become members of the organization and supervise each other."[4]

There is an assumption that the interests of the prison's leadership will guide the decision to undertake a change initiative. Said the report, "Depending on the organizational culture assessment findings, further intervention may be unnecessary. If the values and beliefs of the employees are aligned with the formal values of the organization, then clearly, further intervention relating to organizational culture would be unnecessary. Similarly, if upon conclusion of the assessment, the agency makes it clear that further work in this area will not be undertaken, then obviously the work is complete without benefit of further intervention." Once again, this is not a criticism of CJI. It was not its goal, nor was it the purpose of NIC in funding this work, to foment an insurgency. But the goal of having the leadership decide what they wanted and then trying to help them get it proved to be a wasted effort. The approach NIC and CJI articulated and attempted to implement turned out to be another technical problem-solving approach to addressing an adaptive cultural problem.

The report did recognize that cultures are complex and that managing them effectively, much less bending them to suit management's goals, is no easy task. "Cultures are not static entities. As circumstances change, new practices are developed and old practices discarded . . . even values may be redefined and fundamental assumptions altered . . . Cultural change is not a quick fix. Moreover, the intended changes seem never to be perfectly realized and often accompanied by undesirable byproducts." The report does not specify what exactly these undesirable by-products are, but it makes clear that they are anything that the prison's management did not intend.

The assumption of the Leading and Sustaining Change Project was that the changes to be implemented had already been defined by the process of choosing issues identified in the assessment and agreed upon by the warden and executive staff at the prison. The opportunity for the staff to have a say in defining the goals of any change process was limited to what they told the assessment team. According to the report, "One of the intermediate outcomes/outputs of the assessment should be the identification of the problem and a recommendation of an intervention intended to have an impact on reducing that problem." The project strategy recommended that the result of the assessment be shared with the staff by, for example, having the assessment team leader do town-hall-style meetings or briefings. The point of these meetings with staff is that "the interaction promotes their buy-in and tends to generate renewed energy. It helps to understand what the leader is doing with the information and how quickly the stage is being set to address the issues."

The report also recommends that the designated change advisor be on-site for at least part of the assessment, especially for the closeout briefing with management. This way he or she can listen to the findings firsthand at the same time that management does. This, the report says, "enables the Change Advisor to gauge the reactions of the staff as they are briefed and this experience has been viewed as invaluable in helping the Change Advisor facilitate various interventions and strategies." From this point, it becomes the role of the change advisor to "guide and mentor the prison and its leaders throughout the change process, which by its very nature is likely to occur over several years . . . the Change Advisor will guide the warden in determining what needs to be done and the sequence in which it should be accomplished. In turn, the prison staff will work collaboratively with the Change Advisor to formulate plans, engage in the actual change activities, and follow through on their progress."

Just in case it was not clear who would be in the driver's seat, the 2009 report added, "The first order of business, once the issues and the solutions have been identified through the assessment, is for the Change Leader (i.e. the warden) to be prepared for the task at hand." It continued, "Since transformational change requires the presence of a Change Leader, and since wardens and other prison officials are very unlikely to possess those skills, one of the major roles of the Change Advisor is to help the warden (and perhaps others) become a Change Leader of the leading and sustaining change effort in the prison . . . the warden will need to demonstrate change leadership skills in order for the process to take hold in the organization and for the results to become imbedded in the culture."

Transforming the warden, therefore, becomes the essential first step in transforming the prison culture. According to the report, "This insight is critical, as all too often, when organizations and individuals speak of their passionate desire for a change in workplace culture, they often overlook that in many instances, individual behavior must change first. In these situations, it is not uncommon for employees, supervisors, managers and even executive staff stating, 'Oh, I didn't realize I would have to change too—I thought it was everyone else!'" Once the warden has "developed the mindset that leading the change process is his/her job, then the rest of the organizational change process can begin . . . Success in transformational change is all about developing the capacity to lead effectively. The Change Advisors were asked to work closely with the warden, mentoring him/her and providing him/her with the feedback necessary to move the process of change steadily forward."

Once equipped with the proper mindset, the warden can begin guiding the change process. The first step, according to the report, is to "develop a team of key individuals who will plan and direct it." This team should include staff from every level of the organization, both formal and informal leaders, anyone whose cooperation is essential, and even "mavericks who are committed to the organization but not to its current culture." The team's first task is to "develop a consensus on the desired changes, to identify the full range of elements that will require change, and to develop a strategic plan for effecting those changes." This group is not being invited to reinvent the change effort itself; the goals and parameters of the change have already been set; their job is to develop and implement an action plan. Says the 2009 report, "Using the assessment report as a guide, this group works to design a corrective action strategy for improving operations, addressing specific problems, and improving the quality of life for both staff and inmates. The goal of the activities engaged in by this team is to significantly change the culture as recommended in the assessment report."

The purpose of the team is also strategic. Says the report, "Involving key people from various units and levels in planning strategic change is essential to gaining support for it." As the team deliberates, the contours of the major groupings within the organization and how each views the changes are revealed. The report continues, "This data can then be examined to identify common themes by which the intended changes might be explained and justified, reasons for resisting the changes, and bargains that may be struck in return for support."

There is nothing atypical about the approach the Leading and Sustaining Change Project laid out. Its strategy was well articulated and not unlike the usual problem-solving approach. The problems and their solutions had been predefined by objective means using experts. The general parameters of the strategic plan had been developed with and approved by the leadership. All that had to happen now was for the rest of the organization to somehow be enticed, manipulated, and pushed into doing what the leadership had decided it should do.

In the 2009 report to NIC, the CJI included a brief review of eight "change management profiles" summarizing eight projects it had carried out in the area under a series of cooperative agreements titled "Leading and Sustaining Change." Each project followed the model of using change advisors, change leaders, as well as many work, planning, and implementation committees and subcommittees. Almost always, some kind of staff appreciation program was included. Very rarely did the staff participate in any meaningful way in defining problems or responses. Instead, they were empowered to carry out the various plans and projects others had defined for them.

The results were disappointing. In each case, the cultural change initiative ran through the laundry list of problem-solving strategies and techniques, only to have each one eventually run out of steam. Because these change projects relied on the warden as *the* change leader, they floundered whenever there was a leadership change or a shift in the leadership's attention. When NIC attempted to evaluate the Prison Culture Project, it found that little had happened. The eight projects are summarized next, and how they got offtrack should not come as a surprise.

Eight Examples of Leading and Sustaining Change

Case 1 was a maximum-security facility with a lengthy list of problems, including low morale, staff shortages and high turnover, sick leave abuse and unexcused absences, and one of the highest rates in the system of the use of force. An assessment team identified a long list of issues, including fragmentation, anxiety, stress, inconsistency, favoritism, distrust, and poor communication among staff. The team made a number of recommendations, including taking "proactive steps to focus on staff needs" and finding a new warden "whose management style matches the current needs." Little happened at this prison, however, because "in this particular instance, the concept of establishing a Change Advisor was not yet fully developed" (presumably the idea did not appeal to the current warden). The change effort ended and produced a report that merely "contained a series of preliminary recommendations as well as suggested intervention strategies for further review and consideration."

In case 2, another high-security prison, the problems identified by central office included pervasive staff sexual misconduct and an atmosphere of racial discrimination. The assessment team found familiar conditions at this prison—conflicting subcultures that included compounds with different missions, corrections traditionalists versus staff with more progressive approaches, and conflict between staff supporting diversity versus staff stuck in what the report called a "Cultural Blindness/Resistance" mindset.

In this prison, the intervention was what the report described as "a 'textbook' case of exceptional culture change management." The change advisor took part in the assessment and attended a debriefing session with the warden and executive staff. She then worked closely with the warden, participating in town-hall-style meetings with staff and advising on the creation of a team to work on the change effort. Over the following year, the intervention focused on team building, communication, professional relationships, collaboration with stakeholders, and training. According to the report, the intervention also focused on "structures, systems, staffing, procedures, processes, and resources that were all part of the systemic environment and having a direct influence culture change."

Nearly a year after the assessment, the change advisor summarized the progress, writing, "We modeled a process of identifying and addressing broad institutional issues through the assessment and subsequent consulting," and said that the warden had begun routinely talking to and reaching out to staff for feedback and ideas. The change advisor added that coaching was still available and that planning and staff training were ongoing to help define goals and solve problems. In the view of the change advisor, the results of the yearlong effort had been impressive; management had shown a willingness to "reach out in difficult circumstances and build a bridge or be open to those who try" and had become "proactive about involving others in the process of addressing challenges."

In case 3, still another maximum-security prison, the original request for assistance was made by central office, which identified the problems as a racial imbalance between staff and inmates, ineffective communication between staff and inmates, a lack of supervisory leadership and experience, and staff attendance issues. The culture assessment team identified several "underlying factors contributing to negative outcomes," including unclear or conflicting understanding of the mission, confusion and polarization among staff, an ad hoc approach versus a more structured style and failure to follow the chain of command, lack of staff recognition, and angst, anxiety, and apprehension among staff.

In one of the most ambitious efforts undertaken in this project, a multi-part change initiative was developed that included a number of town-hall-style meetings, the formation of the Culture Change Steering Committee (later renamed the Employee Forum [EF] for Change), a plan for coaching the warden, and "several activities in support of the ongoing change management." According to the report, the outcome of all this work included "the development of exceptional working relationships between members of the Employee Forum and the identification of a number of issues at [the prison] which could be improved by members of the EF, i.e., employee recognition, refrigerator/microwave replacements, yard coverage, ventilation system, and drinking water in the break room, etc." The report concluded, "The Forum improves communication between groups and provides a source of ongoing improvements."

Case 4 was a facility originally designed for high-custody/special needs inmates, but now housed inmates at all custody classification levels. The problems at the prison included the "failure of staff to operationally adapt" to the mission change, uncertainty about whether the change was permanent, and micromanagement by central office. The result was an extremely fragmented organization with a culture characterized by fear, alienation, confusion, distrust, and lack of professionalism. A change advisor was recruited to work with the warden, focusing on "employee recognition efforts, change in leadership styles, and employee benefits." The advisor worked on-site for one to three days every month for three years.

After the completion of a new cultural assessment that confirmed the findings of the first, the change advisor proposed that a cultural change plan be developed to focus on "making it clear to employees that management was concerned about them" and focusing on "enhancing their professionalism." The first step was to empanel an ad hoc advisory committee that met quarterly with the warden and change advisor. The second part of the plan was to create two recognition programs. The first allowed anyone on staff, not just supervisors, to nominate another staff member for an award. (The awardees were given choice parking places, they were recognized in the prison's newsletter, and their pictures were displayed in the administration building. The employee of the year got a gift certificate.) In the second recognition program, institution staffers were randomly selected to participate in a meeting, facilitated by the change advisor and members of the ad hoc advisory committee, to make suggestions about policies and procedures that could be changed. The suggestions were reviewed by the warden, who then "issue[d] a written directive in which he state[d] whether he [would] implement or not implement any or all of the top three suggestions proposed by each group." The report concluded, "This program is not only important in terms of the suggestions proposed, but it also empowers staff" (which was apparently reward enough, because no other incentives were involved). According to the report, the change advisor, after three years of working with the prison staff, reported that "he has been very pleased with the progress made, adding it is 'probably the most successful intervention in which I have participated in as a consultant.'"[5]

Case 5 was a maximum-security facility designed to provide both medical and intensive mental health care and housed inmates of all custody levels with chronic medical and mental health issues. The request to NIC for assistance came from the new warden, who sensed that "below the surface" there were problems with staff, who he described as "disgruntled and frustrated." The cultural assessment found that the prison was being run through a number of cliques that exercised broad control over the facility and that there was a deep-seated belief that central office did not appreciate the mission or work of the prison and its staff. Following the initial assessment, there was a lengthy delay before the change advisor was finally brought in, by which point so much had changed it was unclear what should be done. Unfortunately for the change effort, there followed an extended period of leadership changes, which included the warden's leave of absence due to illness, an extended period with an acting warden, and finally the appointment of a new warden. While the change advisor continued to work with the warden, the report concluded that the experience at the prison served as "an example of how discontinuous change and leadership upheaval can stall progress."

In case 6, the prison was originally designed as a large low-/medium-security facility, but since its activation it had undergone several mission changes. The request for assistance from NIC came from the director of corrections, who identified a number of issues, particularly allegations of sexual harassment and unfair treatment of staff as well as unprofessional conduct by managers. The cultural assessment of the prison showed the familiar pattern of a basic endorsement of a hieratical culture but coupled with a preference for a more humane working environment. At this prison, the change advisor was hired before the assessment was undertaken and was present for the last day of the assessment and attended the closeout session with the warden and his executive staff. Soon after the assessment was completed, several activities were initiated to promote staff morale. These included the formation of the Employee Retention and Satisfaction Committee, the publication of a staff newsletter, monthly "Impact Awards," the recipients of which were given designated parking spaces, and quarterly staff barbecues.

Over the space of several months, there were more discussions between the warden, the change advisor, and the CJI staff, which resulted in a list of areas for future work. During the period when these discussions were taking place, the department got a new director, who also put a high priority on staff retention and satisfaction. While the change in leadership and emphasis was welcomed by the warden and staff, there was "a lot of uncertainty with regard to budget, job cuts, institution closings, and staff transfers" as a result. According to the report, "As a result of their fear and uncertainty over their jobs," the rank-and-file staff, warden, and executive staff "seem to have also withdrawn somewhat from the culture change work." With budget concerns taking on a new importance under the new director, "the culture change process appeared to have taken a 'backseat' to the more pressing operational and financial worries." Finally, the warden canceled a planned meeting with the change advisor that was intended to formalize a cultural change plan. At this point in the process, the warden was transferred to a new prison and a new warden was appointed.

Yet another new warden arrived on the scene. He was also enthusiastic about the cultural change work; a new assessment was done, discussion continued with the change advisor, and key members of the executive staff participated in a 360-degree leadership inventory. At this point the warden was transferred, and a new warden, the third since the culture work had begun, came in. The new warden, like the previous two, was "excited to become engaged with the staff." Since this warden knew the prior warden well, the change advisor recommended that a formal mentoring arrangement be developed, to which they both "heartily agreed." The report concluded, "Given that much has taken root at [the prison], the Change Advisor continued working with both current and former leadership to develop a plan to phase out his direct support of the institution."

In case 7, the prison housed more than twice as many female inmates, at all security levels, as the facility had been designed to hold when the cultural assessment and change project began. The warden requested help in addressing a long-standing issue of staff sexual misconduct. Following the assessment, a request was made for follow-up technical assistance, which resulted in a 360-degree leadership inventory for key managers at the prison and the delivery of a three-day training program titled "Promoting a Positive Prison Culture," which had been developed by Carol Flaherty-Zonis, a trainer and consultant funded by NIC. Other aspects of the cultural change efforts at this prison included town-hall-style meetings, the formation of a change team, management training, and more planning.

The report concluded, "Knowing institution culture and attempting to understand how it works was the first step. The management team moved way beyond that and began using the culture assessment as a springboard for much larger change." Based on the results of the culture work at the prison, a set of goals was developed to guide the coming year. A list of the goals was distributed with employee paychecks to guarantee that every staff member was aware of them. According to the report, "With the goals, they established a vision for the institution in terms of our core leadership practices for all supervisors and managers." The report made no mention of the severe crowding in this prison, nor did it discuss whether any of the steps taken had in any way reduced it or mitigated its effects.

Case 8 was a maximum-security facility, parts of which were more than 125 years old. A cultural assessment was requested by the department director, who cited a long-standing problem of staff resistance to management attempts to increase gender and racial diversity. Staff attitudes, according to the director, were leading to a high turnover rate among female and minority staff and a staffing pattern with extremely low representation of both these groups. Labor-management relations were so strained that most of the staff refused to participate in the cultural assessment process. The assessment team, though unable to gather qualitative and quantitative data, still concluded that "based on numerous statements made by staff about the Department's recent initiative to expand the diversity of the correctional officer workforce, the team did affirm the existence of the 'presenting problem'—a lack of diversity at the facility."

A decision was made to redefine the project as a technical assistance consulting effort in which the "general findings and suggestions were provided to the Warden and the Director privately." The culture intervention at this prison, therefore, became an effort to develop a more positive *managerial* culture. The new plan involved using an on-site coordinator (instead of a change advisor) to do an assessment of just the managers. After the assessment a culture team was formed, with members elected by the managers. It met biweekly for seven months to develop a strategic plan for cultural change, which it presented to the other managers at an all-day meeting. An implementation team was formed to review the plan, and after its approval, the plan was forwarded to the executive team and then, upon its approval, presented to the managers at a general meeting.

At the time of the 2009 report, the prison had been working on this plan for about two years. During that time, managers had taken part in a two-day training program on strategic planning in a cultural framework.[6] They had also worked to make their meetings more participatory, developed a plan and obtained approval for a process to "facilitate the integration of new managers," and proposed a plan to better manage risks. Plus they submitted requests for more technical assistance, including a 360-degree management assessment, coaching for managers, and diversity training.

Meanwhile, the on-site coordinator continued to work with the prison and the rest of the department. For example, he had worked with the planning committees to develop "performance metrics for culture change efforts" and begun collecting data to examine selected indicators of conditions before and after the changes had been implemented. He had also overseen the formation of a new committee made up of staff members and "charged with soliciting proposals, reviewing them, fleshing them out, and assisting in implementation" of changes and improvements. As of the date of the report, thirty-five written proposals had been submitted for review.

The NIC Prison Culture Project Evaluation

The National Institute of Corrections made one attempt to evaluate the Prison Culture Project. Dr. James M. Byrne of the University of Massachusetts, Lowell, Dr. Faye Taxman of Virginia Commonwealth University, and Dr. Don Hummer of Penn State, Schuylkill, conducted the evaluation under a cooperative agreement with NIC. It reviewed the work done under the Culture Project over a two-year period from September 2003 to September 2005.[7] The evaluators examined the effects of the culture initiative in nine prisons on levels of violence or disorder and changes in the staff's perceptions of prison culture, based on quarterly surveys. Each of the prisons received a different mix of services under the project; eight of the nine had had a cultural assessment performed (one site received training but never had an assessment). Of the eight sites that were assessed, five participated in a change project.[8]

The evaluation began by criticizing the theoretical approach of the Culture Project. The authors wrote, "Stated simply, there is no body of existing scientific evidence that can be referenced to support the dual notions that (1) prison 'culture' is one of the primary causes of prison violence and disorder, and that (2) changes in prison culture (i.e. movement from a negative to a positive culture) will result in improvements in the performance of prisons in the control of violence and disorder . . . it is clear that the conceptual framework underlying this initiative was developed based on the combined *experiences* of NIC staff and its contracted service providers; it was not based on an evidence-based review of the research on 'best practices' in this critical program/policy area" (emphasis in original).

Lacking an evidence base with operationalized definitions, the evaluators sought to clarify the thinking behind the Culture Project. They wrote, "Although NIC program developers did not explicitly define either positive or negative prison culture, it appears that 'negative' prison culture was believed to be associated with a variety of staff-related (staff morale, staff sexual misconduct, lack of diversity), management-related (ineffective communication, convoluted mission, lack of leadership), and offender-related (racial tension, prisoner drug use, escapes) problems." They quoted Randy Corcoran, then the project manager at NIC, who told them the basic assumption of the project was that "if we change staff culture, inmate culture will follow." The evaluators noted that the focus of the Culture Project was exclusively on staff culture and that inmate culture was not directly addressed. They added, "The idea that rates of violence and disorder in prison can be lowered *without* specifically addressing inmate culture is a central tenant of this NIC-ICI initiative" (emphasis in original).

The evaluators collected both staff perception information and records data on violence in the prisons. The staff information came from surveys at the prisons using a modified version of the OCAI-P plus a scale on organizational justice and another on organizational learning.[9] The records data concerned what the evaluators considered the ultimate "bottom line" of the study: changes in interpersonal, collective, institutional, and intrapersonal violence. They also conducted telephone interviews with the change advisors. The evaluators noted that, while the change advisors were highly experienced in working with organizations, the advisors felt that their limited role in working with wardens had limited the kinds of problems they could address. They also thought that they should have had time on-site early in the process in order to familiarize themselves with the culture and history of the prison.

The evaluators concluded that the Prison Culture Project suffered from a fundamental flaw. They wrote, "Overall, our review revealed significant problems related to both the level and quality of implementation . . . our review of implementation underscores the value of clearly *defining the problem* (i.e. developing a problem oriented approach to addressing prison violence and disorder) and then linking specific interventions (and intervention combinations) to the problem(s) being addressed" (emphasis in original). The evaluators saw the lack of a clear link between and among the different interventions as a significant design flaw.

Impact of the Prison Culture Project

The evaluators encountered significant problems in getting complete survey data from all nine sites in the evaluation. Staff survey data were available from six of the sites, but only two sites had both baseline survey data and at least one later survey to allow for comparisons. The results were decidedly mixed. In the site where the survey was done at the beginning of the project (T1) and again a year later (T3), the results were not what the evaluators expected. The report said, "Surprisingly, the only statistically significant difference in mean scores between T1 and T3 was in staff perceptions of the family dimension, which appeared to *diminish* in importance over time. During this same one year period, staff perceived the culture becoming more hierarchical. Since there is no evidence that *either* dimension is associated with improved organizational performance, we are limited in the inferences we can draw here about organizational culture and organizational change" (emphasis in original). At the second site, the evaluators found no statistically significant differences between the mean scores of survey respondents in the first survey and those in a second one seven months later. It did appear that "the organization was becoming less hierarchical and more 'like a family' over time."

At the first site, however, the staff were found to be significantly more positive about "procedural justice" (the belief that the management of the prison is fair in deciding rewards or benefits) and in "distributive justice" (the belief that good work is recognized and rewarded). At the second site, however, the results were reversed; the staff were significantly more negative about procedural justice (they were lower on distributive justice, too, though the finding was not statistically significant) but demonstrated a significant increase in their sense of control in managing their jobs.[10]

The official records data that the evaluators sought for their pre-/post-test analysis was available for only two sites. At one of these sites, which had received all of the interventions (assessment, training, and a change advisor) and had the longest follow-up period (twenty-three months), a trend analysis of total incidents showed a drop in inmate misconduct in the six months immediately following the assessment and a further decrease in the eight months following the training. Violent incidents and administrative violations followed a similar trend. The evaluators noted that, because they used a quasi-experimental design and had no control group for comparison, "it is impossible to determine if the significant effects demonstrated here, or those potentially revealed in future analyses, may be causally linked to [the NIC Culture Project]. It is entirely possible that significant effects may be resultant from intervening variables such as a change in inmate or staff composition, changes in policy that affect incident reporting practices, or a change in data collecting for incident reports, just to name a few. We must be extremely cautious also in basing conclusions on data from one institution."

The evaluators ended the report with a number of observations and recommendations. They concluded that the Culture Project as a whole did not have a strong empirical foundation and that it ignored a number of available innovative problem-solving strategies that "appear to be based on a much firmer empirical foundation." They went on to say, "The challenge for NIC and other agencies interested in culture change (both staff- and inmate-based) is to develop an array of *evidence-based* problem-solving strategies and then integrate these strategies into current staff-based culture change initiatives . . . Ultimately, we suspect that specific problem-solving interventions designed to reduce the levels of violence and disorder in prison will need to address issues related to both staff and inmate cultures . . . The research literature on the link between various organizational change strategies and subsequent organizational performance emphasizes a simple truism: there is no 'magic bullet' for organizational change; each organization is unique and different approaches work in different settings. Despite this caveat, it is possible to identify a few core principles of effective interventions at the organizational level" (emphasis in original).

The evaluators' confidence in the eventual triumph of evidence-based problem-solving techniques is admirable. I completely agree that various "proven" best practices for solving problems is the best place to start whenever we want to solve a technical problem. But what if we have already tried and failed to solve the problem with these practices; should we simply keep trying the same thing, expecting a different outcome?[11] The truth is that, while the great-grandchildren of the Enlightenment philosophers and the grandchildren of the Progressive Era may cringe at this notion, the armies of reform will not be led by subject matter experts. This is because such experts are very often hammers that see every issue as a nail. As it turns out, cultural change is not a nail.

If you are a leader, whether formally or informally, at any level in an organization and you want to encourage cultural change, the reals have to match the ideals. It is not sufficient to tell people that you value their input. You have to actually listen to them, treat them and what they say with genuine respect, and seriously consider what they have to say in as nonjudgmental a way as you can. This is what the Dialogue practices and principles teach you to do. After you have listened, you have to sometimes acknowledge that their ideas and the way they want to do something are better than your ideas and the plans you proposed. This is the essence of empowering staff by practicing what you preach, as opposed to making all the decisions and "empowering" your staff to sort out the details of how to execute your directions.[12] Harold Clarke, director of the Virginia Department of Corrections, says, "I cannot empower people; they must choose to empower themselves" within an organizational culture that allows them to do so.[13]

CHAPTER SIX

Dialogue

If David Bohm is the godfather of Dialogue, then Peter Garrett is the father of the Dialogue practices and of Prison Dialogue. While Bohm provided the theory, Garrett and others perfected the practice. Garrett is a tall, lanky Englishman who, when I first met him in 2012, vaguely reminded me of the actor Stewart Granger. I could picture him in an African safari movie. As it turned out, I was not far wrong, because I soon found out that he had grown up in Africa and that the experience had a profound effect on his world view.[1] Born in the United Kingdom, Garrett was two years old when his family left by ship for Rhodesia, now Zimbabwe, where his father had opened an insurance company. He lived there until he was sixteen, when, much to his regret, his family moved back to the United Kingdom. While he did all his schooling to the upper levels in Rhodesia, what had the largest influence on him was the country itself. School was held only in the morning, so he spent his afternoons and weekends outdoors in the bush. Said Garrett, "Quite a bit of my thinking is based on the fact that when you get into the bush, into the wild, everything is quite deeply interconnected and it is evident that it is. When you see a bird take flight, you know something has happened which in turn affects something else . . . when you see a wisp of smoke, or whatever, you know that the relationships between the different parts are quite deeply connected. The more awareness you have, the safer you are in that situation."

As a teenager Garrett went on three expeditions organized by the Rhodesian Schoolboy's Exploration Society, which left a lifelong impression on him. Led by university professors, the boys traveled to remote areas and unexplored (by white people) areas of the country to help map them and document the local geology, plants, and wildlife. Garrett always went with a group led by an archeologist named Cook, who began each expedition showing the boys how to make stone age implements, such as axes and scrapers. Before they could go on the expedition, they were required to make a stone ax themselves that could be used to cut down a small tree. What impressed Garrett was that, having learned how to make stone implements, they would go into unmapped areas to find real stone age implements. How they would do that, according to Garrett, was to ask themselves, "'If I were a stone-age person, where would I go?' I'd go up on that hill where I could see all around. So we would go there and sure enough, we'd find the implements." By looking at the landscape in the way that craftsmen of past millennia would have looked at the same place, they found what they were looking for.

The insight Garrett drew from those experiences in the African bush imagining how prehistoric people had made decisions led him to think about hunter-gatherer societies. Garrett noted that prehistoric people, much like the Bushmen of the Kalahari today, did not need to spend all their time hunting and gathering. This left them a lot of time to talk to each other. In addition, hunting animals requires sitting together and talking about those animals. Said Garrett, "It takes wisdom and a lot of respect for animals to catch them, so the conversations are more about the nature of the animals, how they run, how they relate to each other, how you got hold of them in the past and so on. And it's quite a respectful process because you are dependent on them, and they're pretty clever and don't particularly want to be caught. So in that kind of conversation about the animals and understanding them, each person is involved, because it takes more than one person to catch a buck, for example, and to cook it and eat it. So each person starts to think about their role in that . . . The idea is you talk about it, and each person has a common understanding of it, and each person knows what their part is in succeeding."

While Garrett left Africa when he was sixteen years old, he later returned for a time, managing and working on two different farms in South Africa. His two children, a daughter and a son, were born on those farms. They were delivered by a midwife who refused to take payment, although she did agree to accept a dress made by his wife, Jenny. The experience of farming, said Garrett, renewed his "sense of physical interconnectedness." In a 1987 interview, David Bohm revealed a similar sense of connection. He said he felt "a sense of nature being whole very early. I felt internally related to trees, mountains, and stars in a way I wasn't to all the chaos of the cities. When I first studied quantum mechanics I felt again that sense of internal relationship—that it was describing something that I was experiencing directly rather than just thinking about . . . In quantum mechanics I came closer to my intuitive sense of nature."[2] It is not surprising that when he first heard Bohm speak, Garrett immediately felt an intuitive understanding of his ideas about wholeness.

Garrett did not start out intending to be an experiential trainer or consultant in Dialogue, much less in Prison Dialogue. He says that his involvement started as a serious but part-time hobby. After he returned from farming and other work in South Africa, Garrett worked in London in a number of management and marketing jobs in the building and hotel business before later setting up his own import/export wholesale business. He was working in property development when he began devoting a significant amount of time to developing dialogue work. Still in his spare time, he did community group work that led him to organize a residential conference at Warwick University on "integrity," to which he invited people from many fields and disciplines. One of them was David Bohm. Bohm gave a presentation at the conference about wholeness and fragmentation that made such a strong impression on Garrett that he organized a second, three-day private conference for forty people, which became the basis for Bohm's book *Unfolding Meaning*.

Twenty years later, Garrett still remembered vividly the original presentation and the way in which Bohm used the growth of an oak tree to illustrate the idea of unfoldment. The process of an acorn growing into an oak is one in which the earth, water, and air move through the acorn to form the tree and then return back into the environment as the tree dies and decays. Said Garrett, "So really the environment is unfolding in the form of a tree, and then the tree enfolds back into the earth as it collapses and decomposes." Garrett, the onetime farmer, observed, "So it was more about the fact that there is a wholeness to everything rather than distinct trees and a piece of land . . . the land is unfolding into the form of a tree through a seed and so on . . . [Bohm was] . . . trying to position the process of enfoldment as being the primary and continuous state of reality—rather than thinking in terms of separate objects and kind of fragmenting that wholeness into bits, which the mind usually does."

During the 1987 interview, Bohm was asked about the concept of enfoldment. Bohn answered, "Everybody has seen an image of enfoldment: You fold up a sheet of paper, turn it into a small packet, make cuts in it, and then unfold it into a pattern. The parts that were close in the cuts unfold to be far away . . . Enfoldment is really very common in our experience."[3] The snowflake pattern that appears when you unfold the paper was always there and is now revealed. If you refold the paper it does not go away; it is enfolded in the paper. Our tacit knowledge is enfolded in the same way in that it is revealed when we have dialogic communication. In the same interview, Bohm said, "Meaning enfolds the whole world into me, and vice versa—that enfolded meaning is unfolded as action, through my body and then through the world . . . So any transformation of society must result in a profound change of meaning. Any change of meaning for the individual would change the whole because all individuals are so similar that it can be communicated."

The initial exposure to Bohm's thinking led Garrett to partner with him in arranging a series of private conferences to explore how fragmented ways of thinking and talking about a world that is actually a whole affect our communication with each other. Bohm's stature, along with Garrett's organizing and group work skills, proved to be a good match.[4] The format of these conferences was an agenda-free dialogue. Said Garrett, "So we said if we have no purpose, no aim, nothing we're trying to achieve apart from understanding the way the thinking works, then we should have no agenda and no leader, and see what happens." Over a number of years, a loose network of people in the United States and United Kingdom participated in seminars and dialogue groups to get a better understanding of the process.[5]

Two events took place in the early 1990s that turned Garrett's hobby into his vocation. The first was that the property development industry went into decline and, as property value fell, there was not much money to be made in the business. During that time, David Bohm became seriously ill and later died. Garrett began tracking down some of the people Bohm had worked with and made contact with a psychotherapist named Patrick de Maré, who was associated with the Group Analytic Society of the Tavistock Institute.[6] As it happened, de Maré introduced Garrett to a probation officer named Dave Parsons, who wanted to start a Dialogue group in a high- and maximum-security facility, HMP Whitemore in Cambridgeshire.[7] Parson was familiar with Dialogue, having read a paper Garrett had coauthored in 1991 with David Bohm and Donald Factor titled "Dialogue: A Proposal."

When Garrett was invited to work in a maximum-security prison, he reacted the way most people do before their first visit. He said, "I would say I went into prisons reluctantly or very cautiously . . . I was keen to pursue the Dialogue work, but having to visit a maximum-security prison and to be briefed before doing so made me pretty cautious and pretty worried about what I might meet." The first Dialogue group started at Whitemore in September 1993 and ran weekly for the next seven years. The groups usually had about twenty participants, fifteen of them inmates and the rest staff. According to a case study description prepared for the twentieth anniversary of Prison Dialogue, "The prison culture was fragmented and dehumanized, commonly resulting in violation and violence . . . The prison at that time was struggling to keep good order and discipline, and suffered staff and prisoner assaults, hostage taking, murders, minor rioting and an escape."[8] So this UK prison was similar to the ones in the United States assessed by the Prison Culture Project. Over the next twenty years Garrett and his business partner, Jane Ball, would work in and with a dozen prisons in the United Kingdom well as the four departments of corrections in the United States led by Harold Clarke.

Garrett's early experiences in working with prison staff and inmates took place alongside his involvement with training and consulting in the private sector. The original emphasis in Dialogue had, in Garrett's view, tended to mythologize the agenda-free, leaderless group as an end in itself. He felt strongly that there was a need to take Dialogue beyond thinking about dialogue to practical applications of Dialogue. He wanted to use Dialogue and unfoldment as a way of talking and thinking together that was closer to the natural processes of learning and discovery. According to Garrett, "If you get into the sense of enfoldment and unfoldment, you can talk forever, because thoughts keep coming into your mind, and you keep developing them and so on and they grow. If you don't get into that kind of flow, it becomes broken up, and you get into disagreements and arguments and so on." This is why Dialogue is usually energizing, not exhausting.

The common problem, as Garrett saw it, was that something was necessary to keep the "flow" of groups from flowing on forever and never getting anywhere. He saw the need for some way to get feedback so that people and groups could stay on track, and that led him to think about Dialogue within organizations.[9] Here he found the opportunity to bring his sense that people are interconnected to a familiar area. As a businessman, he found that he particularly liked "working for organizations where you have to get paid, because if you're making no difference, they won't pay you and you can't work there, so it's kind of a good feedback system." Garrett began to work with William Isaacs, who had participated in the conferences he had organized in the United Kingdom and Switzerland. Isaacs was from MIT's Sloan School of Management, had received a grant from the Kellogg Foundation to develop further the idea of Dialogue, and was using Dialogue with corporate clients.[10] For several years, Garrett partnered with Isaacs in a leadership development program. Other faculty members at different times were David Kantor, Peter Senge, Otto Scharmer, Edwin Schein, and the Canadian extemporary pianist Michael Jones, among others. This was the program Harold Clarke participated in.

By that time, Garrett was running three different two-hour Dialogue groups every Tuesday at Whitemore Prison and participating most months with Isaacs and others in Dialogue training and leadership development. The arrangement allowed him to compare the ideas they were trying out in the MIT work with what he was learning every week at the prison. I once asked Garrett if he was trying out in the prison the ideas he got from the MIT training, but he told me it was the other way around: "I felt that the quality of learning I got with academics was more theoretical and less useful. The prisoners and staff were talking about more real things and were less able to disguise what was going on intellectually." Garrett added, " People say that a good theory makes for easy practice, but I found it to be the other way around; good practice makes for good theory!"

Garrett recalls one incident in the early days of his prison work that impressed upon him how different the stakes can be in a prison than in academic institutions. In UK prisons, kites from inmates (notes to staff intended to be kept confidential) are written up in security information reports (SIR). Once, an officer gave a copy of an SIR to another inmate that identified a particular inmate as a snitch. The inmate came to the Dialogue group to try to clear his name and avoid the retaliation he knew was waiting for him. He did not succeed and was seriously hurt when other inmates later assaulted him. Garrett said that the inmates' goals were "about personal safety, about their reputation, about maintaining sanity through very long sentences, about bullying, about depression." Unlike the situation with his MIT colleagues, "none of these were in order to publish academic papers." About the development of Prison Dialogue, Garrett said, "The key piece, the practices, were developed . . . from the early work in the high- and maximum-security prison. My practice in the prison was based on respect. Because I offered respect, it opened the door for people to be genuine, and as they were genuine they got listened to. And so the door to that work is respect, from my point of view." That insight would become a touchstone for the work he would do with inmates and prison staff.

Garrett would eventually find in Jane Ball a business partner who could match his own commitment, and equal his enthusiasm, for the Dialogue work. Ball, like many successful working mothers, seems to have mastered the knack of combining indefatigable energy, unflappable confidence, and a need for very little sleep. She also seems immune to jetlag. More important, she has an easy way of working with a wide range of people (and is great at remembering names). Growing up in the United Kingdom, she moved with her family often and felt as though she was "always trying to fit in."[11] After finishing her degrees in politics, philosophy, and economics at Oxford, Ball spent five years operating a clinic/shelter for homeless people in London. As her interests in social issues broadened, she earned a master's degree in criminology from Edinburgh before returning to London and then Warwickshire. She met Garrett while doing social work in a high-security prison in 1999 and a year later began working with him, later becoming a partner in their firm, Dialogue Associates. Their offices are in the rural town of Chipping Campden.[12] Ball joined the firm in time to participate in the work Garrett had begun with Harold Clarke while he was still in Nebraska. She and Garrett worked together with Clarke in his subsequent assignments around the United States. Meanwhile, Ball and Garrett continued to work in prisons in the United Kingdom.

The Dialogue training Garrett and Ball deliver is highly experiential, with all of the skills and practices being acted out, in contrast to the usual way, in which a lecture is followed by exercises typical of most training for adults. The experience tends to feel a bit chaotic and is certainly more physically taxing than other types of training. There is a lot of moving around. Garrett had come away from his experiences with Bohm conscious of "the interconnectedness of everything at an inner level and I felt I had that at a physical level . . . that's why I'm keen that a learning process should be both conceptual and visceral. If you can get that then you know what it means; that's been my translation . . . bring the two together in a way of connected learning, if you can."

During the period I worked with Garrett and Ball in Virginia, I participated several times (first in March 2012) as different groups of staff received the Dialogue training. Because Dialogue training, as delivered by Garrett and

Ball, is much more an experience than an instructional practice, the best way I can give you a feel for it is to describe my experience. The description in the next section is drawn from the notes I took during that first, two-day training session. (It was also during that first week that I had my first interview with the companionable Mr. Garrett, a lengthy session that began over drinks and lasted through and long after dinner.)

Dialogue Training

Garrett and Ball's training in Dialogue is itself dialogic and an extended exercise of dialogic practices in its presentation and structure. It begins with one of the frequently used techniques in Dialogue, the check-in. Every Dialogue training, like Dialogue meetings, begins with a check-in to get everyone into the room and focused on what is happening there and at that time. This is not simply one of the usual ice-breaker exercises or games intended to relax people; it is the first step in the training. One of the central themes of Dialogue is full participation in the most active sense of the word; everyone must be engaged in the process, and through engagement, all should be actively involved in designing and redesigning the process as it unfolds.

A basic tenet of Dialogue is that if people are not engaged, there must be a reason. The assumption is that everyone present is intelligent, committed, and capable of making a valuable contribution. If anyone is not engaged, the appropriate response is to inquire into the reasons for the nonengagement, not to reject those who are not engaged, or to label their nonengagement as resistance, or to deliberately exclude those who are not team players. Reacting in one of these inappropriate ways is one of the most common reasons that Dialogue groups fail. It is important to stay with the group when the tension begins to rise. It is exactly at that point, when there is just enough collective discomfort to nudge people into a shift, that everyone has to stay engaged. Often, the best thing is for everyone to keep quiet for a minute or two. One writer called this "letting the silence do the heavy lifting."[13] More often, someone makes a joke to dispel the tension or launches into a monologue that allows the group as a whole to pretend nothing awkward has happened. This is one situation in which bystanders in the room need to pipe up and point out how the group just skipped over the opportunity to do something important.

Dialogue sessions are conducted in a circle so that every person can see every other person in the group. Because people have to be able to see and hear each other easily, a Dialogue group is easiest with only twenty or thirty participants. The usual setting for meetings, at a table with people on two sides and the leader at the head of the table, does not work for Dialogue. The process begins at check-in because it provides every participant with the opportunity to talk and also listen to the others.

There are several ways to do a check-in, but one of the most effective is to have the person who will talk next be picked by whoever has just spoken. This requires that everyone in the group pay attention to the person who has already talked (and to remember people's names, too). The process brings each person's voice "into the room" and gets each person focused on what is happening there rather than thinking about what might be happening elsewhere. "Voice" in Dialogue means more than speaking aloud. There is something essentially human about face-to-face communications between people, and only a small part of the meaning of what is being communicated is carried by the bare words.[14]

"Voice" refers to our way of expressing ourselves when we are genuine and authentic. Voice is a practice; it is something you do, not something you act out based on a set of communication techniques or strategies you have been trained to use. There is nothing mysterious about using your genuine voice, although it is sometimes difficult to do. The truth is, you already know how because you learned how to use your voice as you grew up. It is how people who care about each other often talk with one another. You can tell when you are using your voice in this sense because it feels different from other ways of communicating. It flows more smoothly. It is energizing rather than tiring. If you have spoken for any length of time and feel tired, you have not been using your voice. And fragmentation, among partners, within families, and in organizations, makes talking together a struggle because it is difficult for people to find their voice.

A practice complementary to voice is that of listening. Listening means paying full attention to what others are saying in order to understand what they mean. This is different from just processing the informational content of their statements while you wait for your turn to talk. On the other hand, your practice of listening is limited when others are not using their genuine voice; if they are not using their voice, there is less to listen to. With nothing genuine happening in the room, it is even hard to focus your attention for long. Significantly, however, when people are listened to, they are encouraged to find and exercise their voice. And conversely, when people are not listened to, they find it much harder to speak for any length of time and feel tired by the process. How many meetings have you attended that left you completely exhausted even though all you did was sit there and talk?

One exercise Garrett and Ball use in their training to give participants a feel for voice and listening involves using voice and not-listening. All the participants are put into groups of four, and one person is asked to simply talk about a favorite subject. It can be a hobby, a particular area of interest and expertise, family, travel, or whatever else the person likes and has no trouble talking about. This participant is asked to just talk on, no matter what. The other three participants are asked to do three things in sequence: listen attentively, then shift to listening while also thinking about three emails they need to send (no one ever seems to have trouble thinking of at least three), and finally get out their mobile device and actually send the emails (while trying to follow the person who is still speaking about his or her favorite subject). The listeners, of course, cannot really listen to the speaker while they are distracted. What is interesting is that the speaker cannot really speak when his or her audience is so obviously not paying attention. The speaker literally loses his or her voice. The speaker falters even before the mobiles come out; as soon as the others are not listening closely, the speaker becomes less engaged. Most speakers finally fall silent (or remember an email they themselves want to send and get out their mobile device, too).

Voice and listening are two of the four practices required for people to engage in productive conversations or Dialogue. A third practice is what Garrett and Ball call "respect." Respect is taking other people and their views seriously and, by doing so, making clear that they and what they say is important for you to hear. You demonstrate your respect by listening. Respect is not the same as admiration or condoning others' actions; you can respect a person and his or her views in this sense even if you do not trust or like the person. But it is impossible to practice respect while demeaning or dismissing the other person. Instead, you must to some degree exchange yourself with others by "standing in their shoes." To do this, you must accept the basic assumption that other people are doing the best they can, given the situation in which they find themselves. This is true even if they are inmates. While this may seem difficult, especially in places where competition or conflict is high, if people are able to practice using their voice more genuinely and listening to each other, respect will emerge.

None of this can happen between people unless they also use the fourth practice, which Garrett and Ball label "suspension." When we practice suspension, we honestly inquire into the assumptions and implications of *our own* views and biases. In an important sense, the concept of suspension captures an essential element in Dialogue. When we practice suspension, we set aside, at least for the moment, our habit of judging others from the perspective of our own or our group's interests and concerns. We cannot have a dialogue with anyone while remaining convinced that our personal beliefs, judgments, interests, and views are, by definition, the only right ones. A key practice in Dialogue is the art of collectively suspending. That means inquiring into the assumptions and implications of what we think and believe in our culture. When this works, the tacit knowledge that underpins our cultural assumptions (beliefs, values, attitudes, etc.) is openly shared and, very often, is changed.

By using our genuine voice, seriously listening, giving respect, and suspending judgmental assumptions, we can develop true dialogues with others. When people are communicating together and using all four practices skillfully, they develop a shared meaning and a common feeling about where they are and what they might do next to change their situation should they decide to do so. When we do this together, Garrett says, "that is the process of getting a common understanding, a common sense, and each person has a unique role in carrying it out. It's not like the decision-making process we have now. Because of our numbers, because of the way we're organized, we have some people in control of others. We have strategies, visions, policies, and plans. We have people policing each other to make sure they deliver what is required of them . . . So we now have a very fragmented society . . . the experience is very fragmented." When fragmentation is healed through Dialogue, voice, listening, respect, and suspension become the natural basis for interactions. Life is easier. We accomplish together things we could not do before.

Problem Solving, Culture Change, and Communication

The two broad categories of organizational change, technical problem solving and cultural change, are fundamentally different in their orientation. Problem solving is focused primarily on rearranging the operating environment by altering policies and practices in ways that improve the efficiency and efficacy of a system as it is. Cultural change is much more internally focused in that it seeks to alter the way the living culture of an organization functions on a daily basis. When an organization undertakes cultural change, it enters uncharted territory. The hallmark of cultural change is that no one knows exactly what the outcome will be or what route is needed to get there. This occurs when something happens, be it an opportunity, a challenge, a threat, or a change in consciousness. It requires a novel solution that must be understood and supported by everyone who will be involved and affected by the change. The types or modes of communication that work well enough for dealing with problem solving do not work for this kind of adaptive cultural change. Instead, it requires Dialogue.

According to Garrett and Ball, Dialogue becomes especially important when cultural change is called for and three conditions are present. The first is that there are multiple stakeholders, all of whom will have to actively support, acquiesce to, or at least allow a process to proceed. Second, there are significant power differences among these stakeholders. Third, there are also differing cultural assumptions among them (i.e., whether or not the culture is fragmented). Dialogue must take place at each step in the process. It must take place before key decisions are made and again before actions are implemented. Dialogue must also take place whenever significant issues arise (as they certainly will) as a way of addressing the issues themselves instead of adopting a renewed push to force compliance. And it is especially important that, after changes have been implemented, the process of collective learning continue through Dialogue. This often requires discipline by management to avoid the usual temptation to jump in with a quick fix for a problem that is really a symptom of fragmentation. The use of Dialogue in prisons over the past twenty years has demonstrated that it can work to generate real cultural change.[15]

In their training, Garrett and Ball review the different modes of communication and illustrate through exercises how each one works, where it works best, and, most important, how it feels to people in different roles. Some modes of communication are best used for technical problem solving. In monologue, for example, one speaker holds the floor and controls the flow of communication. In formal situations, the speaker faces the audience from a stage or behind a lectern and addresses them while they sit, more or less passively. Even when the speaker invites comments or questions, he or she still controls who speaks and decides which remarks from the audience will be given a response. The audience, meanwhile, can see only the speaker's face, not the faces of others in the audience. For the purposes of instructing others, directing them to do something, making a speech, or even giving a musical performance, this mode of communication is usually the most effective way of communicating. But it produces passivity in the audience; monologues drain energy out of groups. Very few people actually like to be lectured in this way (and if you add a few dozen PowerPoint slides, monologues can induce a coma).[16]

Two other modes of communicating, debate and discussion, allow for more interaction but seldom result in genuine dialogue. In debate, the purpose of the communication is to get issues on the table and allow each side to promote its own views and interests through a competitive process. The point is to win the argument by beating down the opponent. Listening is less a priority than it is a tactic in dissecting the others' arguments. Nobody uses voice in a debate, either. Participants take a position that can be defended or push a point. Discussions are usually less adversarial, but they still focus on presenting people's views and advocating for them. They are a quick way to reach a decision, however, and are for that reason often the most efficient way to manage problem-solving tasks. But they accept as their premise that, for the moment, fragmentation is a fact of organizational life and that we will try to ignore it. Whenever we agree to disagree so we can move on (until the problem comes back) we have decided to punt on fragmentation.

The typical physical arrangement of debates and discussions reinforces these modes of communication. We usually have the two opposing sides line up opposite each other, as in a debate, or arrange people around a table, which limits participants' line of sight. Both limit the ability of participants to develop a shared understanding of what they are discussing or what they should do about it. Debate and discussion also run the risk of missing the point by rushing to judgment without fully examining the issues, and often many participants are left acquiescing to a decision they will not actually support. They retreat from the field determined to fight another day, and the problem you thought had been fixed does not stay fixed.

Communication Actions

All communication, regardless of its particular mode, is made up of individual acts. Following the systems of psychologist David Kantor, Garrett and Ball describe conversation as being made up of four basic actions: moving, following, opposing, and "bystanding."[17] Whenever anyone makes a proposal, that person is making a move. Others have the option of responding by either (1) making a move of their own (i.e., making an alternative proposal), (2) following the mover by supporting his or her proposal; (3) opposing the proposal directly; or (4) being a bystander (observing the effect of the proposal on others and the interaction that follows). Bystanders are not dropouts—they are engaged in the interactions, but they are not taking one of the other roles at the moment. Often they perform the important function of describing the dynamics they see in the group, and this added awareness can be very helpful, particularly when things are stuck and/or in a repetitive loop.

When people take one of these roles, they get a visceral sense of what it feels like to be in that role. In the training, standing up and simply pointing in one direction, posing like Washington crossing the Delaware, gives a person a sense of what it means to make a move. Even more instructive is when a second person follows by standing right behind the first person and pointing in the same direction. The feeling is even stronger when more people line up behind the leader. It feels good to look over your shoulder and see a line of people backing you up. But if just one of your followers moves around to oppose you, holding his or her hand out to block you, the experience is dramatically different. Having done it several times, I can tell you that just having someone stick his or her hand in your face and say something like, "I oppose you!" feels unpleasant at the gut level. And this is when all I am doing is pointing at a blank wall. In a budget meeting, when a project I want to do is being discussed, the phrase "I have some concerns" feels like someone shoving a hand in my face.

In the course of any interaction, different people may take different actions and from the flow of those actions the dynamic of the group emerges. If one person makes a move, suggesting that the whole group do something, for example, and everyone else immediately follows, a decision has been reached (although possibly reached too quickly). A swift decision like this feels very different from a situation where one person makes a move and everyone else immediately opposes it and/or takes the role of a bystander. In addition, the mode of communication imposes a structure on the interaction that will determine how easy or difficult it is for different people to take one or another action. You cannot make a move when you are sitting in an audience that is being lectured to. The mode of communication also serves to either highlight differences or lessen the effect of power on interactions.

During Dialogue training, Garrett and Ball routinely have participants arrange themselves into the physical configurations people take when they experience different modes of communication. Like moving and following, sitting in a group staring up at one person who does almost all of the talking is a completely different experience than one-on-one, face-to-face interactions. Who can move or oppose if you are just one person in an audience, especially when you cannot see how anyone else is reacting to the speaker? If two groups are facing off, each side is similarly constricted. Sitting at a long table while the boss talks or having two groups already in conflict line up on opposite sides of the table will physically reinforce some modes of communication and inevitably distort the meaning of what is said and the significance of what is heard.

But beyond feeling good about each other and the process, why would we want to develop true dialogic communications with others? When people work together, they need to think and talk together. Different ways of talking and thinking together work better depending on the task at hand. Some ways of communicating are better adapted to planning and executing technical changes to solve specific problems. But when cultural change is required, those modes of communication do not succeed. Usually they make things worse.

Building a Safe Container

A higher level of communication takes place when discussions are turned into Dialogue by the use of the four dialogic practices: voice, listening, respect, and suspension. Such conversations create a "container," or social space, where people can begin to examine ideas *together* in a process that is inclusive, builds relationships, and encourages engagement. These conversations become more skillful as they develop, and assumptions are clarified so that shared understandings can emerge. Conversations do have limits; they may become unfocused and sometimes allow people to avoid making decisions, especially tough ones.

At such times, when there is a need for the kind of cultural change that requires full engagement and will lead to solutions that are owned and will be supported by everyone, true Dialogue becomes essential to success. Dialogue is used by organizations to develop solutions that are genuinely aligned with their mission and are sustainable. For Dialogue to work in this way, it must take place with all the right people involved (or a microcosm of the relevant groupings) and at the right time. Dialogue, however, takes time and effort; it is a process that must be cultivated at a pace that allows people to absorb the changes occurring in and around them. This does not mean that the process needs to be so slow that no one feels uncomfortable. Dialogue is, by definition, challenging for everyone involved. The main risk in Dialogue at this stage is not that it will go too slowly, but that we will become impatient with people or groups that are reluctant or oppose the effort and leave them behind. In the end, we will make up the time we spend keeping them in the process because we will not have to retrace our steps later in order to bring them back.

When the Dialogue process works best, it becomes truly generative. Within the safe container the organization has built, generative dialogue based on dialogic practices and actions emerges. Within this space, free interaction allows innovative solutions to emerge from the shared understandings that have developed through people thinking and talking together. "Shifts happen," said one participant in the Virginia training; shifts in operating paradigms, frameworks of thought, and organizational culture can all be generated through the process of generative dialogue. This, really, is not so new an idea—after all, does not Proverbs 18:21 say, "Death and life are in the power of the tongue"?

Leading Energies

For some people, the process of Dialogue can be disorienting because it is so different from our usual way of talking to each other in organizations and seems to be uncontrolled. As energizing as the process may feel, at first blush it can often seem ungrounded or naively utopian. What grounds the process and keeps it from spinning into the organizational theory stratosphere is what Garrett and Ball call "leading energies." Even when the Dialogue actions and practices have been successful in producing generative dialogue, the work still needs the right focus and energy to fully succeed. The leading energies are a way of guiding people through complex conversations on complex issues. The four leading energies have been labeled "visionary," "citizen," "performance," and "wisdom" and are derived from the work of Kantor. Different dialogic conversations can be about any one or more of these.

Visionary and citizen dialogic conversations paint a picture of the future and define each person's role in creating it. Garret says, "A vision can do a whole lot of work." To exercise vision and focus its energy, people must imagine what they ideally want to happen in the future. Doing that together also requires them to make a realistic commitment to getting to that future. In contrast to a visionary conversation, a citizenship conversation is about each person's understanding of what he or she can do to contribute to the realization of the vision. This requires each person to know what his or her own job really is and how it fits into the organization as a whole. Like other parts of the dialogic process, citizen conversations take time, interest, and often courage. To understand people and what they do, what they really want, and what they fear requires a sincere commitment by everyone. When the work of building the container and using Dialogue to think and work together has been properly done, even difficult subjects become manageable.

As people get a clearer idea about the organization's vision and their different roles in creating it, there needs to be Dialogue around performance. Performance-based management, data-driven decision making, and evidence-based practices are all familiar territory to contemporary organizations. But they take on added dimensions in the context of a dialogic process because Dialogue about performance is about ensuring that commitment is delivered. It is not only about each individual person's or unit's output; it is also about how each person's and unit's input contributes to the successes of the whole organization. A performance conversation focuses on what exactly needs to be done and, just as important, what exactly the organization should stop doing. One of the things most organizations need to stop doing is increasing fragmentation by measuring performance only in terms of each unit's output, rather than also measuring each unit's *contribution* to organizational success.

Finally, Dialogue needs to be wise. By wise dialogic conversation, Garrett and Ball mean the type of Dialogue that takes place in the midst of complexity, uncertainty, or ambiguity and that leads to an understanding of what is critical. For example, a wisdom conversation asks, "What is the single shift that, if undertaken, would make the most difference?" It requires a review of the organization's history, a search for similar challenges in the past, and a critical reexamination of what was learned from those experiences. To do this, people need to stand back, get a broader perspective, and fuse their shared meaning and understanding.

Power, Decision Making, and Dialogue

While Dialogue finds its roots in the work of David Bohm, the application of Dialogue and the analysis of power and fragmentation in organizations are Garrett's contributions. The dialogic processes, practices, actions, and energies appear deceptively simple, but applied together in the context of an organizational culture, they gain a remarkable power to effect transformation.[18] They seem to be especially useful for organizations on the control end of the control/flexibility dimension in the Competing Values Framework (hierarchical and market). Garrett's unique experiences working in private-sector market cultures and public-sector hierarchical ones like prisons, against the backdrop of his grasp of the holistic nature of organizations, gave him an intuitive understanding of how these organizations worked and could be changed.

According to Garrett, "I began with a question, 'What do organizations organize?' They clearly organize workforces to do things . . . you can do things in an organization you can't do on your own . . . What I am making a play for is to recognize clearly that what organizations do is to organize power. That power is concentrated at the top of the organization and is distributed in quite a specific way by the delegation of authority to make decisions. Some of it is formal, where you are appointed to a role and you have a certain accountability to make a decision. Some of it is informal because you become a powerful player in the organization by reputation or whatever." Garrett says that if a hierarchical organization wants to address the fragmentation of its culture by using Dialogue, it will have to find ways to recognize and moderate power.

This is what Dialogue within a safe container does. Garrett says that moderating power, whether formal or informal, "means senior players have to find a way of reducing their power at certain points, and junior power players have to step up and find a way of increasing it." Dialogue works very well in organizations that have two features: clearly defined power structures and pervasive fragmentation into silos and competing subcultures. Hierarchical organizations organize collective action by giving some people the authority to tell others what to do and decide who gets what, including resources, responsibility, recognitions, and rewards (or punishments). They also determine who can talk openly about what. Cultural change in such organizations will always entail a redefinition of power and authority, although seldom as much as those in power fear or those pressing for change hope. Dialogue is not necessarily a revolutionary process, but it does require that active steps be taken to mitigate the effects on communication that are a product of differences in power.

The second feature of organizations is that they are fragmented by nature. Social organizations were developed to manage the ever-increasing specialization that has been the hallmark of the rise and spread of human civilization. At least from the moment some humans began to grow things to eat instead of hunt for them or gather them, much more specialized roles and functions began to multiply. And with this multiplicity of roles and functions came an increasingly narrow focus by those fulfilling those roles and functions on their own, ever-narrowing circle of purposes and interests. In other words, all the many benefits of more complex social organization, from the family farm, to corporations, to the modern bureaucratic state, come at a significant price.

Living and working in the context of a fragmented social order leaves our own thought and communication fragmented as well. When we try to think and talk together, we face what often seems like an insurmountable wall blocking us from communicating. What Dialogue does is equip us with a few simple skills and principles we can learn and practice that give us ways to think and talk together and make decisions more successfully. Using them, with patience and courage, allows a shared sense of understanding and meaning to emerge. The power of this approach can reach far beyond what happens in prisons, jails, and other correctional settings. The people released back to their communities usually return to places that are also fragmented and in need of healing.

As we know from the cultural assessment reports, correctional staff do not want to eliminate hierarchical structures, but they do want to see more flexibility. Says Garrett, "I'm not making an argument to change that structure. I'm making an argument to be aware of how to moderate it . . . So my work is not to say a CEO should not be a CEO; a lot of them are there for a very good reason because they have skills and ability that others lack. But if they don't moderate their power, they can't change the fragmented situation. My argument is a fairly pragmatic one, which is that the nature of Dialogue, I believe, can address fragmentation, potentially, but it needs certain conditions to be able to do that. One is the moderation of power."

A large correctional organization can have thousands of staff members spread across dozens of offices and institutions, so it is not hard to understand why people have a hard time seeing how they or their facility, unit, or the like fits in with the whole. Part of the problem is that corrections agencies fill many different functions and therefore have many different specialties. They have to do their specific jobs, so they have to concentrate on doing their own part. But, says Garrett, "bright, intelligent, willing, aware people, because of the nature of organization, concentrate on their little piece." This tendency is amplified when an organization concentrates on performance and performance measures. This is the common downside of this approach; it tends to increase fragmentation because people quite naturally narrow their focus on their own unit's performance goals. The larger, more complex, and diversified an organization is, the more important it becomes for people to have a way to grasp the big picture. But since we are talking about a living culture, the big picture is constantly being repainted.

Or, to put it another way, every organization is continually telling itself a story about itself, defining and redefining its identity. In Garrett's words, "I would say that in any organization, including a prison, the identity is continually being retold by the people in that organization. So people are continually, in the language and phrases and the way they construct that story, retelling it. And if you listen in any organization you'll hear that organization is a victim of circumstance, is very good at some things, is very professional, is unfortunate, is shrinking, is expanding, is compassionate, or whatever it is. And organizations tell their identity again and again and again all the time." But when the organization is fragmented, the stories people tell each other vary from one place to another. A story may make sense from the perspective of one person, group, or prison, but it is divorced from the larger reality of the organization. According to Garrett, "The story varies in different pockets and the routing of that story is informal. And the currency of it is largely unsubstantiated. So a story becomes mythological in nature and carries more weight than fact."

The Prison Culture Project assessment team often found examples of staff holding onto stories that were clearly untrue, based on the available facts. At one prison the team visited there was much overlap between the prison staff and the local community, a small town where everyone knew everybody. Staff reported feeling embarrassed by negative publicity in the local newspapers, which, they believed, attacked them whenever possible. As it turned out, when the assessment team reviewed local newspaper articles that had appeared over the previous four years, it found that the majority of them were in fact positive. In another prison, line staff complained that management did not respect them. The team report said, "Almost to a person, they complained that when walking around, managers talked to offenders and ignored staff." However, in actually observing the interactions of the warden and deputy warden, the team found that they both "knew line staff by name and took time to speak with them despite being mobbed by offenders."

As in the case of staff appreciation programs that staff do not appreciate, the examples of a misperception of the prison's public image and even of the way management interacted with staff point to fragmented stories. The way to address these many differing and often competing stories is through genuine, inclusive Dialogue. Says Garrett, "I'm suggesting there is a place for conversations which are broad and which include a range of the identities of the organization that will enable it to be established as based in fact, based in real history, and therefore it can be tested and challenged in a way that can help integrate that identity. To me that's a kind of dialogic forum."

One of the exercises I have seen Garrett and Ball do with large groups is to have all those participating in a training or workshop line up according to their tenure in the organization or corrections field.[19] Each time, it is remarkable how strongly the perceptions of the organization and its self-identity are influenced by how long each person had been there, who was running it in their early careers, and what major events happened while they were working for the organization. Time and again, I have found organizations where veteran staff are haunted by the past in ways that newer staff do not really understand. A major riot, homicides and suicides (of staff or inmates), hostage incidents, or a major public scandal will often color the perceptions of the leadership and staff in ways they do not often discuss and of which the newer staff who did not experience them are only vaguely aware. This is one way that veteran staff come to have an understanding of the organization and its culture that other staff do not share. People who work in corrections tend to pick up a lot of excess baggage. Negative experiences with leaders and management such as those documented by the Culture Project assessment team are also layered on top of that history.

Each person and group will have a different history, and within each prison there will always be a mix of people who have participated in different ways and for different lengths of time in adapting to the conditions in which they have found themselves. It can be profoundly difficult for people in any organization or group to work through this and get to a common under-standing of their individual and collective mission. The structure that Dia-logue provides can help people in organizations do this work. Says Garrett, "If you get a primary Dialogue process you'll clean that up hugely. You'll also clean up how the official voice sounds—the authenticity of it. So the identity process of Dialogue is quite important, I think, if you can establish it. That's the contribution I would say that one can make to something like a prison system . . . to establish a core whereby it is possible to talk about the identity, challenge it, test it, get harder data on it, and actually disseminate something which has more legitimacy to it, but also creates the potential to improve it in real ways. Without it you are subject to a whole flow of individual agendas and, unfortunately, you tend to suffer that fragmentation in unfortunate ways . . . To my experience, if you get a good dialogue going it has ripples across the organization. It's quite a powerful thing to do, more powerful than imposing a management system or something."

The process of Dialogue works to increase the coherence of both an or-ganization and its parts and also, in the process, increases the integration of each person and group going through that process. Ideally, in a healthy orga-nization, decision making will be informed by each person's or group's sense of their relation to the whole organization. They see themselves as a part of the whole and take into account how what they do will affect or benefit their co-workers and the organization. When the organization and its culture are fragmented, it is hard to make decisions in relation to the whole because you do not have a clear understanding of how the whole organization is operating. Garrett points out, "The nature of fragmentation is you're cut off from being aware of it. Therefore, you make decisions more locally. And what you find is that a lot of them are counterproductive. They affect other people, who in turn affect you." This way of working by a person or group may appear self-centered or territorial, but in very fragmented situations, awareness of what is going on is all local and so decisions are based on local concerns.

Garrett goes on, "I think that after every meeting we should go out feeling . . . a better understanding of the real state of things. And if we do that, of course, it's natural for people to want to contribute to their own and their colleague's well-being. So it does move in a positive direction inevitably. I don't believe there are bad people, but there are a lot of people who are ignoring reality, and we have to find a way of addressing that." Garret continues, "It comes together in its own way. I've found creating a good dialogue process in an organization is a very powerful thing to do. It will shift that organization. You'll find that people who really shouldn't be there will start to move a bit further away. People you thought were really not up to it assume quite significant roles . . . The other thing is that there is a stance behind the dialogue . . . which is kind of a pragmatic and inclusive stance which is based on the fact that everybody is interrelated. If you do include everybody it will work out. If you exclude some, you will suffer for it. And it's not a blind belief; it's a belief for me born out of my original bush experiences and the theoretical work with David Bohm and others about wholeness. I do believe the system is whole. It has its own answers. It's a matter of freeing them up. I feel fairly confident to go into difficult situations and find a solution and have quite enjoyed doing that."

CHAPTER SEVEN

Creating a Healing Environment

There are two bits of advice about leading change that I sometimes quote together. The first is from the psychologist Kurt Lewin, who said, "If you really want to understand something, try to change it." The second is from Woodrow Wilson, who said, "If you want to make enemies, try to change something." It turns out that, when it comes to leading change, both of these quotes are true. Anyone going through a serious process of change will learn a lot about themselves and others, some of it things they would rather not know. One of those things is how much some people dislike change and how many of them will dislike you for pushing it upon them.

This should serve as a note of caution to would-be change leaders, both formal and informal, within an organization. The many leadership books, training courses, and consultancies that explain how to become a transformational leader and change an organization by following a step-by-step plan underrate the psychological, physical, and spiritual toll involved in leading significant change.[1] For one thing, they seldom warn people to think long and hard about whether an organization really needs a cultural change or if its leadership is equal to the task. Cultural change is very demanding work because its goal is not just to fix a problem; it is to fix the culture that is generating the problem. The task of changing a culture is an order of magnitude greater (measured in years of your life) than fixing a problem.

You do, however, have something going for you that most of the advice on heroic leadership tends to underemphasize. You are not alone. If you look at organizations holistically, leadership becomes something that is shared; it is not limited to the people who have certain job titles. In Dialogue, there is an awareness that change can come in a number of ways, that everyone has a contribution to make, and that all must keep in mind that the process needs to be visionary, reflect organizational citizenship, focus on the performance of the whole organization, and remain wise. Leadership is a shared responsibility, not an adversarial relationship. Harold Clarke sees the role of a leader as often facilitating the process, not controlling it.[2] "It's not something that one person is going to create. It's something that is going to be created collectively. So I may be the catalyst, I am the catalyst, that has caused the conversation to begin. But at the end of that conversation, it is not going to be totally my will . . . it is not going to be totally my product. It is going to be a product created by all those engaged in the dialogic process." Clarke said, "I see myself then in a mode of either being somewhat of a teacher or being a facilitator causing folks to think beyond where they are, always keeping in mind the ultimate objective, which is public safety." Clarke concluded, "Again, often being the catalyst and being present, instigating to some degree but then letting the conversation happen without your voice always being the major voice," yields more progress than delivering a series of monologues from the head of the table.

Clarke does not argue that leaders should not lead, but he does believe that they should avoid getting in the way of the process. "I also fully understand that at any given time everybody in that room is not going to agree, so I have to put myself in sort of a neutral position, accepting the information from both sides, inquiring of both sides, or all three sides . . . and then ultimately making a decision—respecting all the sides." In meetings I attended with Clarke and his staff, I noticed a few times, when the group was struggling, that they more or less turned to him as if to say, "What do you think?" Clark's answer was often something like "I'm not going to tell you because I know that's going to foreclose further discussion. So I have my own ideas, but I am not going to share them right now." He wanted them to struggle longer rather than take the easy way of being told by the boss what to think or do.

None of this is to say that fixing problems is a bad thing or that problem fixers are inferior to culture transformers. For one thing, fixers usually succeed while transformers more often fail. Fixing things is good, if it works. But cultural issues are something that, despite repeated and well-designed attempts, never get resolved for good. This is one way to tell the difference between technical problem solving and the need for cultural change; things that ought to be fixable do not get fixed through problem-solving techniques. Problems get solved; culture issues have to be resolved. It is a good idea to try to fix something the usual way a couple of times, but after that you are just teaching people that things cannot be fixed. If this were a theoretical argument, the reasoning would be circular, as in "If you cannot fix a technical problem with problem-solving techniques, then it must not really be a technical problem; ergo, it requires cultural change." But the argument here is not theoretical; it is pragmatic, as in "If one thing does not work, then try something different and see if *that* works."

Seeing if something else works tells you whether a problem-solving approach is enough. Problems can get fixed, but cultures have to heal themselves. In fact, even seeing an organization's culture as the problem starts us on the wrong path. An organization's culture is one of its greatest resources. Cultures contain much of the collective wisdom of the organization (although sometimes they may be locked up in what seems more like pockets of resistance), and it is a good idea to keep as much of that hard-won knowledge as possible. Further, a problem-solving approach to cultural change is an example of trying to change the culture by changing the culture and is another form of fragmentation. It is treating some part of the organization's culture as though it were a separate piece or fragment that can be fixed in isolation from the whole (as in, e.g., blaming the skepticism of line staff on their supposed knee-jerk response to any change).

Cultures are not problems; they are processes, and framing them as problems leads to a whole way of talking about culture and change that is counterproductive. The language of fixing things is filled with terminology that reinforces the idea that the process is being controlled. Action plans are developed by internal experts and external consultants. New policies and practices are rolled out or implemented, resistance is managed, and a new way of doing business is installed and sustained. The language of these initiatives sometimes makes it seem that the organization is being invaded, not transformed from within.

The Healing Environment Initiative in the Virginia Department of Corrections was designed to heal the department from within. In a memorandum of understanding between the department and NIC signed in July 2011, the vision for the project was succinctly described. The memorandum proposed a workforce transformation project in support of a healing environment to "focus initially on leadership and senior management and expand over time to involve and affect the entire organization culture, with both top-down and bottom-up strategies. Senior managers will become learning coaches in the development of a culture embracing trust, collaboration, and teamwork. They will also mentor middle managers who will, in turn, mentor line staff so that staff at all levels will learn and practice behaviors and communication skills that support offender change. In this way, offenders living in this healing environment will be exposed to increasing pro-social learning and will practice communications skills that will improve their chances for success."[3]

Implementation

Implementation models provide a detailed roadmap for solving technical problems that can also be adapted to cultural change initiatives. Implementation has become an evidence-based practice that presents a step-by-step process organizations can use. The National Implementation Research Network (NIRN), originally founded at the University of South Florida and now located at the University of North Carolina, Chapel Hill, has been working to formalize and extend knowledge of implementation science.[4] The NIRN model is very detailed and has been tested against a sizable body of empirical research. It shows what usually works when organizations try to solve problems. It is important to understand how a step-by-step problem-solving model can work in addressing technical problems in order to see how it can be modified to structure a cultural change process.

The steps or stages in an implementation process are a little like the culture types covered in earlier chapters in that they are "things" that we can use as convenient labels but they are not freestanding events. This is a general problem with all stages-of-change models; they easily make each step or stage seem like a stopping point. Then the problem becomes how to get to the next stage by, for example, moving from the "contemplation" stage to the "action" stage, to use the language of one popular model.[5] But, looked at dialogically, the name of any particular step is really a description of what people are talking about, thinking of, and doing at the time. If we have been talking and thinking about a need or opportunity that confronts us and have reached a shared understanding (for now) of what it is, then what's next? How do we get to the next step? We get there by building on our shared understanding to talk, think, and do different things, such as name the problem, give it a definition, and explore its scope. We are changing the direction of our dialogues, not stopping and starting up again. When we are riding a bike and want to make a turn, we do not stop, get off the bike, and turn it in a new direction; we just lean into the curve and keep on pedaling.

The NIRN model defines implementation as the art and science of incorporating into the routine practice of an organization an innovative policy, practice, or program. It requires that an implementation be described in sufficient detail that an independent observer can see a specific set of activities that make up the implementation. A well-designed logic model, for example, lays out the resources, activities, outputs, and outcomes for implementing changes.[6] An organization that forms committees to talk about implementation, but never does anything more than plan, model the process, or assess and coach its members, falls short of implementation by this definition. Paper or process implementations focus on the surface aspects of the culture, but real implementation has to be about the behavior *of* the organization. To implement anything, specific people within an organization must do specific activities that are visible, are verifiable, and represent new patterns of working together. How people interact with each other must change for any visible and viable cultural change to emerge.

The first step in the NIRN model is *exploration and sustainability*.[7] Failing to invest the resources and time necessary to complete this step is what dooms most implementation efforts before they even begin. In the traditional step-by-step model, this is where the leadership, change team, staff work group, or advisory committee defines what the change will be, identifies the recommended evidence-based solution, assesses the feasibility of adoption, and plans how the organization can be readied for what awaits it. This group also decides what resources are available and needed, how the fidelity of the implementation will be monitored and maintained, and what the measures of success will be. Then, of course, the group has to start thinking about getting buy-in and dealing with potential resistance by marketing the idea to staff (this is where talking about how "they" will react comes in).

The step-by-step model assumes that defining the problem and locating a solution are not especially problematic. It is not usually that simple. Cameron and Quinn, in their presentation of the Competing Values Framework, included their own recommendations for starting a process of change that is essentially an expansion of this first step of the NIRN model and helps to flesh it out.[8] The first step in the Cameron and Quinn model involves coming to a general agreement about what the current culture is, and the second involves developing a shared vision of the preferred future culture. These are the actual and preferred cultures perceived by different groups in the organization as revealed, for example, by a cultural assessment. The process must include representatives from all of the groups, both from within and outside the organization, who will be involved in or affected by the cultural change effort. All of this, of course, is what Dialogue has been designed to accomplish. Cameron and Quinn do not discuss Dialogue, but it is easy to see the role it could play in the process.

Cameron and Quinn's next stage entails a review to determine what the change from the current to the desired future culture will and will not mean for the organization and each of its subgroups. This step is designed to create a shared narrative of the history and future of the organization. They write, "The team should identify two or three incidents or events that illustrate the key values they want to permeate the future organizational culture."[9] These are success stories that can be used as examples of the organization at its best, especially stories that highlight expertise and resilience. This, again, is one of the places where Dialogue would play a crucial role. As mentioned earlier, Garrett and Ball often have everyone in a training session line up according to their tenure with the organization. As you go from long-serving veterans to the most recent hires and have each tell their story, an oral history of the organization emerges. It is remarkable to hear how much each person's view of the organization and its culture is a product of that person's first experiences in it.

However the initial groundwork has been laid, the next step in the NIRN model is to launch an *installation* stage for the change initiative, something like a shakedown cruise. During installation, all the necessary people and resources are put into place. If staff need to be hired, reassigned, relocated, trained, equipped, or supplied, this should be done, together with all the necessary bureaucratic adjustments, infrastructure, rules, regulations, and so on. It is a good idea to avoid calling this a pilot program, since this gives people the impression that the changes are contingent on the success of the pilot and, therefore, they do not have to take them seriously yet. The installation stage is also an opportunity for at least some of the people in the organization to become familiar with the proposed changes as they start to feel more concrete. Following this stage, during which most of the bureaucratic bugs have hopefully been worked out, the *initial implementation* is rolled out.

It is at this point that many organizational change efforts start to fall apart. This is because most organizations have not engaged everyone necessary in the whole process, and it is not until the rollout that most people first see and feel the changes taking place. For many people, change in theory is too abstract to arouse much concern, particularly in organizations where change efforts have come and gone many times before. But change in fact is uncomfortable. The truth is that a change usually does not even feel real to many people *until* it starts to become uncomfortable. This happens when activities are changing, patterns of interaction are being disrupted, and the underlying assumptions of the organization's culture are being implicitly challenged. It is also right around this time that tension goes up, voices are raised, and the melodrama spikes. This is also when management is most tempted to charge in to quell the unrest.

It is here that the power of Dialogue becomes more evident. Dialogue approaches resistance as an opportunity for inquiry and seeks to turn conflict into positive energy for change. In Dialogue, resistance is seen as a refusal to become engaged in the process, often for some valid reasons, and the goal of a dialogic inquiry is to turn it into the practice of opposing, through which those reasons are explored. The person or group may still not like the change being proposed, but if they are opposing it as part of a dialogic process they are at least in the game and involved in reaching a resolution. The energy that was locked up in a stance of resistance and that people spent complaining to each other in private conversations can be channeled into an open dialogic conversation that makes a positive contribution to the process.

Dialogue groups are not immune to failure at this juncture, either. People routinely avoid discomfort in their lives, including their work lives. Whenever a group of any kind, dialogic or not, feels the tension rise, the collective desire to reduce it is nearly irresistible. The urge to tell a joke, deny there is any real disagreement, change the subject, or just call for a break and get out of the room is palpable. This is the point at which everyone in the room needs to become a bystander for a few minutes. Garrett and Ball use a convention in which anyone can call for silence by just raising a hand, and others then stop speaking and raise their own hands. When the tension becomes unbearable, everyone's hand should go up.

Going Faster by Going Slower

At any one time in any change process there will be some people, including the leaders, who want to push faster for change and others who feel that change is coming too quickly. "Who's right?" Garrett once asked me. "They're both right!" he answered. "We have to keep negotiating that, and we have to keep feeling it and thinking it and exploring it." There will always be people who are unhappy with what is happening. For some, the changes are too extensive and coming too fast, while for others the changes are insufficient and are taking too long. Dialogically, *both* schools of thought, the "slow-downers" and the "hurry-it-uppers," are assuming the roles of opposers. The most useful response to both of them is to ask, "Why do you feel we are going too fast (or slow) and what do you think we ought to do about that?" They have to be engaged whether or not you find them annoying. People have a right to be annoying. Garrett advises, "We've got to keep moving . . . So the route back to being able to make decisions in relation to the whole is to start to work with those people who are having a negative impact on you." This is a case where we can actually go faster by going slower because we will have already done upfront what we will just have to do later.

Harold Clarke is familiar with this, too. He said, "Every place that I have been there have been folks who quickly jumped at it . . . There are people I think have foresight and people who want to be cutting edge in every jurisdiction." Clarke recalls that in one instance, "when I first started the conversations about Dialogue and open staff meetings and so forth, I was told by members of the team, 'People aren't going to talk. They're just not going to talk because there's too much baggage in the room.'" On that occasion, Clarke brought Peter Garrett to work with senior staff members, particularly two who were engaged in an acrimonious relationship, and then with the executive team as a whole. Clarke said that, by the time he left that post, "the executive team was excited about the conversations we were having, and the openness in the meetings, and so forth."

Instead of following Garrett and Clarke's advice, the leadership in most organizations, when confronted by a rough initial implementation, usually tries to plow through to full implementation by "going to scale." The purpose of this expansion is to somehow nail down the changes while this can still be done. Most of the initial implementation, however, has taken place in areas that were deliberately chosen because they were change-friendly. When the full implementation comes, on the other hand, it means expanding into less hospitable parts of the organization, and the battle becomes an uphill struggle. Still, the logic goes, if the organization can soldier on, and whatever the collateral damage there may be, it might still reach the final stages on the step-by-step implantation model.

For those organizations, often battered and bloody, that do reach the summit, the NIRN model promises a brighter future. Once the changes have become an accepted part of the organization, then, according to the NIRN model, the *innovation* stage begins. This stage is thought to emerge from the process of full implementation when staff finally stop coping with the changes and start making further improvements. As good as this sounds, it begs the question of why an organization would wait until the end of a process to reach the innovation stage. Why not use Dialogue to generate innovation from the start?

Finally, if the organization has come this far, the NIRN model proposes a last stage of *sustainability*, during which the effects of the changes finally settle into the organization's culture. The achievement of sustainability is the Holy Grail of the change management industry, and one of its myths is that this goal can actually be reached. The idea is that someday the work will be done and the transformed organization will glide into a bright future carrying the leadership's legacy with it. But sustainability is an illusion; the current leadership's successors will have to work every bit as hard to keep the organization moving as their predecessors had to work to get it pointed in a new direction. Cultures are adaptive, and the ever-changing world requires an ever-changing culture to both respond to and, in turn, change its environment. Incorporating Dialogue into the way an organization does business means that there is no end point to the process. The true value of doing things dialogically is that the organization constantly learns how to use Dialogue routinely to respond to daily issues as they arise.

The paradox of changing organizational cultures is that we do not change them when we try to change them at the surface level. They change when we change our behavior and find that a new way of doing things works better than the old way did. Discomfort and even resistance, including sharp conflict within the organization, are part of the process; they are the growing pains that attend any significant change. And they have to be respected, explored, and treated with compassion, not managed or overcome. Steps like installation and initial implementation are useful because they are opportunities to encounter and constructively work through issues. Taking the time and energy to do so will provide an organization with the essential knowledge to proceed to full implementation.

Dialogue assumes that dialogic communication creates or strengthens, and thrives within, a safe container for communication. During a meeting in early 2013, the Council for a Healing Environment of the Virginia Department of Corrections reflected on what they meant by a "safe container." As their check-in, they asked each person to suggest one word that helps describe a safe container.[10] Out of their dialogue, they concluded that a strong and safe container is needed "not just for Dialogue; it is essential for all Healing Environments." Such a container is where "each person can genuinely and respectfully say what he or she thinks and feels, and is listened to openly so that challenging issues can be raised and considered in depth . . . Everyone takes responsibility for contributing to the progress of the group through voicing, listening, suspending judgment but also by moving, opposing, following, by-standing, using inquiry and holding each other accountable."

The group decided that, to maintain a sense of safety, people in the group should deal with issues within the group rather than outside of it and not talk behind others' backs. They also decided that "employees always have responsibility for reporting inappropriate or dangerous behaviors that risk life, health, safety, and the well-being of those in the larger container of the Department." By 2013, the Healing Environment Initiative had been going on for more than two years. But the staff were still defining, redefining, and refining their basic ideas of what it entailed. This was as it should be. There is no point in the process where the dialogue should stop.

Implicate Change Model

The step-by-step implementation model does not have to be thrown out with the bathwater. It can be supplemented with a model of dialogic change that overcomes the pitfalls of applying a straight problem-solving approach to cultural change. Step-by-step approaches sound like marching forward on a predictable path, but Dialogue works best when the way forward is uncertain. Instead of a preset path, Dialogue encourages a series of dialogic conversations to emerge out of the process and cascades through the organization. It is designed to work in places where there are power differences and multiple stakeholders. And, as the name implies, a dialogic change approach builds in, from the very beginning and throughout the process, the use of Dialogue.

Garrett and Ball, as they worked in prisons over a twenty-year period, developed their model for adaptive change in organizations: the Implicate Change Model.[11] The model is built on the premise that cultural change can be brought about only when everyone is involved by using Dialogue skills and principles for talking and thinking together. Among the things the Implicate Change Model does is make what is usually called sustainability an essential element of the planning and implementation of any change, not an afterthought. Under this approach, you do not have to go back after you have started implementing something to get buy-in or to deal with resistance. This is the approach of going faster by going slower. It saves all the time and energy of going back and asking people what they want (after you have already irritated them by deciding for them what they want in the first round). This is one reason to keep in mind that when *you* want *others* to change because *you* believe that it will be good for *them*, the real trouble usually starts. This is what happened repeatedly in the Leading and Sustaining Change cases when people discovered that some committee had already decided what was good for them.

Garrett and Ball contrast their model with the more typical step-by-step approach taken by organizations trying to bring about change. The usual sequence is: (1) a new leader announces a reorganization; (2) the new way of doing business is "rolled out in a series of road shows and workshops" designed to get staff to buy into a plan they had nothing to do with developing; (3) people pretend to go along with the plan while they try to figure out what it means for them; (4) complaints about how staff don't "get it" start to drain enthusiasm for the effort, which now seems much harder than anyone expected; (5) passive resistance delays implementation while a "We be here when you be gone" logic spreads; (6) overt resistance and obstructive behavior appear; (7) leadership tries to force compliance in order to overcome the resistance; (8) delays increase costs and undermine the argument that the promised benefits are worth it; (9) the change process is only half done when a new leader is appointed; (10) see step 1 (repeat until the threat of innovation has passed).

As an alternative, Garrett and Ball lay out a few principles about organizational change that summarize the fundamentals of their approach. The first is the recognition that change is always an *adaptive* process (i.e., it has to actually help people do things they want to do). The second principle is that you have to assume that most people believe there is a better way to do things and are naturally interested in change (although they usually resist change being forced upon them). The third principle is that people are assumed to be naturally intelligent and compassionate and want to participate meaningfully in any process that will affect them. This is important, because if you cannot assume at least this much about most of the people in your organization, there is no point in trying to lead a change effort. It is also important to understand that people in an organization are more deeply interconnected than any organization's leaders (or outside consultants) can understand without actually talking to and listening to them. Recall that the NIC Prison Culture Project demonstrated time and again that leaders believe they know what their staff feel and think, but they are nearly always wrong.

Garrett and Ball point out some of the realities of change in organizations. One is that change takes time, but in the long run it comes more quickly when it is allowed to develop naturally through a dialogic process. Another reality is that whenever you find yourself talking about what "they" will do or think, you have just identified someone who needs to be brought into the dialogue. There is also the basic truth that organizations are power structures, and that means that fragmentation is pervasive. Finally, the more stakeholders who are involved, the more skill it takes to talk and think together. This means everyone, not just the leadership, change agents, consultants, other assorted facilitators, or subject matter specialists, needs to have the skills required to engage in the work.

The Implicate Change Model continues to be developed by Garrett and Ball, and more details are available on their website.[12] Briefly, the core of the model is to set up iterative cycles of engagement and interaction to move the process forward. An organization begins by identifying a need or opportunity and uses Dialogue to get a shared sense of what it represents for the organization as a whole. Collectively, people then name the issue, explore its scope, and give it a working title. Next, they determine who all the stakeholders are and what their needs or interests are (by talking with them, not speculating about what those needs or interests might be). Once all the

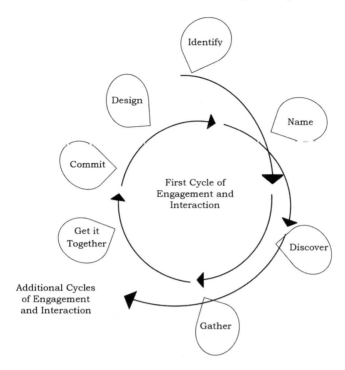

FIGURE 7.1: The Implicate Change Model Cycles of Engagement and Interaction

stakeholders have been identified, they attend a gathering to think and talk together. With everyone in the room, the next topic of Dialogue is to get it together and align the interests of each stakeholder group. Then everyone has to commit to the business at hand. Finally, each cycle ends by designing the next cycle in an ever-widening circle of engagement and interactions. The whole process is depicted in figure 7.1 to show how the cycle can be executed repeatedly as needed.

There might be only one cycle, with a smaller group dealing with a specific issue. But a cycle may have to be repeated when, for example, those involved find at the end of the first cycle that not everyone who needs to be engaged has been. Or those in the next cycle may move on to a different dialogue about what is next in the process. The step-by-step implementation model can be conceptualized in a hybrid form where each of the steps is a different cycle as the focus of the dialogue evolves. The hybrid model is illustrated in figure 7.2.

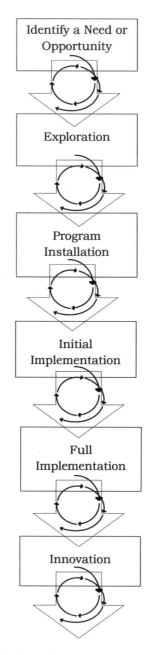

FIGURE 7.2: Hybrid Model of Step-by-step Implementation and the Implicate
Change Model

The hybrid model captures the notion that the implementation process is actually composed of different dialogues taking place in a sequence based on the task at hand. The point here is that talking, thinking, and doing are not discrete steps. That would make the process itself fragmented instead of holistic.

The Virginia Healing Environment Initiative

The Commonwealth of Virginia has a population of 8.2 million people, 64 percent of whom are white, non-Hispanic. The median income in Virginia is $63,636, higher than the nation's median of $53,046, and the percentage of Virginians living below the poverty level is 11.1 (compared with 14.9 percent nationally).[13] The average daily population for corrections from 2010 to 2012 was almost 90,000, with about 30,600 inmates housed in forty-five secure facilities and another 59,000 people under community supervision in one of its forty-three probation and parole districts.[14] The Virginia Department of Corrections employs about 11,500 people systemwide. In 2012, Virginia had an incarceration rate of 451 per 100,000 residents, compared with a national incarceration rate of 480, and estimated its recidivism rate at 23.4 percent, among the lowest in the country and a notable decline from an estimated 28.3 percent for the 2004–2007 period.[15] At the time Clarke arrived in Virginia, the state had already been involved in an ambitious statewide reentry program.[16] Begun in 2010, the Virginia Adult Reentry Initiative was a far-ranging and ambitious effort to change the way the Department of Corrections worked with people returning from prison. As part of this initiative, the department implemented a number of changes, including individualized case plans based on standard assessments, evidence-based programs, and outreach to the community.

Clarke says that, when he first got to Virginia, he made a point of drawing on the experiences of his previous leadership positions by not immediately telling the department exactly what to do. He said, "So, when I first floated the idea in Virginia, it was December of 2010, a month after I arrived on the scene and my first meeting with all of the wardens, and superintendents, and all of the chiefs, and all of the members of the executive staff—a joint meeting. And after talking about our mission and our vision and the important stuff for reentry, and the integrated reentry model, then I said, 'Ok, there's something else I want you to think about. I want you to think about how we are going to accomplish all of these technical things we have spoken about. How are we going to accomplish that?' I said, 'I have an idea; that is that we create a healing environment in every district office, in every prison, in headquarters. And as a result of creating that healing environment, we are going to be able to address the needs of staff, and offenders, and the public alike.'"[17]

The reaction he got from the leadership in Virginia on that day was much like the one he got twenty years before, when he first proposed the idea of healing corrections. It was a kind of stunned, "What!?" What happened then, as it had in the past, was that people asked Clarke, "Define it. Tell us what to do . . . [and then] . . . basically sat and waited for me to tell them what to do." Clarke says what he had already learned was that "telling them what to do is not getting at the buy-in; it's telling them what the leader wants. And then they're just going to do what that leader wants. But as soon as that leader walks away, so does the initiative. It's not part of them. It's not something that they own."

For all the apparent complexity of the Implicate Change Model, its use is simplicity itself. That is because Dialogue is not a theory; you train people in Dialogue by having dialogues with them. While the practices and principles can be taught, Dialogue can be learned only by doing. So the basic strategy for embedding Dialogue in an organization is to deliver the training I described in chapter 6 to a wider and wider circle of people, starting with leadership and expanding throughout the organization. In Virginia, this meant first training the leadership team of about thirty people, made up of the director, deputy directors, central office department heads, and regional directors, both for institutions and for community corrections. On the heels of this training, there came more training for the extended leadership team, which included wardens, superintendents, community corrections district heads, and additional department heads, about 120 people in all.

The training began in March 2012 with two days of training for the leadership team and a daylong event for the extended leadership team that was designed to introduce them to the basic concepts of Dialogue. This was the beginning of a series of quarterly weeklong visits in which Garrett and Ball would work with the leadership team, the extended leadership team, and the Healing Environment Council.[18] Training for yet another group was later squeezed into the schedule. These were twenty-four department staff members (chosen from more than three hundred volunteers) to be trained as Dialogue practitioners to assist in the initiative and train staff in the field.

In a letter to all Department of Corrections employees in the spring of 2012, as the training was beginning to take off, Clarke summarized the initiative as he saw it.[19] He wrote that since he had introduced the concept of creating a healing environment the previous year, "there have been many discussions regarding a 'healing environment' and what it actually means for DOC. While our Executive Team developed the overarching description, 'a healing environment is one that fosters positive change and growth and increased public safety in our communities.' I believe the healing environment is best described at the local unit level." Clarke went on to say, "There are several key components of a healing environment. The first is an energetic and positive environment for staff and offenders which results from attitudes and behaviors we bring to and exhibit at work. The second part includes promoting practices that ultimately result in better public safety, less recidivism, fewer victims, and a safer, more productive work environment. The third critical factor involves each of us playing a crucial role in fostering understanding and communicating the elements of a healing environment with emphasis on the unique characteristics of that environment in our units."

During 2012, the entire extended leadership team received the two-day Dialogue training. To keep the number of participants manageable, a third of the extended leadership was trained during each of the quarterly sessions. In 2013, the same group was brought back, but this time with their deputies, again one-third during each of the quarterly trainings for two days. All of these sessions were also attended by the executive leadership from each of the three regions and central office. Late in 2012, the first set of Dialogue specialists was recruited. These specialists received quarterly training on-site at the department's Academy for Staff Development near Richmond and intensive coaching by Garrett and Ball in between the face-to-face training sessions. In late 2013, these Dialogue specialists "graduated" and became Dialogue coaches, taking up the role of helping to train the next wave of more than sixty new specialists.

An important feature of the training is the development of a proposal by each unit head, either a warden, superintendent, or community corrections district chief, of a local healing environment initiative. The local healing initiatives were not reviewed or approved by upper management. They were presented and discussed during the training and then taken back to the individual facilities or district offices to be further developed by the local leadership and staff working together. The Dialogue specialists are tasked with training staff in Dialogue skills and practices and serving as resources for staff in working dialogically on their healing initiatives. The result is that the department-wide Healing Environment Initiative is "scaled down" to the local level, where hundreds of staff members are introduced to Dialogue and how it can be used to address a local issue or concern.

Healing Environment Initiatives

The local healing environment initiatives varied from one site to the next. In a confidential survey of the wardens, superintendents, and community corrections district chiefs that I conducted in early 2014, they described a wide range of activities or efforts they were pursuing. About 40 percent of the initiatives they described were various kinds of staff recognition, programs to motivate or improve staff morale, and organizational development or program improvements. A few of these were reminiscent of the kinds of staff recognition or morale booster programs that were common in the Leading and Sustaining Change efforts. Quite a few of these had catchy names, such as "New Beginnings," "Operation Pick Me UP," "Sharing the Load," "Team Up," "Be CAREful Out There," "Working Together to Achieve Success," "Finding the Rhythm," and "Think and Operate Above Your Pay Grade!" While some referred to creating healing environments or using Dialogue the primary focus of their initiative was elsewhere.

In more than 60 percent of the initiatives described in the survey, however, there was clearly a focus on improving communications and creating a healing environment. In most cases the use of Dialogue, either as training or in working dialogically, was a central theme. One unit head reported using Dialogue to "create a more supportive and caring work environment—Healing Environment is stressed daily." Another group was "creating an environment that promotes healthy conflict and achieves accountability . . . we need to engage in open, honest and passionate communication. Through productive, unfiltered dialogue we can cultivate ideas, sharpen one another, and achieve staff engagement, commitment and accountability." Still another said, "The Healing Environment initiative is very positive and has grown into the general culture at our Unit. The concept of the Healing Environment is centered around positive communication, respect and professionalism."

One healing environment initiative was called "Communication Rocks!" The unit head said, "We have been using our new dialogue skills to change the way we talk to each other. We have dialogue groups that meet to discuss any issues that arise and we try to involve as many staff as we can." Another said, "We are actively teaching, monitoring, encouraging, and modeling the initiative at meetings and during administrative rounds. We are using dialogue as one skill to reach understanding with staff and offenders." A district chief said, "The Healing Environment Initiative in our district has been embraced by the staff. They continue to be supportive of each other and the ideas presented by one another." Said another, "Our [healing environment] initiative is basically to recognize that this is something to embrace as it's just the right thing to do and to recognize the reward you feel when you can help someone by providing them with an environment that is supportive of them." In one district, the healing environment initiative was named "Heart Speak." The initiative, according to the chief, "focuses on allowing increased avenues for staff to express themselves in order to have their voices heard and their true internal feelings expressed."

According to the survey, the initiatives enjoyed strong support from the wardens, superintendents, and community corrections district chiefs. Among this group 88 percent agreed or strongly agreed with the statement "I have seen specific benefits at our facility/office as a result of our Healing Environment Initiative." In response to the statement "I have seen changes in attitude, positive or negative, among the leadership at our facility/office that I believe are the result of the Healing Environment Initiative," 93 percent of wardens and superintendents and 88 percent of district chiefs agreed or strongly agreed, with all saying the changes had been positive. In response to similar statements about changes in attitude and behavior among staff, 88 percent said they had seen changes in attitudes, and 78 percent said they had seen changes in behavior. A majority of the wardens/superintendents also said they had seen changes in inmate attitudes (57 percent agreed or strongly agreed) and even in inmate behavior at their institutions (68 percent agreed or strongly agreed). The district chiefs also said they had seen shifts in the attitudes of people under community supervision (75 percent agreed or strongly agreed) and in their behavior (53 percent of district chiefs agreed or strongly agreed).

The wardens, superintendents, and community corrections district chiefs also reported substantial support and a high level of participation in the healing environment initiatives by their staff. When asked how many staffers they felt were "completely supportive" and "actively engaged" in the healing environment initiative at their facility or office, 64 percent of wardens/superintendents and 84 percent of district chiefs said "most" or "all" were supportive and engaged. When asked how many person-hours they estimated were being dedicated to their healing environment initiative, 53 percent said 20 hours or less, while 28 percent said 51–100 hours, and 18 percent said more than 100 person-hours per month were being spent on the initiatives. Among the department's extended leadership of wardens, superintendents, and community corrections district chiefs there was, then, strong support for the use of the initiatives and recognition that they were having a positive effect, that they had wide staff support, and that the burden on staff time was manageable.

Staff Perceptions of the Healing Environment Initiative

With funding from cooperative agreements with NIC, the Urban Institute also conducted an evaluation of the Virginia Healing Environment Initiative. By the end of 2013 it had conducted two surveys of Virginia Department of Corrections full-time employees. The first wave was conducted during March to May 2012. All 11,135 full-time employees in the department were contacted by email and invited to participate in the online survey. A total of 4,724 staff members (42 percent of the total) eventually responded. The second wave was conducted over a seven-week period between July and September 2013. As with the first administration, the survey invited all full-time staff ($N =$ 11,583) to participate and 4,520 (37 percent) did so. A total of 2,608 respondents participated in both of the first two waves of the survey.[20] A third wave was conducted late in 2014.[21]

In the staff surveys both knowledge of and support for the Healing Environment Initiative was strong, and in many cases grew from the first to the second wave.[22] In the first wave, 63 percent of staff said they had heard about the initiative, while 97 percent said they had heard about it in the second wave more than a year later. Overall, 88 percent of second-wave respondents agreed or strongly agreed with the statement "I believe in the value of the Healing Environment Initiative, compared with 77 percent in the first wave. The pattern of strong, and increasing, support for the initiative was reflected in other statements about it. In 2013, 86 percent of staff agreed or strongly agreed with the statements "The Healing Environment Initiative is a good strategy for this organization," and "The Healing Environment Initiative serves an important purpose" (compared with 74 and 76 percent, respectively, who agreed or strongly agreed the year before).

One subject that, not surprisingly, came up among staff at all levels was how the Healing Environment Initiative would affect safety in the prisons. In the surveys, between two-thirds and three-quarters of staff said their job was a dangerous one. In 2012, 65 percent agreed that "My job is a lot more dangerous than other kinds of jobs," 74 percent agreed that "I work in a dangerous job," and 65 percent said, "In my job, a person stands a good chance of getting hurt." It is interesting that these perceptions remained virtually unchanged from the first wave to the second wave fourteen months later. What did change was the perception among staff that the changes taking place in the department were making their jobs less safe. In early 2012, 67 percent of staff agreed that "All the changes going on around here have made my job much more dangerous." By mid-2013, only 23 percent of staff agreed that the changes were making their job more dangerous.

In fact, it appears that correctional work was becoming safer during this period. The total number of institutional charges for infractions of facility rules by inmates fell from 36,348 in 2010 (a rate of 11.8 per 1,000 inmates) to 29,803 (a rate of 10.0 per 1,000) by 2012. In 2013, there were 29,676 infractions, reflecting an increase in more serious infractions (almost 400 more), while less serious ones continued to decline (about 500 fewer). There had been four serious assaults on staff in 2010 and six in 2011, but only three in 2012 and none in 2013. There also had been one or two escapes each year in 2008–2011, but there were none in 2012 or 2013.[23]

Not only inmates were behaving better.[24] The total number and rate of disciplinary actions against staff declined steadily over the 2010–2013 period. There were 400 disciplinary actions taken against staff in 2010, a rate of 34 per 1,000 staff. In 2011 there were 269, and by 2013 the number had fallen to 226 (a rate of 19.5 per 1,000). The decline was consistent across all

levels of disciplinary actions, with serious, medium, and low levels all reduced. There were even fewer on-the-job injuries among staff, with 1,238 reported in 2010, 1,139 in 2011, and 1,013 in 2012.[25] Staff still had complaints;
the healing environment is not a paradise for all employees. There were 46
grievance hearings in 2010, 62 in 2011, 36 in 2012, and 55 in 2013. Not everyone is happy with change.

In the survey I conducted of wardens, superintendents, and district
chiefs, I asked about staff members who were not on board with the Healing
Environment Initiative. When respondents were asked, "How many of your
staff are resistant to your Healing Environment Initiative?" 75 percent overall
(92 percent of wardens/superintendents and 56 percent of district chiefs) said
that "some" were resistant. Later in the survey, they were asked two questions that shed some light on what they thought about the willingness, or
lack thereof, of staff to become engaged. The first question was "What would
you say are the main reasons why staff at your facility/office do not become
engaged in your Healing Environment Initiative?" and the second was "What
would you say are the main reasons why staff at your facility/office do not
become supportive, by-stand, or are resistant when it comes to your Healing Environment Initiative?" There were 130 codable responses to these two
questions from the survey respondents (some gave more than one response).
Of the fifteen themes identified through a content analysis of these responses,
three clusters accounted for about 60 percent of the items.

Despite the training these wardens, superintendents, and district chiefs
had all received in Dialogue practices, they tended to blame recalcitrant staff
for their failure to participate more in the local healing environment initiatives. There was no indication in the brief survey that dialogic inquiry was
being employed to find out why all staff were not engaged. According to about
20 percent of the responses, staff were too used to and comfortable with the
old way of doing business and the existing culture to be open to the initiative.
About 22 percent blamed the lack of involvement on the character or personalities of individual staff members, who they described as lacking empathy,
rigid and adverse to change, "creatures of habit," or reacting negatively to
something they thought was too "warm and fuzzy" (like the hard hats in the
culture studies). Another 18 percent of responses referred to mistrust, fear,
or anxiety, and apathy or frustration. About 11 percent of the responses cited
the demands of the workload and job stress, while 10 percent mentioned a

need for more training or education to help staff understand the initiative better.

The point is that these leaders in the Virginia Department of Corrections, the wardens, superintendents, and district chiefs actually running its prisons and district offices, did not become extraordinarily empathetic or report some kind of epiphany about the holistic nature of our world. They were still wardens, superintendents, and district chiefs doing their jobs. And yet they and their staff were doing something that was producing clear and measurable changes in the way they thought and acted. Whatever they were doing was even influencing what the inmates and those under community supervision were doing. Safety and security in the institutions and public safety in the Commonwealth were improved.

What were they doing to produce these shifts? It appears that, for one thing, they talking a lot about creating a healing environment, and that message was actually cascading through the organization. In the Urban Institute's survey of staff, they were asked if they had heard about the Healing Environment Initiative. In the first wave, 63 percent said they had heard about the initiative, but by the second wave 97 percent had heard of it. What is more interesting is what they reported about how they had heard of the initiative. Between the first and second waves, there were increases in the percentage of staff who reported hearing about the initiative from every direction—in communications from Director Clarke (37–69 percent), from their warden, superintendent, or district chief (26–55 percent), from their supervisor (24–57 percent), in training (26–68 percent), and from other staff (16–42 percent). Most important, when asked what activities they had participated in where the Healing Environment Initiative was discussed, 62 percent of staff in the second wave said they had participated in Dialogue circles, compared with just 8 percent only a little more than a year before, when the first wave data were collected.

A good example of how the ideas of a healing environment and the use of Dialogue were being spread through the department is what Harold Clarke was doing during this time. Clarke said he knew that everyone was not "a hundred percent on board," but that "people were polite and they listened." Clark went on to say, "I took great pains to go out most of the time with [executive staff] . . . When we go into a region we will sit and we'll talk sometimes for three or four hours with the team in that region and answer any questions that they have just openly and just trying to be as sincere and candid as you possibly can in addressing issues with people." This, I believe, is the kind of staff appreciation program that can actually work. It recognizes the expertise of staff in the most sincere way—by genuinely listening to them and talking with them. This is because the program does not simply show appreciation or recognition in some ceremonial or symbolical way; real appreciation and recognition are concretely expressed in action.

Changing the Culture by Not Trying to Change the Culture

What happened in Virginia is an example of changing the patterns of communication and interaction among and between staff. Clarke did not tell people he appreciated and respected them; he just treated them in an appreciative and respectful way, and he made clear that he expected them to do the same to each other.

In earlier chapters I discussed the culture that staff in prisons across the United States told the cultural assessment team they preferred. They almost always wanted a more clan-like organizational culture to mitigate the effects of the hierarchical culture they said existed in their institutions, but without replacing that culture entirely. They did not want much less structure or internal focus, but they did want a more flexible environment. I also suggested that a better way of describing (an ideal) correctional culture would be to focus on high-reliability organizations and what corrections has in common with other organizations with similar missions. Characteristics such as a preoccupation with failure, reluctance to simplify, and sensitivity to operations are all common, if not unique, to such organizations (when they are working properly). But two other characteristics are also necessary for a high-reliability organization to work. These are deference to expertise, the learning that comes from hands-on experience, and a commitment to resilience evidenced by organizational pride and esprit de corps.

A corrections department that is a high-reliability organization, therefore, is a hierarchical organization with some clan-like cultural elements. Such an organization is able to maintain its internal structure and focus, but maintain an operational posture that will allow it to respond in a crisis. If there is often a degree of tension between structure and flexibility, that is because the mission of corrections and the challenges of its operating environment create conflicting and constantly shifting demands. Corrections, as a profession, knows this, and correctional culture preserves that wisdom. But cultures are dynamic, and anything we have known before always needs to be relearned. Or, more precisely, we need to teach each other as we work together.

By now, I assume you know what my prescription is for creating the conditions in which this is possible. It is to use the practice of Dialogue to heal the pervasive fragmentation so common in organizations and, by so doing, create a healing environment. Reflecting on his experience in Virginia to date, Harold Clarke said, "I think that we have a more concerted effort in Virginia, and we have people who are prepared and willing to run with it. That's making a lot of difference . . . Plus we have had more time to think about it as well. And we have gotten better at it. And one of the things that I have come to realize over time is that it's important to put the idea out there, that it is very important to tie it to our ultimate mission, but also not to describe it for everyone. Let them decide how they think it ought to be described."

CHAPTER EIGHT

The Future of Imprisonment

I began this book with the story of a tragedy, the violent deaths of Nathan Leon, Tom Clements, and Evan Ebel over the space of a few days in March 2013. And I quoted Clements, who asked how what we do in prisons can be made to "square up" with our broader responsibilities beyond simply running them in a safe and secure manner, to use the common refrain. In retrospect, it is clear that what we have done is use our system of justice to shield (most of) us from global changes as they have unfolded during our lifetimes. Our world has changed and continues to change, yet our habitual ways of coping with it leaves us with more questions than solutions. Many of the strategies we have tried have ended up deepening our problems, not resolving them. This book seeks to describe a path that can lead us toward more illuminating answers.

I have argued that we are trapped in what I call the big squeeze of too many people within our justice system, too few resources to cope with the challenges confronting us, and a self-defeating public policy debate in an atmosphere so polarized and fragmented that even modest reform efforts yield only limited results. While I admire deeply the hope for reform that periodically springs up among the optimists, it is not something I can fully share. This is because, while most of these reforms are well intentioned, well designed, and usually well executed, they cannot alter the dynamic of a fragmented system. In fragmented systems, our attempts at problem solving metamorphose into deeper problems because the processes that produce the problems in the first place remain unaltered. This is how it happens that, even though we aspire to stop being part of the problem, we never seem to get to the point where we become part of the solution.

The first step to a solution is to make our fragmented systems more coherent by working to heal them through connecting with each other in more constructive and meaningful ways in order to make our system of justice whole. The culture of corrections is one place where I believe such a transformation is possible and that, when successful, would alter the cultural dynamic within our justice system and eventually between it and the larger society. Prisons and jails are the cultural epicenter of our use of punishment, and change within them will have a profound impact outside them. A genuine dialogue within corrections and between it and the other pieces of our justice system can be the catalyst for a national dialogue. In the end, our society's relationship to the people who work and live within our justice system, as well as all those who are outside but are still affected by it, must be transformed.

To start this process, American corrections must transform itself from the inside out. By changing its own culture, it will heal itself and become a healing force in our society. Transforming correctional cultures will mean changing how we talk and think together. One very powerful way of doing that is through the practice of Dialogue. With it, a healing environment can be developed in prisons, jails, and community corrections agencies that will create a different future—one in which corrections is part of the solution. Being part of the solution, however, means that the profession of corrections must do more than simply heal itself.

It can do this by actively participating in a genuine dialogue that reaches far beyond the walls of our prisons and jails or community corrections offices. But a national discussion cannot be another national monologue delivered by corrections experts, politicians, media, or advocates in all their various forms and political persuasions. Dialogue assumes and requires that everyone who lives in or with any system be represented. To leave anyone out of the process is to reinforce and perpetuate the fragmentation that dialogue is designed to heal.

I have already given a short list of all those who are directly involved in the justice system: those accused or convicted of a crime, victims of all kinds (both direct and indirect), the correctional workforce at all levels, and their families, friends, neighbors, and communities. The longer list includes law enforcement, prosecutors and the defense bar, the courts, service providers, social service agencies, and community organizations. It also includes those in the broader community who have a sincere interest in the health, safety, and well-being of their neighbors. If a genuine dialogue could take place among and between even some of the people from each of these groups that allowed us to think and talk together about what we want from our justice system and society for ourselves and others, would we not see more clearly how to create a brighter future?

Harold Clarke once told me he had found that many staff members, particularly those working in specific prisons, believed that a healing environment is all about staff and taking care of them. He said, however, that "the offenders are also part of that environment as well; the public is impacted by that environment. So if you are going to have an environment that is totally healing it needs to be impacting everybody who comes within that environment, including public, offenders, staff, and everybody else."

Talking about Punishment

Michael Tonry, a professor of criminal law and policy at the University of Minnesota and among the most prolific writers in the area, begins his essay on punishment by noting, "We are not very good at talking about punishing offenders."[1] This may not be entirely true, since we seem to be enthusiastic about the subject, especially during election campaigns and after a particularly shocking crime. But we are not good at asking why we are punishing people in the first place. The number of books and articles on the subject that manage to avoid the word "punishment" is a testament to our ambivalence about the idea (if you were ever sent to your room by your parents, you thought you were being punished, not "sanctioned," by them). We ought to have a much clearer idea about why we punish people, and that must include an honest acknowledgement of the many reasons for doing it. Broadly speaking, there are two general reasons any society punishes people: instrumental and expressive.

The usual logic offered for the use of punishment is instrumental. When lawmakers decide to make something a crime or to increase the punishment to be meted out for one already on the books, the reason they most often cite is the instrumental one of making society safer. At the same time they might, for expressive reasons, punish people in order to define some acts as unacceptable. Some punishments are expressive in another sense; they are statements about the proposer's ideology, self-image, or political persona. With this kind of expressive punishment, it is not especially relevant whether it will do any good to impose the punishment; it may even be harmful. What is important is that someone's sense of outrage demands of us that we do it anyway.

Expressive punishment seeks to satisfy an ideal of justice; it tries to set things right in the eyes of the community by taking an eye for an eye. When it drives punishment, it is the symbolism itself, not the purpose of changing people's behavior, that counts. Crime makes people mad. It invokes fear and anxiety. People are deeply resentful when someone has intentionally harmed them or others, and they especially hate it when anyone gets away with a crime without suffering the consequences. We feel a need to express our outrage, and in our rage we demand punishment. But rage, as understandable as it is, does not bring out the best in us. This is where the "recognition of history, the imperfections of men, and the limits of reason," to recall President Obama's phrase, comes into play. Our all too human failings are familiar to us, but so too can be our strengths when we do discover the best in us.

The punishments imposed by our society will serve different purposes to various degrees, and every debate about crime and corrections seems to get hung up on which should take priority. One reason discussions on punishment get stalled is that the sides in any debate emphasize different purposes. The second reason the debate gets stuck is a common unwillingness to acknowledge that expressive punishment happens routinely in American society, just as it does in other societies. We do sometimes punish people because we are angry or afraid, or do not like them. We also know that race, ethnicity, and class (all sources of fragmentation in our society) play a significant role in who gets punished and how much they get punished. Finally, of course, a society may punish people in order to maintain a political or economic status quo. This has clearly happened in this country in the past, and some argue that it continues to do so.[2]

Tonry noted that even among those who do the most talking about the subject of punishment are different groups talking about different things. Practitioners usually take a practical approach and concern themselves with what works to control the behavior of different people under different circumstances. Policy makers, both elected and appointed, are more likely to be preoccupied with crime, especially changes in the level of crime or high-profile crimes, public opinion, and what that may mean for their political fortunes or survival. Social scientists, who tend to talk a great deal, want to describe exactly what is happening, precisely how it has changed, is changing, or could change, and to explain in causal terms why it is all working in this way. Meanwhile, social theorists, critics, and philosophers argue over deterrence, retribution, just desserts, and justice. All of the other people involved in corrections usually just want to talk about their personal experiences and struggles so they can make sense of it all.

It is time that we became serious about the struggle to make sense of it all. David Bohm had something to say about seriousness, too. He argued that if you are just trying to defend your opinions or avoid facing unpleasant realities, you are not being serious: "A great deal of our lives is not serious. And Society teaches you that. It teaches you not to be serious—that there are all sorts of incoherent things, and there is nothing that can be done about it, and that you will only stir yourself up uselessly by being serious."[3] In a fragmented world, everything seems too hard to attempt, too daunting to achieve, too entrenched to ever change. And yet, it does, somehow change. Bohm went on to say, "There is no pat political answer to the world's problems. However, the important point is not the answer—just as in dialogue, the important point is not the particular opinions—but rather the softening up, the opening up of the mind, and looking at all opinions."[4]

Gazing into the Abyss

The philosopher Friedrich Nietzsche wrote that "if you gaze for long into an abyss, the abyss gazes also into you." The politics of crime and our reaction to it has become a dark abyss. The rhetoric of law and order, including its endless attack ads about who is softer on crime, has become a permanent fixture of the political landscape because it still works with voters. At the same time, America's strange fascination with crime and criminals produces an endless stream of popular dramas, reality shows, round-the-clock coverage of this year's trial of the century, and an "if it bleeds, it leads" style of journalism.[5] How can stories about crime and criminals dominate our news and entertainment if we hate them? Coming up with a serious answer to this question requires us to gaze into the abyss and to honestly look to see who or what is gazing back. It may be our own fears.

We do not like our own fears. In fact, we usually do everything we can to defend ourselves against them.[6] We often do that by protecting ourselves from emotional pain, anxiety, and the impulses that arise from them that we do not want to acknowledge, even to ourselves. For example, if you are at work and feel particularly frustrated and unappreciated, or if you think you are getting screwed in general, you might have a strong impulse to punch somebody. It might not be anybody in particular, just somebody. This impulse sets up a conflict with what you learned and internalized about all the wrong things to do. For most of us, punching people is definitely on the list of wrong things to do. Almost always, hopefully, the idea of going postal at work and what would happen next is enough to keep us from actually punching someone (although a verbal jab or two might slip out).

But we still feel anxiety, which can become so uncomfortable that we resort to various ways of tinkering with our own thinking to defend ourselves. Among our favorite ways of doing this are denial (convincing ourselves we do not really want to punch anybody or, if we do, it is not that big a deal), displacement (shifting our desire to punch one person, like our boss, to somebody else, like the secretary who told us what the boss wanted; verbal jabs count on this one), and projection (believing it is the other person who really wants to punch *us*). People who routinely commit crimes are typically heavy and highly creative users of these defenses, except that when they use them we label them criminal thinking styles.[7]

An especially interesting defense against anxiety-producing or unacceptable emotions is to replace them with their direct opposites.[8] If you buy this idea, it is not too hard to imagine people hating criminals because they really would like to be a criminal, too. Getting what you want by just taking it, controlling everyone around you, even punching people simply because you feel frustrated and unappreciated or are getting screwed may not sound too bad. This is, after all, the basic storyline of countless movies and television shows. Watching people do such things and worse as a form of entertainment or listening to every detail about a horrific crime and the person who did it sounds a lot like the vicarious experience of *being* a criminal. Turning around and angrily demanding severe punishment for the people who *are* criminals sounds a lot like psychological defensiveness. This is what I meant by looking into the dark abyss and finding it looking right back at you.

Patricia Caruso, former director of the Michigan Department of Corrections, watched and participated in the changes in corrections as they played out in her state, from the building booms of the 1980s and 1990s to the economic busts that followed. The experience convinced her that our society in general and our criminal justice system specifically must redefine what we mean by success. For one thing, says Caruso, "we need to lock up people we're afraid of, not people we're mad at."[9] The disconnect between crime rates and incarceration rates we have witnessed in the past twenty years represents a shift away from "afraid-of" policies designed to affect public safety to a "mad-at" approach that reflects our need to cope collectively with our fears.[10]

A process of softening up, opening the mind, and looking at all opinions, as suggested by Bohm, is not how we usually describe the current state of affairs in our public policy debates on crime and punishment. The more common description is "partisan" or "ideological." Ideologies are cultural things made up of values, beliefs, attitudes, and so on arranged into interlocking structures that can function as defenses against a fragmented world. They are the cognitive equivalent of an articulated exoskeleton; like a lobster in a restaurant tank trying to avoid the searching hand of the chef, they protect us from uncomfortable realities. They create a more or less serviceable order out of what we think we know; they are our personal attempt to impose coherence on a fragmented world. But the underbelly of ideologies is the emotionally charged, tacit knowledge that holds the ideological structure in place. Rational analysis, data-driven arguments, and appeals to Enlightenment values seldom touch this level of knowledge. Instead, it is the gut shot of an emotionally powerful experience that drives its knife through the gaps in an ideology's defenses.

Nothing transforms a person's perceptions and opinions about the criminal justice system so much as personal involvement in it. Getting arrested yourself or having someone close to you, like a son or daughter, arrested is an eye-opener. So is learning the story of someone you thought you knew well and finding out that he or she served time. Meeting someone who looks like they do, talks like they do, and could *be* them, but is living in the shadow of a past arrest or conviction, is often a shock to those who think they do not know any ex-offenders. The truth is that, given the reach of our criminal justice system, everyone does know someone who has been involved on the receiving end of punishment. We do not know that because he or she does everything possible to avoid telling us.

The Resettlement Journey

Getting yourself arrested, or having your children arrested (as tempting as that may sometimes seem), as a way of raising your consciousness about the justice system may be a bit too much. Peter Garrett and Jane Ball, however, have developed a powerful way for people to gain at least some sense of what that experience is like. They call it the "Resettlement Journey," and it is a way for people to come to a shared understanding of how the system works by watching it acted out. I have seen Garrett and Ball use the technique with correctional staff in Virginia several times, and it has always made a strong impression on the participants. It turns out that even the people working in the system do not have a clear understanding of how the whole thing works or how it is experienced by people going through it. They can find out, however, by hearing the stories of the one group of people who have moved all the way through and then back out of the system: the people who have been incarcerated.

Garrett and Ball developed the approach working in prisons in the United Kingdom. What is usually referred to as "reentry" in the United States, is called "resettlement" in the United Kingdom. This serves to stress the idea that just reentering society is not that same as settling into a new life. The shift in tone from "reentry," which sounds like a space capsule dropping from the sky, to "resettlement" is evident in Garret and Ball's description of what they call the "Line of Sight Vision." In their discussion of case studies in Dorset from 2006 to 2010 they describe the vision in this way: "The concept was that for successful resettlement, prisoners needed a clear and visible route, or line of sight, from prison to independent resettlement in the community. People were more likely to be successful in their resettlement journey if there were manageable steps along the route, without unrealistic hurdles, if they could see what was coming up, and if there was an opportunity to think through with other people what was going to happen . . . The image is the line of sight as you are driving down a road—your journey is more likely to be safe, successful and enjoyable if you know where you are going, know where you have to take a turn, can see junctions clearly ahead and have time to anticipate what to do."[11]

In November 2010, Garrett and Ball facilitated a "Line of Sight" workshop at HMP Guys Marsh, a medium-security prison in the south of England. The workshop participants included current inmates, people in resettlement, corrections staff, police, magistrates, and local treatment or service providers who had all been involved in the work in Dorset. More than sixty people were invited for the six-hour workshop. The case studies described the process as follows: "In the afternoon groupings were positioned around the room to represent the Line of Sight and the offender resettlement journey—from the local prison, to the training prison, and in the community from the direct access hostel and day center for those whose lives were unsettled, through supported accommodation to independence. The prison gate was marked across the floor. Two Prison Dialogue facilitators walked two ex-offenders in resettlement from the community where they were arrested, into prison, back out on their release and along the Line of Sight. Along the way they talked about their experiences and what helped and what hindered their progress, and the agencies were invited to talk about their role in the journey."

When this exercise is done in the Virginia Department of Corrections, staff members representing each part of the organization arrange themselves around the room, with community corrections at one end, a demarcation line marked with duct tape to show the prison gate, and each level of security arranged from low to maximum arrayed on the other side of the room. Two or three people who have been incarcerated and have volunteered to come back are literally walked through this representation of the system as they tell their story of how they themselves experienced the system. Often, the volunteers served a lengthy sentence, and many of the other participants had met them earlier in their careers. The experience, for both the volunteers and the staff, is always profound.

It is not difficult to imagine how this technique could be taken into the larger community and expanded. It would include all of the people who are involved in the whole process of crime and punishment. In other words, it would include those accused or convicted, victims, correctional workers, families, friends, communities, and so on, as well as the usual stakeholders: law enforcement, lawyers, judges, treatment and social services, and so on. Finally, it would include politicians and policy makers, reporters, advocates, theorists, people who care about their community, and even an academic researcher or two. It sounds like a big group, but engaging everyone means everyone, and there are techniques, such as Future Search Conferences, that can handle big crowds.[12]

During such a conference, an expanded version of the "Line of Sight" resettlement journey could be staged and would involve all the participants. The way they might be arrayed and the path of a person in the process of resettlement might look something like the diagram in figure 8.1.

If this exercise were to be carried out in the afternoon, after the whole

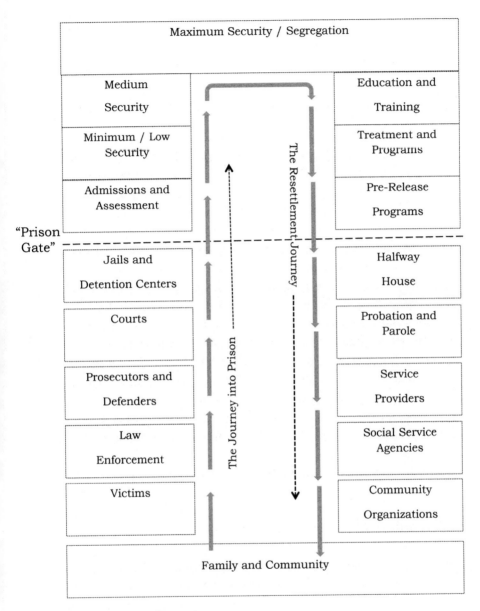

FIGURE 8.1: The Resettlement Journey

group had received a half-day introduction to Dialogue training, it could very well produce a profound after-dinner dialogue. Another day or two of genuine Dialogue could start to produce real solutions.

Dialogue and Inmates

The focus of this book is on correctional leaders and the correctional workforce on the grounds that they are the only ones who can actually make real changes in correctional cultures. But what exactly would this transformation mean for the people who live in prisons? Peter Garrett's Prison Dialogue work has, from the beginning, been primarily with inmates. Garrett once told me, "In terms of working in prisons, I've been more concerned to understand people who have suffered severely from fragmentation and need some kind of support to get back into an integrated position . . . So I've been very interested in working with individuals in bringing their lives back together . . . It's quite raw in a prison, and to me, why I particularly enjoyed working with offenders is because it's quite extreme, the fragmentation."[13]

Garrett, recalling his sudden return to the United Kingdom when he was sixteen years old, said he had always felt an affinity with the inmates he met in prisons. That move, which he described as "a huge cultural wrench," left him with an insight into what inmates were experiencing. In prisons, he said, he found "people who had been wrenched from their lives and who were finding it very difficult to adjust culturally in the prison. So I actually found something in common with prisoners that I had in my own history . . . I found it aided my own development work in the prisons, as it happens." In other words (mine again) Garrett had a shared experience with the inmates he was talking with and listening to. It made the dialogue between them beneficial to them both.

Garrett also said that not only had the inmates he worked with in maximum-security conditions "committed a severe crime, but it had caused them severe pain, some of them had killed their partner or their children or whatever, but also they had been interrogated repeatedly about that crime, often shamed in public, and had [been] suffering for it. And that's quite a severe condition to get back to wholeness; and what really interested me was that I found that a process of inquiry about one's own life can lead you to stand in a place of innocence . . . the only place I know to stand in innocence is to inquire into it, because the inquirer can't inquire from a guilty point of view. You may be covered by guilt, but once you get into real inquiry you start to stand in a place where you start to organize it and structure it."

I asked Garrett how engaging in dialogue, which is by definition a social process, can create coherence in a correctional setting. He said, "It does, for a number of reasons. One is that when you stand as an inquirer into your own life, from the point of a serious offender . . . you stand on a little bit of dry ground, which is an innocent position from which to look at it. [The] second thing is that thinking is a collective process—if you think on your own, you'll find it's a bit like the old-fashioned record that goes around and around and slips and repeats itself. It gets stuck. How it does that is you're thinking about the situation, and then you slip into repetitive thought . . . And it builds up and is emotionally held as a repetitive cycle." But, Garrett added, if there is a genuine inquiry into a repetitive cycle of thinking, "you can start to get a more complete process of thinking. Typically, where we start to get into difficulty is where we're on a kind of repeated cycle that increases in intensity until we do something about it." If we can think and talk together through the process of dialogue, we can get to that little bit of shared dry ground that exists in the midst of our otherwise swampy thinking.

The Future of Imprisonment

When I first discussed with Harold Clarke my intention to write this book, I asked him if he thought doing so would be worthwhile. I told him my hope was that other corrections leaders and staff would draw inspiration from it, that they would say, "This can work, and we should heal our organization." I wanted to know if he thought it was realistic to present a model to the field of corrections that could be used to transform it. I was worried that what I saw happening in Virginia could be a case of the right leader getting to the right organization at exactly the right time so that all of the pieces fell into place. So I asked him, "Do you think that the healing environment idea is something that could be transferred to another place and successfully carried out?"

Clarke answered, "I think it's something that can be transferred to other places and carried out successfully, but every place is going to be somewhat different and you may have some challenges that you have to address as you're doing it. Some places are more receptive than others. You're going to find receptivity on a scale, and it's going to be at varying places at varying levels. I think it can be done. I think it's a matter of how you market it as well. In any given jurisdiction, here in Virginia, your ways of marketing to the treatment staff need to be somewhat different than the ways of marketing to the uniformed custody staff. It touches everybody and everybody has a role to play in it."

He went on to say that the most important part is "helping people to understand the role that they're playing in it. I was at, one point, willing to change the words 'healing environment' to anything that they wanted to call it once we were true to what we were trying to do. So I introduced that thought in the executive staff meeting and they almost ran me out of the room. They liked 'the healing environment.' But I gave them the option of coming up with some different words to describe what we were doing . . . They said, 'No way. We like healing environment. We want to stick with those words.' But I think it can be packaged and shared in different jurisdictions, but how it's sold and how you address the unique situations in the different jurisdictions is going to differ from place to place. And so you need to find a way to address that."

Clarke concluded that, while corrections is in the business of creating public safety and knows well how to operate secure institutions, "incapacitation creates temporary public safety, but offenders are going home someday—90 percent in Virginia, 97 percent nationally. We have to do better than to simply incapacitate." Clarke went on to say, "You do better than that by addressing the deficits, the needs of offenders and staff. And to address the deficits and needs of offenders and staff, you have to create the conditions for that to occur. And the conditions that need to be created are those, in my vision, that are readily in existence in a healing environment where the needs of staff and offenders are being addressed. So I am sold on the concept. I think it's a human thing . . . We have to evolve in our industry. If we don't evolve in our industry, it's going to be because of our lack of initiative and because of our lack of courage to do the right thing and our desire to embrace the past."

I asked Peter Garrett the same question, but in another form. I had noticed that people in Virginia were having trouble defining a healing environment, and I suggested to him that they were running into trouble because they were attempting to define it as a "thing" instead of conceiving it as a place or process. I suggested that the organization could instead be thought of as a "super-sized safe container" that is created and maintained by a dialogic process throughout the organization. Garrett answered, "I like your thinking about the Healing Environment as a place and a system-wide container within which a prisoner is offered the opportunity to recover individually and socially within prison, and then in relation to family and community on release. In my view a key element of such a container is the quality of dialogue (talking and thinking together) amongst and between staff and prisoners. There is also a physical element to the container, which is rightly more tightly held for higher-security offenders and more relaxed for lower-risk offenders, and which offers the chance for physical, mental, emotional, and spiritual reintegration (or healing) to occur during the time people are in our care."[14]

Garrett concluded, "I don't have a fairy tale view, but I do have a view that without managing fragmentation humanity will destroy itself. I don't anticipate changing the course of humanity single-handedly . . . What I do think is that there is a problem that requires some wisdom and I think I've done some research with others that's started to look at that and how to tackle that, and that's why I persist with the dialogue work and look to inspire others to get involved in it."

NOTES

Introduction

1. G. Packer, *The Unwinding: An Inner History of the New America* (New York: Farrar, Straus and Giroux, 2013). See also C. Murray, *Coming Apart: The State of White America, 1960–2010* (New York: Crown Forum, 2012).

2. The project developed the National Archive of Criminal Justice Data, which I ran for its first seven years. See http://www.icpsr.umich.edu/icpsrweb/NACJD/ for information on the archive. My doctoral dissertation, about the fear of crime (University of Michigan, Sociology Department), used data from the archive.

3. This is as good a time as any to remind readers that my views and opinions are my own and do not represent those of the U.S. Department of Justice or any of its agencies. Also, I have nothing to say in this book about federal policies or the Federal Bureau of Prisons (FBOP), for two reasons. One is that the federal system and the FBOP are so unlike the other systems in the United States that describing them or how they differ from state and local systems would require a book in itself. The other reason is personal—I have been in the civil service and involved with the FBOP for so long that, even aside from any conflict-of-interest issues, I do not believe I could write a completely objective account of what they do.

4. For a recent example of the criticism of these types of popular and well-funded initiatives, see J. Austin, E. Cadora, T. Clear, et al., *Ending Mass Incarceration: Charting a New Justice Reinvestment* (Washington, DC: American Civil Liberties Union, 2013), accessed April 14, 2013, http://www.aclu.org/criminal-law-reform/ending-mass-incarceration-charting-new-justice-reinvestment.

5. See D. Bohm, *On Dialogue* (New York: Routledge, 1996); D. Bohm, *Wholeness and the Implicate Order* (New York: Routledge, 1980).

6. D. Bohm, *Unfolding Meaning* (New York: Routledge, 1985), 23.

7. Bohm did not insist on universal harmony, either. He thought there were many practical problems that are best solved by being broken down. He said, "I want to make a sharp distinction between a part and a fragment. There are some things that should be smashed up, so I'm not totally against smashing up." See *Unfolding Meaning*, 28.

8. K. Appiah, *The Honor Code: How Moral Revolutions Happen* (New York: W. W. Norton, 2010). See also K. Appiah, "What Will Future Generations Condemn Us For?" *Washington Post,* September 26, 2010.

9. Personal interview, June 29, 2012.

10. For a description of the project, see C. Innes, *The Norval Morris Project at the National Institute of Corrections* (2014), http://www.nicic.gov/Library/028201. For

more information on the project, see the National Institute of Corrections website, http://nicic.gov/Norval. The project's planning and logistical support was provided by Justice Systems and Training (J-SAT) of Boulder, Colorado, under the leadership of Bradford Bouge. For more information, see the J-SAT website, http://www.j-sat. com/.

11. The average length of time in office of all active state department of corrections directors is computed by the staff of the Association of State Correctional Administrators. At each semiannual meeting, a chart is displayed in the meeting room and always attracts a good deal of interest from the rather competitive directors. At the meetings in Tampa, Florida, on February 1–2, 2014, the average tenure reported was 3.8 years.

12. Peggy Holman, who participated in the Norval Morris Project as a facilitator, has written about ways to generate emergence. See P. Holman, *Engaging Emergence: Turning Upheaval into Opportunity* (San Francisco: Berrett-Koehler, 2010).

13. To make the book easier to use, I have worked to repress the effects of my prior professional training. As a semireformed researcher, I cannot help myself from writing a lot of endnotes. My training has left me with an obsession with documenting things. The endnotes serve to park the more detailed information, list my sources, and avoid loading the text with too much wonkish researcher talk. I am also mindful that I am contributing to the historical record, and some details of how things happened are not available elsewhere. At the same time, as a writer, I take words seriously. I use many ideas that are very close cousins of others (see the endnotes), but I do not use the same terms because I do not want the theoretical baggage that goes with them.

14. J. Dewey, *The Quest for Certainty* (Chicago: University of Chicago Press, 1929), 7.

15. The Dalai Lama has written about crime and justice from the perspective of a secularized Buddhism. See H.H., the Dalai Lama, *Beyond Religion: Ethics for a Whole World* (New York: Houghton Mifflin Harcourt, 2011). See also H.H., the Dalai Lama, *Ethics for the New Millennium* (New York: Riverhead Books, 1999); O. Flanagan, *The Bodhisattva's Brain: Buddhism Naturalized* (Cambridge, MA: MIT Press, 2011). The Dalai Lama was a panelist at an event in 1979 titled the "Art Meets Science and Spirituality in a Changing Economy: From Fragmentation to Wholeness" and can be seen in a video sitting beside David Bohm nodding in agreement as Bohm explained Dialogue (accessed September 10, 2014, http://www.cultureunplugged.com/play/8247/Art-Meets-Science-and-Spirituality-in-a-Changing-Economy).

1. How Many Tragic Ironies Are Too Many?

1. Text of Hickenlooper's letter to the Colorado Department of Corrections on the killing of Tom Clements, *Denver Post*, March 20, 2013, accessed September 18, 2014, http://www.denverpost.com/ci_22830292/text-hickenlooper-doc-killing-tom-clements.

2. F. Bruni, "Redemption's Advocate" (2013), accessed March 22, 2013, http://bruni.blogs.nytimes.com/2013/03/21/redemptions-advocate/.

3. The Colorado Department of Corrections had actually conducted a well-designed study of the effects on inmates of confinement in segregation. The study revealed that the number of inmates who showed improvements in their level of psychological functioning was greater than the number of those who experienced adverse effects (20% vs. 7%) and that most remained stable during their confinement. See M. O'Keefe, K. Klebe, A. Stucker, and W. Leggett, *One Year Longitudinal Study of the Psychological Effects of Administrative Segregation* (Colorado Springs: Colorado Department of Corrections, 2010) (for the full report, see http://www.doc.state.co.us/sites/default/files/opa/AdSegReport_2010.pdf); J. Metzner and M. O'Keefe, "Psychological Effects of Administrative Segregation: The Colorado Study," *Corrections Mental Health Report* 13 (2011): 1–2, 13–14. Also see S. Grassian, "Fatal Flaws in the Colorado Solitary Confinement Study" (2010), accessed September 18, 2014, http://solitarywatch.com/?s=fatal+flaws+in+colorado.

4. The day after Clements's death, Governor Hickenlooper signed into law a new gun control bill designed to expand background checks on gun purchases and make such "straw" purchases harder. The legislation had been in the works since a number of mass shootings had occurred, including one at an Aurora, Colorado, theater in 2012 in which twelve people were killed and fifty-eight others were injured. See M. DeLuca, "Colorado Gov. Hickenlooper Signs Landmark Gun-Control Bills," NBC News, March 30, 2013, accessed May 2, 2013, http://usnews.nbcnews.com/_news/2013/03/20/17387348-colorado-gov-hickenlooper-signs-landmark-gun-control-bills?lite; J. Brown, "12 Shot Dead, 58 Wounded in Aurora Movie Theater During *Batman* Premier," *Denver Post*, July 21, 2012, accessed September 18, 2014, http://www.denverpost.com/ci_21124893/12-shot-dead-58-wounded-aurora-movie-theater.

5. C. Sandell, "Evan Ebel's Ankle Bracelet Failed Days Before Colorado Killings," ABC News, April 2, 2013, accessed May 2, 2013, http://abcnews.go.com/US/evan-ebels-ankle-bracelet-failed-days-colorado-killings/story?id=18865250.

6. P. S. Banda and N. Riccardi, "From a Young Age, No One Could Tame Evan Ebel," Associated Press, March 28, 2013, accessed March 28, 2013, http://news.yahoo.com/young-age-no-one-could-tame-evan-ebel-081218146.html.

7. Both quotes, as well as the one from the Decatur police chief, come from S. Greene, "Evan Ebel, Suspect in Tom Clements Murder, Was Concerned about Transition Back into Society," *Colorado Independent*, April 28, 2013, accessed May 1, 2013, http://coloradoindependent.com/127596/clements-murder-suspect-ebel-was-anxious-about-walking-free-documents-show. (The brackets appear in the original.)

8. In its February 2014 meetings, the Association of State Correctional Administrators began the process of creating an award to recognize Clements's legacy.

9. J. Austin, "Reducing America's Correctional Populations: A Strategic Plan," *Justice Research and Policy* 12 (2010): 1–32.

10. The phenomenon of exploding correctional populations and the accompanying direct and indirect economic and social costs has generated a large literature. See T. Clear, *Imprisoning Communities: How Mass Incarceration Makes Disadvantaged Neighborhoods Worse* (New York: Oxford University Press, 2007); D. Garland (ed.), *Mass Imprisonment: Social Causes and Consequences* (Thousand Oaks, CA: Sage, 2001); B. Useem and A. Piehl, *Prison State: The Challenge of Mass Incarceration* (New York: Cambridge University Press, 2008); M. Jacobson, *Downsizing Prisons: How to Reduce Crime and End Mass Incarceration* (New York: New York University Press, 2005); M. Maurer and L. Chesney-Lind (eds.), *Invisible Punishment: The Collateral Consequences of Mass Imprisonment* (New York: New Press, 2002).

11. One estimate is that about 30 million parents and children have been directly affected by incarceration over these past thirty years. See L. Glaze and L. Maruschak, *Parents in Prison and Their Minor Children* (Washington, DC: Bureau of Justice Statistics, 2009).

12. The demands of working in correctional settings have a number of negative physical and psychological effects, including depression and work–family conflict, negative emotions and coping styles, and even elevated rates of suicide and post-traumatic stress disorder. See C. Obidoa, D. Reeves, N. Warren, et al., "Depression and Work–Family Conflict among Corrections Officers," *Journal of Occupational and Environmental Medicine* 53 (2011): 1294–1301; S. Stack and O. Tsoudis, "Suicide Risk among Corrections Officers: A Logistical Regression Analysis," *Archives of Suicide Research* 3 (1997): 183–186; M. Dollard and A. Winefield, "A Test of the Demand-Control/Support Model of Work Stress in Corrections Officers," *Journal of Occupational Health Psychology* 3 (1998): 243–264; S. Spinaris, M. Denhof, and J. Kellaway, *Posttraumatic Stress Disorder in United States Corrections Professionals: Prevalence and Impact on Health and Functioning* (Florence, CO: Desert Waters Correctional Outreach, 2012); and P. Finn, *Addressing Corrections Officer Stress: Programs and Strategies* (Washington, DC: National Institute of Justice, 2000).

13. S. Konda, H. Tiesma, A. Reichard, and D. Hartly, "U.S. Correctional Officers Killed or Injured on the Job," *Corrections Today* 75 (November/December 2013): 122–125.

14. L. Ferrero-Miliani, H. Nielsen, P. Andersen, and S. Girardin, "Chronic Inflammation: Importance of NOD2 and NALP3 in Interleukin-1b Generation," *Clinical and Experimental Immunology* 147 (2006): 227–235.

15. B. Bogue, "How Principles of High-Reliability Organizations Relate to Corrections," *Federal Probation* 73 (2010): 22–27.

16. K. Cameron and R. Quinn, *Diagnosing and Changing Organizational Culture* (San Francisco: Jossey-Bass, 2006).

17. L. Carroll, *Organizational Culture: An Overview of Perspectives, Methods, and Findings* (Middletown, CT: Criminal Justice Institute, 2000).

18. Following Susan Hunter's untimely death in March 2014, the Susan M. Hunter Correctional Scholarship was established by the Association of State Correctional Administrators as a lasting tribute to her commitment to the field of corrections. See http://www.asca.net//projects/20 for more information.

19. All of the assessment reports are filled with identifying information and are confidential; they are not available to the public.

20. At the time of his death, Morris was the Julius Kreeger Professor Emeritus of Law and Criminology at the University of Chicago Law School. He was internationally recognized as a leader in criminal justice and prison reform and was among the most influential writers of his time, having authored, coauthored, or edited fifteen books and hundreds of articles over a fifty-five-year career. Morris played an instrumental role in creating the National Institute of Corrections during the 1970s and was a charter member of its advisory board until he passed away. See www.nicic/norval for more information on NIC's Norval Morris Project.

21. Jacobs made the remark at the first planning meeting for the Norval Morris Project on August 23, 2004, in Denver.

22. See J. Jacobs, "Norval Morris as Penologist: An Exception Who Proved the Rule," *Federal Sentencing Reporter* 21 (2009): 261–264; N. Morris, "Impediments to Penal Reform," *University of Chicago Law Review* 33 (1966): 627–628.

23. N. Morris and G. Hawkins, *The Honest Politician's Guide to Crime Control* (Chicago: University of Chicago Press, 1970), N. Morris, *The Future of Imprisonment* (Chicago: University of Chicago Press, 1974).

24. See the J-SAT website at http://www.j-sat.com/ for more information.

25. Clarke served from 1990 to 2005 as director of the Nebraska Department of Corrections, then led the Washington state system from 2005 to 2007 and the Massachusetts system from 2007 to 2010. He was appointed director of the Virginia Department of Corrections in November 2010. Clarke also served in a variety of elected positions in the American Correctional Association and the Association of State Correctional Administrators, including that of president of both organizations. In 2014, he received the American Correctional Association's highest career award, the E. B. Cass Award, for distinguished service.

26. The detailed material on Clarke and his career is drawn mainly from an interview with him on June 29, 2012. Additional material comes from numerous personal conversations and/or his statements in various meetings we attended together.

27. See M. Weisbord and S. Janoff, *Don't Just Do Something, Stand There: Ten Principles for Leading Meetings That Matter* (San Francisco: Berrett-Koehler, 1997); M. Weisbord, and S. Janoff, *Future Search: An Action Guide to Finding Common Ground in Organizations & Communities* (San Francisco: Berrett-Koehler, 2000).

28. See Virginia Department of Corrections, *Virginia Adult Reentry Initiative: The Four Year Strategic Plan, Executive Summary, July 2010–June 2014* (2010), accessed September 18, 2014, http://vadoc.virginia.gov/documents/reentryInitiativeExecSummary.pdf.

29. See http://dialogue-associates.com/ for information on Garrett and Ball's private-sector work and http://www.prisondialogue.org/ for information on the nonprofit Prison Dialogue organization, founded by Garrett, which they also actively support.

30. These figures were supplied by W. D. Jennings, administrator, Research and Management Services Unit at the Virginia Department of Corrections and are drawn from his research (personal communication, March 27, 2014) and from Virginia Department of Corrections, *State Responsible Offender Population Trends, FY2008–FY2012* (2013), accessed September 18, 2014, http://vadoc.virginia.gov/about/facts/research/new-statsum/offenderpopulationtrends_fy08-fy12.pdf.

31. Bohm, *On Dialogue*; Bohm, *Wholeness and the Implicate Order.*

32. Bohm, *On Dialogue*, 10.

33. "Art Meets Science and Spirituality in a Changing Economy: From Fragmentation to Wholeness" (1979), accessed September 18, 2014, http://www.youtube.com/watch?v=Dg9QoXv4Geo.

34. Bohm, *On Dialogue*, 12–13 (emphasis in original).

35. F. Peat, *Infinite Potential: The Life and Times of David Bohm* (New York: Basic Books, 1997).

36. D. Bohm, *Quantum Theory* (New York: Prentice Hall, 1951).

37. D. Bohm and F. Peat, *Science, Order & Creativity* (New York: Bantam Books, 1987).

38. B. Hiley and F. Peat (eds.), *Quantum Implications: Essays in Honour of David Bohm* (London: Routledge & Kegan Paul, 1987), 48.

39. For example, Daniel Kahneman, a psychology professor at Princeton, details many of the ways that our bias in perception and thinking leads to distorted understanding. See D. Kahneman, *Thinking, Fast and Slow* (New York: Farrar, Straus and Giroux, 2011).

40. Peat, *Infinite Potential.*

41. D. Bohm, D. Factor, and P. Garrett, "Dialogue: A Proposal" (1991), accessed May 31, 2012, http://www.world.std.com/~lo/bohm/0000.html.

42. Personal interview, March 22, 2012.

43. P. Senge, *The Fifth Discipline: The Art and Practice of the Learning Organization* (New York, Doubleday, 2006).

44. Personal interview, May 30, 2013.

45. D. Fixsen, S. Naoom, K. Blase, et al., *Implementation Research: A Synthesis of the Literature* (Tampa: University of Southern Florida, National Implementation Research Network, 2005), 5. See also the NIRN website, http://nirn.fpg.unc.edu/.

2. The Big Squeeze in American Corrections

1. P. Angle (ed.), *The Complete Lincoln-Douglas Debates of 1858* (Chicago: University of Chicago Press, 1991); emphasis in Angle.

2. Every book on contemporary American corrections seems to begin with a litany of mind-boggling statistics, as though the authors feel compelled to remind themselves and their readers of how incredible the transformation over the past few decades has been. Justice statistics is a constantly changing, amorphous system that is a mix of conscientious effort, incomplete data from a complex, decentralized sys-

tem, and constant spin from defenders and skeptics alike. The best data still come from the steady stream of reports from the Bureau of Justice Statistics; see http://bjs. ojp.usdoj.gov/.

3. The long-range prospects for state and local governments actually appear to be dim; the U.S. Government Accounting Office projects a significant decline in their fiscal position over the next fifty years, absent significant policy changes. See U.S. General Accounting Office, *State and Local Governments' Fiscal Outlook, April 2013 Update* (GAO-13-546SP) (Washington, DC: U.S. General Accounting Office, 2013).

4. To examine the effects of crime rates, incarceration rates, and fiscal factors in more detail, I use the example of state corrections because most of the money in corrections is spent by the states on prisons and the available data are both more readily available and more consistent over time. The Bureau of Justice Statistics produces a number of reports on correctional populations and trends. The figures available at the time of this writing covered 2012. See A. Carson and W. Sabol, *Prisoners in 2011* (Washington, DC: Bureau of Justice Statistics, 2012); L. Glaze and E. Herberman, *Correctional Populations in the United States, 2012* (Washington, DC: Bureau of Justice Statistics, 2013); L. Maruchak and T. Bonczar, *Probation and Parole in the United States, 2012* (Washington, DC: Bureau of Justice Statistics, 2013); and P. Guerino, P. Harrison, and W. Sabol, *Prisoners in 2010* (revised) (Washington, DC: Bureau of Justice Statistics, (2011).

5. E. Carson and D. Gulinelli, *Prisoners in 2012: Advanced Counts* (Washington, DC: Bureau of Justice Statistics, 2013); E. Carson, *Prisoners in 2013* (Washington, DC: Bureau of Justice Statistics, 2014).

6. The data on violent crime trends come from the Federal Bureau of Investigation's Uniform Crime Reports, better known as the FBI UCR, "Index Crimes." The advantage of using violent crime rates is that they have been more or less consistently defined and the law enforcement response to violence has become more uniform over time. The same cannot be said for other types of crime, such as drug or sex crimes. The experiences of individual states and local jurisdictions have varied enormously, of course, but these, at least, give us a national picture.

   The FBI publishes its Uniform Crime Reports (UCR) data in *Crime in the United States* annually, with semiannual preliminary reports and other special reports (http://www.fbi.gov/about-us/cjis/ucr/ucr). In the UCR, violent crime is composed of four offenses: murder and non-negligent manslaughter, forcible rape, robbery, and aggravated assault. Violent crimes are defined in the UCR program as those offenses that involve force or threat of force. Drug crimes are not included among these index crimes, and I have avoided discussing the effects of the war on drugs because it appears to me to be more a historical anomaly than a part of the long-range trends.

7. F. Zimring, *The Great American Crime Decline* (New York: Oxford University Press, 2007); A. Blumstein and J. Wallman, *The Crime Drop in America* (New York: Cambridge University Press, 2000); J. Travis and M. Waul, *Reflections on the Crime*

Decline: Lessons for the Future? Proceedings of the Urban Institute Crime Decline Forum (Washington, DC: Urban Institute, 2000).

8. National Conference of State Legislators, State Budget Actions 1999, Special Fiscal Report, National Conference of State Legislators, Denver, 2000.

9. National Conference of State Legislators, State Budget Actions 2000, Special Fiscal Report, National Conference of State Legislators, Denver, 2001.

10. National Conference of State Legislators, State Budget Actions 2001, Special Fiscal Report, National Conference of State Legislators, Denver, 2002.

11. The best sources of up-to-date information on correctional budgets and expenditures are reports from the National Association of State Budget Officers (http://www.nasbo.org/). The numbers I cite here are from their annual State Budget Actions reports. Another source of state budget information and projections is the National Conference of State Legislators (http://www.ncsl.org/).

12. It was the health of state finances that allowed states to build many things, including schools and parks, as well as prisons. See W. Spelman, "Crime, Cash, and Limited Options: Explaining the Prison Boom," *Criminology and Public Policy* 8 (2009): 29–77.

13. T. Kychelhahn, *Justice Expenditures and Employment, FY 2002–2007*, Statistical Tables (Washington, DC: Bureau of Justice Statistics, 2011).

14. National Association of State Budget Officers, *State Spending for Corrections: Long-Term Trends and Recent Criminal Justice Policy Reforms* (Washington, DC: National Association of State Budget Officers, 2013).

15. T. Kychelhahn, *Local Government Corrections Expenditures, FY 2005–2011* (Washington, DC: Bureau of Justice Statistics, 2013).

16. M. Tonry, "Crime and Justice, 1975–2025: Sentencing," Presented at the American Society of Criminology Annual Meetings, Chicago, November 16, 2012.

17. See S. Scheingold, *The Politics of Street Crime: Criminal Process and Cultural Obsession* (Philadelphia: Temple University Press, 1991).

18. D. Rothman, *Conscience and Convenience: The Asylum and Its Alternatives in Progressive America* (New York: Aldine de Gruyter, 2002).

19. A. Blumstein and J. Cohen, "A Theory of the Stability of Punishment," *Journal of Criminal Law and Criminology* 64 (1973): 198–207.

20. M. Tonry, *The Fragmentation of Sentencing and Corrections in America* (Washington, DC: National Institute of Justice, 1999).

21. Bureau of Justice Assistance, *1996 National Survey of State Sentencing Structures* (Washington, DC: Bureau of Justice Assistance, 1998).

22. A. Blumstein and A. Beck, "Population Growth in U.S. Prisons, 1980–1996," in M. Tonry and J. Petersilia (eds.), *Crime and Justice: A Review of the Literature*, 26: 17–61 (Chicago: University of Chicago Press, 1999).

23. Pew Public Safety Performance Project, *The Impact of Incarceration on Crime: Two National Experts Weigh In* (Washington, DC: Pew Center on the States, 2008).

24. Ibid. See also W. Spelman, "The Limited Importance of Prison Expansion," in A.

Blumstein and J. Wallman (eds.), *The Crime Drop in America*, 97–129 (New York: Cambridge University Press, 2000); W. Spelman, "What Recent Studies Do (and Don't) Tell Us About Imprisonment and Crime," in M. Tonry (ed.), *Crime and Justice: A Review of Research*, 27: 419–494 (Chicago: University of Chicago Press, 2000); W. Spelman, "Specifying the Relationship Between Crime and Prisons," *Journal of Quantitative Criminology* 24 (2008): 149–178.

25. In 2009, Alfred Blumstein and Ken Nakamura published the results of their groundbreaking study on redemption. Past research had shown that the likelihood of recidivism declines steadily over time and that people who stay out of trouble for three years are unlikely to ever reoffend, even if you track them for twenty years. Blumstein and Nakamura estimated how long a person must keep a clean record before the person's probability of reoffending drops to the point where it is about what might be predicted just from the person's age and gender. For example, using data from New York, they showed that the offense and the age of first arrest both had an influence on how long it takes for the average risk of a rearrest to fall to the base risk level from the age–crime curve. The longest period, nine years, was for sixteen-year-olds arrested for robbery, while the shortest period was four years for twenty-year-olds arrested for the same offense. With a subsequent grant from the National Institute of Justice, Blumstein and Nakamura extended their analysis with data from Florida and Illinois. They found that a reasonable redemption time estimate was about four to seven years for a violent offense, four years for a drug offense, and three to four years for a property offense. After that, a person who had committed a crime in the past would be no more likely to commit a new crime than his or her peers. See A. Blumstein and K. Nakamura, "Redemption in the Presence of Widespread Criminal Background Checks," *Criminology* 47 (2009): 327–359; A. Blumstein and K. Nakamura, "Extension of Current Estimates of Redemption Times: Robustness Testing, Out-of-State Arrests, and Racial Differences," Final Report Submitted to the National Institute of Justice, January 2012.

26. Personal interview, July 21, 2012. Caruso has also served in leadership roles in the Association of State Administrators, the American Correctional Association, and the Association of Women Executives in Corrections.

27. R. Apel and D. Nagin, "General Deterrence," in M. Tonry (ed.), *The Oxford Handbook of Crime and Criminal Justice*, 179–206 (New York: Oxford University Press, 2011); A. Blumstein, J. Cohen, and D. Nagin, *Deterrence and Incapacitation: Estimating the Effects of Criminal Sanctions on Crime Rates* (Washington, DC: National Academies Press, 1978); J. Gibbs, *Crime, Punishment, and Deterrence* (New York: Elsevier, 1975); F. Zimring and G. Hawkins, *Deterrence: The Legal Threat in Crime Control* (Chicago: University of Chicago Press, 1973).

28. D. Gordon, *The Justice Juggernaut: Fighting Street Crime, Controlling Citizens* (New Brunswick, NJ: Rutgers University Press, 1991).

29. Federal Bureau of Investigation, *Crime in the United States, 2011* (2011), accessed January 3, 2014, http://www.fbi.gov/about-us/cjis/ucr/crime-in-the-u.s/2011/crime-

in-the-u.s.-2011/tables/table-29; H. Snyder, *Arrest in the United States, 1980–2009*, Bureau of Justice Statistics (2011), accessed January 3, 2014, http://www.bjs.gov/content/pub/pdf/aus8009.pdf.

30. J. Pfaff, "The Micro and Macro Causes of Prison Growth," *Georgia State University Law Review* 28 (2012): 1–35, accessed April 1, 2013, http://ssrn.com/abstract=2181062.

31. A. Carson and D. Golinelli, *Prisons in 2012: Trends in Admissions and Releases, 1991–2012* (Washington, DC: Bureau of Justice Statistics, 2013).

32. N. Morris, "The Contemporary Prison," in N. Morris and D. Rothman (eds.), *The Oxford History of the Prison*, 202–234 (Oxford: Oxford University Press, 1995).

33. T. Clear, *The Beginning of the End of the Great Punishment Experiment* (March 26, 2013), accessed September 18, 2014, http://www.nccdglobal.org/blog/the-beginning-of-the-end-of-the-great-punishment-experiment. See also T. Clear and N. Frost, *The Punishment Imperative: The Rise and Fall of the Great Punishment Experiment* (New York: New York University Press, 2013).

34. Clear, *Beginning of the End*.

35. L. Glaze, *Correctional Populations in the United States, 2010* (Washington, DC: Bureau of Justice Statistics, 2011). The Bureau of Justice Statistics also reported that in 2011 the number of prisoners in state or federal prisons was 1,598,780. This was a 0.9% decline from the year before (when it was 1,613,803). By the end of 2011, there were 492 sentenced prisoners per 100,000 U.S. residents incarcerated (it had peaked in 2007 with a rate of 506 per 100,000). The advanced counts for 2012 showed a total of 6,937,600 people in the correctional population. See Carson and Sabol, *Prisoners in 2011*; Glaze and Herberman, *Correctional Populations in the United States, 2012*.

36. For reports from the early 2000s that predicted a watershed from the earlier recession, see J. Wool and D. Stemen, *Changing Fortunes or Changing Attitudes? Sentencing and Corrections Reform in 2003* (New York: Vera Institute of Justice, 2004); D. Wilheim and N. Turner, *Is the Budget Crisis Changing the Way We Look at Sentencing and Incarceration?* (New York: Vera Institute of Justice, 2002); J. Greene, *Positive Trends in State-Level Sentencing and Corrections Policy* (Washington, DC: Families Against Mandatory Minimums, 2003).

37. R. Subramanian and R. Tublitz, *Realigning Justice Resources: A Review of Population and Spending Shifts in Prison and Community Corrections* (New York: Vera Institute of Justice, 2012).

38. E. Lauren-Brooke and J. James, *Reallocating Justice Resources: A Review of 2011 State Sentencing Trends* (New York: Vera Institute of Justice, 2012); A. Austin, *Criminal Justice Trends: Key Legislative Changes in Sentencing Policy, 2001–2010* Vera (New York: Institute of Justice, 2010),

39. Pew Public Safety Performance Project, *Prison Count, 2010: State Population Declines for First Time in 38 Years* (Washington, DC: Pew Charitable Trusts, 2010). Pew has produced a steady stream of publications intended to raise the consciousness of the American public by pointing out how many people are imprisoned. See Pew Center on the States, *One in 100: Behind Bars in America, 2008* (Washington, DC:

Pew Center on the States, 2008), Pew Center on the States, *One in 31: The Long Reach of American Corrections* (Washington, DC: Pew Center on the States, 2009).

40. N. Porter, *On the Chopping Block, 2013: State Prison Closures* (Washington, DC: Sentencing Project, 2013).

41. A video of the speech and full transcript are available at http://nij.ncjrs.gov/multimedia/video-nijconf2012-laub-petersilia.htm .

42. Petersilia did not say during her speech which of Zimring's or Tonry's writings she had in mind, but in a personal communication to me she identified them as R. Gartner and F. Zimring, "The Past as Prologue? Decarceration in California Then and Now," *Criminology & Public Policy* 10 (2011): 291–325, and M. Tonry, "Looking Back to See the Future of Punishment in America," *Social Research* 74 (2007): 353–378.

43. Council of State Governments Justice Center, *Lessons from the States: Reducing Recidivism and Curbing Correctional Costs Through Justice Reinvestment* (New York: Council of State Governments Justice Center, 2013).

44. See, e.g., J. James, *Justice Reinvestment in Actions: The Delaware Model* (New York: Vera Institute Center for Sentencing and Corrections, 2013). The Urban Institute, with funding from the Bureau of Justice Assistance, is tasked to work with selected local jurisdictions applying the JRI model. According to Urban's website, the project "employs data and collaborative decision making to help jurisdictions lower crime, reduce local criminal justice spending, and control growth in correctional populations . . . The overarching goal of local justice reinvestment work is to reduce county correctional costs and reinvest resources in high-stakes communities to yield a more cost-beneficial impact on public safety and community well-being." Accessed September 18, 2014, http://www.urban.org/center/jpc/justice-reinvestment/.

45. N. LaVigne, S. Bieler, L. Cramer, et al., *Justice Reinvestment Initiative State Assessment Report* (Washington, DC: Urban Institute, 2014), 31–32.

46. Austin, Cadora, Clear, et al., *Ending Mass Incarceration.*

47. Several of the report's authors played key roles in or were prominent supporters of the creation of the Justice Reinvestment movement. The original funding of the effort was provided by Open Society to Austin's Justice for All and the Council of State Governments Justice Center. The Justice Center tripled in size during the period and eventually became a separate organization.

48. Council of State Governments Justice Center, *Justice Reinvestment in Oklahoma: Overview* (New York: Council of State Governments, 2011); Council of State Governments Justice Center, *Justice Reinvestment in Oklahoma: Analysis and Policy Framework* (New York: Council of State Governments, 2012); Council of State Governments Justice Center, *Justice Reinvestment in Oklahoma: Strengthening Supervision and Reinvesting in Efforts to Reduce Violent Crime* (New York: Council of State Governments, 2012).

49. P. McGuigan, "Governor Mary Fallin Rebuffs Justice Reinvestment Implementation Funds," *City Sentinel*, February 26, 2013, accessed May 10, 2013, http://city-sentinel.com/2013/02/governor-mary-fallin-rebuffs-justice-reinvestment-implementa-

tion-funds/. Fallin, anticipating a reelection campaign in 2014, apparently felt that Justice Reinvestment sounded too soft on crime.

50. LaVigne, Bieler, Cramer, et al., *Justice Reinvestment Initiative State Assessment Report*, 103.

51. See the Council of State Governments website, http://csgjusticecenter.org/jr/ok/, (accessed February 17, 2014).

52. Oklahoma Department of Corrections, 2013 Annual Report, accessed February 17, 2014, http://www.ok.gov/doc/documents/annual%20report%202013%20for%20 web.pdf.

53. Whether or not there were any actual savings to reinvest, Oklahoma still appropriated state funds in fiscal year 2013 in the amounts of $2 million for the law enforcement grant program, $700,000 for a felony jail screen, and another $1 million for probation agencies.

54. Jones's comments in this chapter are taken from a personal interview, July 20, 2012, and a telephone interview, May 11 2013.

55. See www.oregoncf.org for information on the Oregon Community Foundation.

56. Personal interview, April 4 2012.

57. J. Austin, "Reducing America's Correctional Populations: A Strategic Plan," *Justice Research and Policy* 12 (2010): 1–32.

3. Cultural Styles

1. "Interactionalism," also known as "symbolic interactionalism," traces its intellectual roots back through Herbert Blumer to George Herbert Mead, to American Pragmatism, and to John Dewey and Charles Sanders Peirce. In Blumer, symbolic interactionalism has three general principles: (1) people act toward other people or things according to the meanings those people or things have for them; (2) the meanings are derived from interactions with others in a social context (i.e., a culture); and (3) these meanings are maintained and changed through the ongoing processes of interpretation and reinterpretation. See G. Mead, *Mind, Self, and Society: From the Standpoint of a Social Behaviorist* (Chicago: University of Chicago Press, 1934); H. Blumer, *Symbolic Interactionism: Perspectives and Methods* (Englewood Cliffs, NJ: Prentice Hall, 1969); H. Becker and M. McCall (eds.), *Symbolic Interaction and Cultural Studies* (Chicago: University of Chicago Press, 1993).

2. E. Schein, *Organizational Culture and Leadership*, 3d ed. (San Francisco: Jossey-Bass, 2005).

3. These "shared understandings" have been recognized and given other labels by different writers. Hofstede refers to "collective consciousness" and "collective programming," Schein talks about "underlying shared assumptions," and Sackman identifies them as group values. See G. Hofstede, *Culture's Consequences: International Differences in Work-Related Values* (Newbury Park, CA: Sage, 1980); E. Schein, "Coming to a New Awareness of Organizational Culture," *Sloan Management Review* 25, no. 2 (1984): 3–16; S. A. Sackman, *Cultural Knowledge on Organizations: Exploring the Collective Mind* (Newbury Park, CA: 1991).

4. "Social constructionalism" has been a particularly fertile area of theory, research, and debate in the United States at least since Peter Berger and Thomas Luckman published *The Social Construction of Reality* (New York: Anchor Books, 1966). For social constructionists, reality itself is negotiated by people, but then becomes a given to those who follow the original period of development. The perspective has influenced thinking about crime, punishment, and prions in work such as Michel Foucault's *Discipline & Punish: The Birth of the Prison* (New York: Vintage Books, 1995). See also M. Brown, *The Culture of Punishment: Prison, Society, and Spectacle* (New York: New York University Press, 2009); D. Garland, "Concepts of Culture in the Sociology of Punishment," *Theoretical Criminology* 10 (2006): 419–447; J. Ford, "Organizational Change as Shifting Conversations," *Journal of Organizational Change Management* 12 (1999): 480–500.

5. See David Bohm: Friday Evening Seminar, November 30, 1990, accessed September 18, 2014, http://www.youtube.com/watch?v=6vtD1HhlIls.

6. See W. McGuire, "The Nature of Attitudes and Attitude Change," in G. Lindzey and E. Aronson (eds.), *The Handbook of Social Psychology*, 136–314 (Reading, MA: Addison-Wesley, 1969); A. Eagly and S. Chaiken, "Attitude Structure and Function," in D. T. Gilbert, S. T. Fiske, and G. Lindzey (eds.), *Handbook of Social Psychology*, 269–322 (New York: McGraw-Hill, 1998); A. Eagly and S. Chaiken, "The Nature of Attitudes," in A. Eagly, and S. Chaiken (eds.), *The Psychology of Attitudes*, 1–21 (New York: Harcourt Brace, 1993).

7. See D. Katz, "The Functional Approach to the Study of Attitudes," *Public Opinion Quarterly* 24 (1960): 163–204; M. Lapinski and F. Boster, *Modeling the Ego-Defensive Function of Attitudes*, Communication Monographs 68, no. 3 (2001): 314–324.

8. Anthony Greenwald and Mahzarin Banaji, two academic research psychologists, write, "Implicit attitudes are introspectively unidentified (or inaccurately identified) traces of past experience that mediate favorable or unfavorable feeling, thought, or action toward social objects." See A. Greenwald and M. Banaji, "Implicit Social Cognition: Attitudes, Self-esteem, and Stereotypes," *Psychological Review* 102 (1995): 4–27; see also B. Gawronski, W. Hofmann, and C. Wilbur, "Are 'Implicit' Attitudes Unconscious?" *Consciousness & Cognition* 15 (2006): 485–499.

9. M. Polanyi, *The Tacit Dimension* (Chicago: University of Chicago Press, 1966), 4. See also M. Polanyi, *Personal Knowledge: Toward a Post-Critical Philosophy*, rev. ed (London: Routledge, (2002).

10. Bohm, *Unfolding Meaning*, 18.

11. E. Schein, *The Corporate Culture Survival Guide* (San Francisco: Jossey-Bass, 1999).

12. See D. Fixen, S. Naoom, K. Blase, et al., *Implementation Research: A Synthesis of the Literature* (Tampa: University of Southern Florida, Louis de la Parte Florida Mental Health Institute, 2005).

13. D. Denison, "What Is the Difference between Organizational Culture and Organizational Climate?" *Academy of Management Review* 21 (1996): 619–654.

14. A number of change models assume that people need to be prodded into accepting changes and that a crisis or challenge to the group will motivate change. John Kotter's change model, for example, sees complacency as a major reason change efforts

fail. He discusses at length the necessity of establishing a sense of urgency by, if necessary, creating a crisis or intentionally setting goals too high to meet. The underlying assumption here is that people have to be pushed into change. See J. Kotter, *Leading Change* (Boston: Harvard Business School Press, 1996).

15. See K. Lewin, *Principles of Topological Psychology*, trans. F. Heider and G. Heider (New York: McGraw-Hill, 1936); see also K. Lewin, "The Conflict Between Aristotelian and Galileian Modes of Thought in Contemporary Psychology" [1931], in D. Adams and K. Zener (trans.), *A Dynamic Theory of Personality, Selected Papers of Kurt* Lewin, 1–42 (New York: McGraw-Hill, 1935).

16. A. Marrow, *The Practical Theorists: The Life and Work of Kurt Lewin* (New York: Basic Books, 1969), 30.

17. L. Carroll, *Organizational Culture: An Overview of Perspectives, Methods, and Findings* (Middletown, CT: Criminal Justice Institute, 2000).

18. K. Cameron and R. Quinn, *Diagnosing and Changing Organizational Culture* (San Francisco: Jossey-Bass, 2006). These dimensions did not appear out of nowhere. They were developed through research that started with a list of effectiveness criteria first compiled by Cambell in the 1970s and analyzed by Quinn and Rohrbaugh using multidimensional scaling techniques. The dimensions that emerged from that analysis turned out to reproduce almost exactly the Jungian framework of psychological archetypes. That so many models have similar-sounding dimensions may be because they are universal. See J. Cambell, "On the Nature of Organizational Effectiveness," in P. Goodman and J. Pennings (eds.), *New Perspectives on Organizational Effectiveness*, 13–55 (San Francisco: Jossey-Bass, 1977); R. Quinn and J. Rohrbaugh, "A Competing Values Approach to Organizational Effectiveness," *Public Productivity Review* 5 (1981): 122–140; K. Cameron and S. Freeman, "Cultural Congruence, Strength, and Type: Relationships to Effectiveness," *Organizational Change and Development* 5 (1991): 23–58; and C. Jung, *Psychological Types* (London: Routledge & Kegan Paul, 1923).

19. An example is the reentry movement within corrections, with its emphasis on outcomes such as recidivism and external stakeholders. The change in perspective has had a noticeable effect on many correctional agencies in recent years.

20. Sometimes confusion is created when a writer tries to contrast a "process" view of culture and an "ideal type" perspective on the assumption that these are different things. This is more fragmented thinking; the processes are not different from the types; the types are generated by the processes. It is just easier to talk about types.

21. See D. Denison, *Corporate Culture and Organizational Effectiveness* (New York: Wiley, 1990); D. Denison, R. Hooijberg, and R. Quinn, "Paradox and Performance: Toward a Theory of Behavioral Complexity in Managerial Leadership," *Organizational Science* 6 (1995): 524–540; J. Martin and P. Frost, "The Organization Culture Games: A Struggle for Intellectual Dominance," in S. Clegg, C. Hardy, W. Nord, and T. Lawrence (eds.), *Handbook of Organizational Studies*, 725–753 (London: Sage, 2004).

22. R. Likert, *New Patterns of Management* (New York: McGraw-Hill, 1961).

23. R. Blake and J. Mouton, *The Managerial Grid: The Key to Leadership Excellence* (Houston: Gulf, 1964).

24. Bogue, "How Principles of High-Reliability Organizations Relate to Corrections."

25. See C. Perrow, "Organizing to Reduce the Vulnerabilities of Complexity," *Journal of Contingencies and Crisis Management* 7 (1999): 150–155; K. Weick and K. Sutcliffe, *Managing the Unexpected: Assuring High Performance in an Age of Complexity* (San Francisco: Jossey-Bass, 2001); G. Bigley and K. Roberts, "The Incident Command System: High-Reliability Organizing for Complex and Volatile Task Environments," *Academy of Management Journal* 44 (2001): 1281–1299.

26. This diagram was adapted from K. Cameron and R. Quinn, *Diagnosing and Changing Organizational Culture,* rev. ed. (San Francisco: Jossey-Bass, 2006), 75.

27. Adapted from ibid., 78.

28. G. Sykes, *The Society of Captives: A Study of a Maximum Security Prison* (Princeton, NJ: Princeton University Press, 1958).

29. See J. Irwin and D. Cressey, "Thieves, Convicts, and the Inmate Culture," *Social Problems* 10 (1962): 142–155.

30. C. Innes, "Patterns of Misconduct in the Federal Prison System," *Criminal Justice Review* 22 (1997): 157–174.

31. The idea that prison culture is a myth is not the same as the recognition that inmates do not have a mythology. In their provocatively titled book, *The Myth of Prison Rape: Sexual Culture in American Prisons* (New York: Rowman & Littlefield, 2009), researchers Mark Fleisher and Jessie Krienert give a vivid portrait of the stories inmates tell and believe about sexual assault.

32. E. Anderson, "The Code of the Streets," *Atlantic Monthly*, May 1994.

33. See D. Clemmer, *The Prison Community* (Boston: Christopher, 1940); L. Carroll, *Hacks, Blacks, and Cons: Race Relations in a Maximum Security Prison* (Lexington, MA: Lexington Books, 1974); M. Fleisher, *Warehousing Violence* (Newbury Park, CA: Sage, 1989).

34. The total institution argument was popularized by Erving Goffman in his celebrated book, *Asylums: Essays on the Social Situation of Mental Patients and Other Inmates* (Garden City, NJ: Anchor Books).

35. For a discussion of the "not-so-total" prison, see R. McCorkle, T. Miethe, and K. Drass, "The Roots of Violence: A Test of the Deprivation, Management, and 'Not-So-Total' Institutional Models," *Crime and Delinquency* 41 (1995): 317–331. See also J. Stowell and J. Byrne, "Does What Happens in Prison Stay in Prison? Examining the Reciprocal Relationship between Community and Prison Culture," in J. Byrne, D. Hummer, and F. Taxman (eds.), *The Culture of Prison Violence,* 27–39 (New York: Pearson, 2008).

4. Correctional Cultures: Reals and Ideals

1. H. Read and J. Watson, *Introduction to Geology* (New York: Halsted, 1975).
2. J. van Maanen and S. Barley, "Cultural Organization: Fragments of a Theory," in P. J. Frost et al. (eds.), *Organizational Culture*, 31–53 (Beverly Hills, CA: Sage, 1985).
3. Organizational culture approaches experienced a boom among business writers and consultants early in the 1980s following the publication of a number of best-selling books. See W. Ouchi, *Theory Z: How American Business Can Meet the Japanese Challenge* (Reading MA: Addison-Wesley, 1981); R. Pascale and A. Athos, *The Art of Japanese Management: Applications for American Executives* (New York: Simon & Schuster, (1982); T. Deal and A. Kennedy, *Corporate Cultures: The Rites and Rituals of Corporate Life* (Reading, MA: Addison-Wesley, 1982); and T. Peters and R. Waterman, *In Search of Excellence: Lessons from America's Best Run Companies* (New York: Harper & Row, 1982).
4. R. Corcoran, "NIC Update: Changing Prison Culture," *Corrections Today,* April 2005, 24–27. See also L. Carroll, *Institutional Culture* (Middletown, CT: Criminal Justice Institute, 2003).
5. Peter Rockholtz, who at the time was the project director of the NIC Culture Project, remembers that he wanted to include something quantitative in the cultural assessment, which was then being developed as a purely qualitative protocol. He said that he liked Cameron and Quinn's Organizational Culture Assessment Instrument because it was relatively short, was easy to score, and produced good visuals that could be compared with others. He said it also had very good psychometric properties, had been developed from data that included public-sector organizations, seemed to translate well to the organizational aspects of prisons, and "We got to use it for free." Others on the team—the CJI project manager, Shaina Vanek; the NIC project manager, Randy Corcoran; and the project consultant Leo Carrol, a professor at the University of Rhode Island—all agreed. The "free" part seems to have carried the argument (personal communication, April 30, 2013).
6. In presenting the results of the Prison Culture Project, I always refer to the head of a state correctional system as "the director" and the CEO of a prison as "the warden," whether or not that was the actual title. For the sake of consistency and confidentiality, "commissioner," "superintendent," or other less common titles are not used. In cases where I refer to someone as "he" or "she," the pronoun is a random choice. I also always refer to "headquarters" to indicate the administrative headquarters of the system, even though correctional staff usually have more colloquial, and sometimes very colorful, terms for the headquarters. Also for readability, consistency, and confidentiality, I refer to a few institutions that are actually jails, or have significant unsentenced populations and operate to a significant degree in a jail-like fashion, as prisons.
7. J. Wilson, *Bureaucracy: What Government Agencies Do and Why They Do It* (New York: Basic Books, 1989), 91.

5. Management versus Everyone Else

1. If structural changes to a department of corrections were really undertaken to make it more capable of changing overall, these three would be the most effective: making the role of the department of corrections director as nonpolitical as possible, hiring corrections professionals to do the job and giving them the autonomy to do it, and unifying prisons and community corrections under one umbrella.
2. I have kept Cameron and Quinn's nomenclature because they chose their terms carefully to match those used in the research literature on organizations as they were developing their framework (Kim Cameron, personal communication, February 21, 2014).
3. Cameron and Quinn, *Diagnosing and Changing Organizational Culture*.
4. The report cites two sources for the claim that the utility of cultural control is more efficient than that of more formal mechanisms: C. O'Reilly and C. Chatman, "Culture as Social Control: Corporations, Cults, and Commitment," *Research on Organizational Behavior* 18 (1996):167–200; and J. Pfeffer, *New Directions for Organization Theory: Problems and Prospects* (Oxford: Oxford University Press, 1997).
5. In this prison there were a number of spin-off benefits that might have been related to the general tone of the Change Project's openness to change. One was the establishment of an on-site child care program. A second was a program with a local university that awarded a certificate in public administration, half the tuition costs of which were paid by the corrections department. In addition, at the time the report was being written in 2009, plans were under way to develop an employee assistance program and arrangements had been made for a Ph.D. candidate in counseling to facilitate a ninety-minute family support group twice a month.
6. The program was delivered by Carol Flaherty-Zonis. See C. Flaherty-Zonis, *Building Culture Strategically: A Team Approach for Corrections* (Washington, DC: National Institute of Corrections, 2007).
7. J. Byrne, F. Taxman, and D. Hummer, *An Evaluation of the Implementation and Impact of NIC's Institutional Culture Initiative*, Final Report to the National Institute of Corrections (2005), available from the NIC library at www.nicic.gov. See also J. Byrne, D. Hummer, and F. Taxman, "The National Institute of Correction's Cultural Change Initiative: A Multisite Evaluation," in J. Byrne, D. Hummer, and F. Taxman (eds.), *The Culture of Prison Violence*, 137–163 (New York: Pearson, 2008).
8. In the evaluation report, the sites are not named for the same reason I do not name the U.S. prisons discussed elsewhere in this book; the Culture Project was carried out with the understanding that the results would be confidential.
9. See P. Sweeney and D. McFarlin, "Process and Outcome: Gender Differences in the Assessment of Justice," *Journal of Organizational Behavior* 18 (1997): 83–98.
10. The analysis of shifts in staff views on organizational justice does not appear in the original 2005 report to NIC. It was added to the 2008 version, which appeared in Byrne, Hummer, and Taxman (eds.), *The Culture of Prison Violence*.

11. Albert Einstein is supposed to have said that doing the same thing over and over again and expecting a different outcome is the definition of insanity.

12. See R. Quinn, *Deep Change: Discovering the Leader Within* (San Francisco: Jossey-Bass, 1996).

13. Clarke made the remark during a meeting of the Virginia Department of Corrections, Council for a Healing Environment, April 12, 2013.

6. Dialogue

1. Most of the material on Garrett and his work is drawn from two extended interviews I conducted with him on March 22, 2012, and May 31, 2013. Additional material comes from numerous personal communications, conference calls, emails, and many dinner conversations with him and Jane Ball.

2. F. Peat and J. Briggs, "Interview with David Bohm," *Omni Magazine*, January 1987; accessed April 5, 2012, http://www.fdavidpeat.com/interviews/bohm.htm.

3. Peat and Briggs, "Interview with David Bohm."

4. The private conferences Garrett organized after he met David Bohm included one in Israel, where the theme of the impact of Zionism on the future of Israel emerged, and another in Switzerland titled "Love and Hate." Further conferences, organized around themes that emerged out of the dialogues, took place in Norway, Sweden, Ireland, and the United Kingdom.

5. Among those involved were Don Factor (the son of Max Factor, the cosmetics magnate) and Anna Factor, who shared Garrett's interest in understanding the process of thought and the implications of it for our understanding. Also involved were Sharon and Roger Evans, who began the Psychosynthesis Institute and hosted a weekly meeting in their North London home that Bohm occasionally attended. One early group began meeting around this time in Lancaster and has met more or less regularly for a day every month ever since.

6. Patrick de Maré (1916–2008) was a psychotherapist with a special interest in group psychotherapy. David Bohm was treated by de Maré and was also influenced by his work. See P. de Maré, "Large Group Perspectives," *Group Analysis* 18 (1985): 79–92, accessed December 21, 2013, http://groupanalyticsociety.co.uk/wp-content/uploads/2011/04/de-Mare.pdf.

7. In the United Kingdom, the term "probation officer" refers to both officers who supervise probationers and parolees (post-incarceration).

8. *Prison Dialogue: The Case Studies* (Chipping Camden: Prison Dialogue, 1991). The document was prepared for the twentieth anniversary observance of Prison Dialogue held in Oxford, September 4, 2013.

9. I once asked Garrett what role the idea of fragmentation had played in the development of the application of Dialogue to organizations. He reviewed the resources he had available and noted that in his writings Bohm is concerned, at the level of thought in the individual, with fragmentation caused by the defense of the ego. His most explicit treatment of the subject is in *Thought as a System* and in his discus-

sion of the implications of fragmentary thought at a social level in *Changing Consciousness* by Bohm and the photographer Mark Edwards. Garrett notes that Bohm was not familiar with organizational life apart from universities and did not have much to say about the fragmentary nature of organizations. Garrett sees his own work as the development of those implications for organizational life, particularly in his discussion of the dynamics of fragmentation based on power lines and power centers. Personal communication, May 15, 2013. See P. Garrett, "Yet Another Reorganization," Dialogue Associates (2008), accessed September 18, 2014, http://www.dialogue-associates.com/files/files/YET%20ANOTHER%20RE-ORGANISATION.pdf.

10. W. Isaacs, *Dialogue: The Art of Thinking Together* (New York: Doubleday, 1999).

11. Information on Ball's life comes primarily from an interview, July 8, 2013.

12. See http://www.dialogue-associates.com/, accessed September 18, 2014, for information on Garrett and Ball's firm.

13. S. Scott, *Fierce Conversations: Achieving Success at Work and in Life, One Conversation at a Time* (New York: Berkley Books, 2002).

14. D. Kehoe, *Communication in Everyday Life*, 2d ed. (Toronto: Pearson Education, 2007).

15. The forty-one case studies of all the Dialogue work done in prisons in the United Kingdom and the United States are available at the Prison Dialogue website. Prison Dialogue is the nonprofit charity Garrett and Ball created to advance the Dialogue work. It has enjoyed consistent support from the Mulberry Trust. See http://www.prisondialogue.org/.

16. I have no proof for this last statement, but after my years of federal government service, I firmly believe it is true.

17. D. Kantor and W. Lehr, *Inside the Family* (San Francisco: Jossey-Bass, 1975). See also D. Isaacs, "Dialogic Leadership" (1999), accessed April 4, 2012, http://www.duke-mansion.com/leeinstitute/pdfs/sysThink_01.pdf, and D. Kantor, *Reading the Room: Group Dynamics for Coaches and Leaders* (San Francisco: Jossey-Bass, 2012).

18. In the interest of clarity, Garrett does not typically use the word "culture" when he talks about organizations, but in our conversations he is comfortable with the term as I define it. He said in reply to my question about organizational cultures as I use the idea, "I would absolutely use the concept. The question is unless you ground it in how people behave, it has no difference at all. I've been trying to take the concept of pervasive fragmentation, which is cultural, down to what can be done at a material level which starts a shift there. So I believe, generally speaking, cultural change programs don't hit the ground. This may just be language; you won't often hear me use the word 'culture.'"

19. In the first training for the extended leadership team in the Virginia Prison Culture Project, Garrett and Ball had the senior staff members, mainly wardens and district chiefs, group themselves according to who was the department's director when they first started working at the prison. They repeated the exercise during a workshop at the American Correctional Association meetings in Washington, D.C., August 2013.

7. Creating a Healing Environment

1. See, e.g., B. Bass and B. Avolio, *Improving Organizational Effectiveness through Transformational Leadership* (Thousand Oaks, CA: Sage, 1994); J. Eggers and J. Gray, "Leadership That Is Transforming, " in N. Cebula, L. Craig, J. Eggers et al. (eds.), *Achieving Performance Excellence: The Influence of Leadership on Organizational Performance*, 41–50 (Washington, DC: National Institute of Corrections, 2011).
2. All quotes from Clarke in this chapter come from a personal interview, June 29, 2012.
3. "Memorandum of Understanding between Virginia Department of Corrections and the National Institute of Corrections," U.S. Department of Justice, Washington, DC, July, 2011.
4. D. Fixsen, S. Naoom, K. Blase, et al., *Implementation Research: A Synthesis of the Literature* (Tampa: University of Southern Florida Research Implementation Network, 2005). See the NIRN website, http://nirn.fpg.unc.edu/ http://nirn.fpg.unc.edu/.
5. See J. Prochaska, C. DiClemente, W. Velicer, et al., "Predicting Change in Smoking Status for Self-changers," *Addictive Behaviors* 10 (1985): 395–406; J. Prochaska and W. Velicer, "The Transtheoretical Model of Health Behavior Change," *American Journal of Health Promotion* 12 (1997): 38–48. See also R. West, "Editorial: Time for a Change— Putting the Transtheoretical (Stages of Change) Model to Rest," *Addiction* 100 (2005): 1036–1039.
6. See W. K. Kellogg Foundation, *Logic Model Development Guide* (Battle Creek, MI: W. K. Kellogg Foundation, 2004), accessed March 1, 2014, http://www.wkkf.org/resource-directory/resource/2006/02/wk-kellogg-foundation-logic-model-development-guide.
7. In the original presentation of the NIRN model in 2005, this step was just "exploration," but over the past decade, the developers of the model have placed a greater emphasis on planning for "sustainability" from the inception of the process.
8. Cameron and Quinn, *Diagnosing and Changing Organizational Culture*.
9. Ibid., 97.
10. The words were patient, cohesive, tolerant, hopeful, re-sealable, awareness, accountable, challenging, open-minded, compassionate, perception, supportive, visionary, ownership, simple, thoughts, caring, confident, committed, confidentiality, trust, trustworthy, reliable, sincere, comforting, responsibility, refreshing, explosive, durable, unafraid, integrity, open, empathetic, respectful, honest, genuine, non-threatening, fair, authentic. Source: Meeting Minutes for the Virginia Department of Corrections Council for the Healing Environment, March 23, 2013.
11. See http://www.dialogue-associates.com/power-resistance-change. See also Garrett's essay "Yet Another Reorganization?" accessed September 18, 2014, http://www.dialogue-associates.com/files/files/YET%20ANOTHER%20RE-ORGANISATION.pdf.
12. See http://www.dialogue-associates.com/power-resistance-change.

13. These figures are for 2013; accessed September 18, 2014, http://quickfacts.census. gov/qfd/states/51000.html. For general information on the Virginia Department of Corrections, see http://vadoc.virginia.gov/.
14. Virginia Department of Corrections, *State Responsible Offender Population Trends, FY2008–FY2012.*
15. The recidivism estimate was supplied by W. D. Jennings, administrator, Research and Management Services Unit at the Virginia Department of Corrections. The 2004–2007 estimate is from Public Safety Performance Project, *State of Recidivism: The Revolving Door of America's Prisons* (Washington, DC: Pew Center on the States, 2011).
16. See Virginia Department of Corrections, *Virginia Adult Reentry Initiative: The Four Year Strategic Plan, Executive Summary, July 2010–June 2014.*
17. When Clarke first told me about that meeting during a conference call with his senior executive staff, I reminded him of something I had often heard him say about the "Webe" response (as is in "We be here when you be gone"). From the laughter I heard from the others in the room, I could tell he had already mentioned Webees to them.
18. We eventually developed a routine for these visits in which I would pick Garrett and Ball up from Dulles International Airport on a Sunday or Monday and drive them to Richmond. After a week of nonstop meetings, training and coaching sessions, and consultations with senior leadership, I would drop them off at Dulles for a Friday night flight back to the United Kingdom (it was during this time that I learned they had apparently developed an immunity to jet lag).
19. H. Clarke, "Moving towards the Healing Environment," Letter to all Department of Corrections Employees, April 16, 2012.
20. Original plans called for the surveys to be conducted at twelve-month intervals over a three-year period. As it happened, the disruptions caused first by the March 2013 "sequester" of the federal budget and the sixteen-day partial shutdown of the federal government in October 2013 interrupted the work on the surveys and delayed funding.
21. See J. Buck Wilson, W. D. Jennings, S. Bieler, and S. Rossman, "Creating and Measuring a Healing Environment in Corrections," Presented at the 2014 annual meetings of the American Society of Criminologists, San Francisco. A final report on the three-year evaluation is expected in 2015.
22. J. Buck Wilson and S. Rossman, "Measuring Support for and Influence of the Healing Environment Initiative: Wave 2 Analysis Update," Briefing for the Virginia Department of Corrections Executive Team, Richmond, Virginia, December 3, 2013.
23. These figures were supplied by W. D. Jennings, administrator, Research and Management Services Unit at the Virginia Department of Corrections, and are drawn from his research (personal communication, March 27, 2014) and from Virginia Department of Corrections, *State Responsible Offender Population Trends, FY2008–FY2012.*

24. These figures were supplied by W. D. Jennings, administrator, Research and Management Services Unit at the Virginia Department of Corrections and are drawn from his research (personal communication on March 27, 2014).

25. Virginia Department of Corrections, *State Responsible Offender Population Trends, FY2008–FY2012*, 15.

8. The Future of Imprisonment

1. M. Tonry, "Punishment," in *The Oxford Handbook of Crime and Criminal Justice* (New York: Oxford University Press, 2001), 97.

2. See M. Alexander, *The New Jim Crow: Mass Incarceration in the Age of Colorblindness* (New York: New Press, 2010), and J. Forman, "Racial Critiques of Mass Incarceration: Beyond Jim Crow," *New York University Law Review* 87 (2012): 101–146; M. Tonry, "Crime and Human Rights—How Political Paranoia, Protestant Fundamentalism, and Constitutional Obsolescence Combined to Devastate Black America: The American Society of Criminology 2007 Presidential Address," *Criminology* 46 (2006): 1–34; B. Western, *Punishment and Inequality in America* (New York: Sage, 2006).

3. Bohm, *On Dialogue*, 48.

4. Ibid., 53.

5. Michelle Brown calls this becoming a penal spectator and examines "prison tourism." See Brown, *The Culture of Punishment*.

6. The modern understanding of psychological defense mechanisms started with Sigmund Freud, but it was further developed by his successors, notably his daughter, Anna Freud. See A. Freud, *The Ego and the Mechanisms of Defense* (London: Hogarth Press, 1937). See also P. Cramer, *Protecting the Self: Defense Mechanisms in Action* (New York: Guilford Press, 2006); G. Vaillant, *Adaptation to Life* (Boston: Little, Brown, 1977).

7. See G. Walters, "The Psychological Inventory of Criminal Thinking Styles: Part I. Reliability and Preliminary Validity," *Criminal Justice and Behavior* 22 (1995): 307–325; G. Walters, *Criminal Belief Systems: An Integrated-Interactive Theory of Lifestyles* (Westport, CT: Praeger, 2002).

8. The idea can be controversial. For example, it is sometimes argued that men who feel sexual attraction to other men but cannot acknowledge those feelings are more likely than other men to hate gays. See H. Adams, R. Wright, and B. Lohr, "Is Homophobia Associated with Homosexual Arousal?" *Journal of Abnormal Psychology* 105 (1996): 440–445.

9. Personal interview, July 21, 2012.

10. If you do not like the psychoanalytic tone of this, the research and literature on coping styles can lead you to the same conclusion. This literature describes the difference between "problem-focused" approaches and "emotion-focused" approaches. See R. Lazarus, *Emotion and Adaptation* (New York: Oxford University Press, 1991); R. Lazarus, *Stress and Emotion: A New Synthesis* (New York: Springer, 2006).

11. See Dialogue Associates, "Dorset Threshold Dialogue Governance Board" and "The Line of Sight Workshop," in *Prison Dialogue: The Case Studies* (Chipping Camden: Prison Dialogue, 2013).

12. See P. Holman, T. Devane, and S. Cady, *The Change Handbook* (San Francisco: Berrett-Koehler, 2007).

13. Personal interview, March 22, 2912.

14. Personal communication, April 4, 2012.

INDEX